GREGG SHORTHAND

BASIC PRINCIPLES

GREGG SHORTHAND

BASIC PRINCIPLES

CENTENNIAL EDITION

CHARLES E. ZOUBEK

Gregg Division/McGraw-Hill Book Company

New York   Atlanta   Dallas   St. Louis   San Francisco   Auckland   Bogotá   Guatemala
Hamburg   Lisbon   London   Madrid   Mexico   Milan   Montreal   New Delhi
Panama   Paris   San Juan   São Paulo   Singapore   Sydney   Tokyo   Toronto

Sponsoring Editor: **Elizabeth R. Shelapinsky, Janet Passaro**

Editing Supervisor: **Elizabeth Huffman**

Design and Art Supervisor: **Caryl Valerie Spinka**

Production Supervisor: **Frank Bellantoni**

Production Assistant: **Mary C. Buchanan**

Photo Editor: **Rosemarie Rossi**

Consulting Design Coordinator/Interior Design: **Susan Brorein**

Cover Photography: **Ken Karp**

Photo Credits
Jules Allen: pages xi, 24, 25 (*top, bottom*), 32, 50, 80, 107
(*middle, bottom*), 124, 130, 158, 211, 213, 228, 234, 236.
Will Faller: pages xii, 25 (*middle*), 37, 52, 53 (*middle, bottom*),
70, 77, 106, 107 (*top*), 118 , 132, 133 (*middle*), 147, 184, 185,
194, 203, 209, 237 (*middle, bottom*), 257, 260, 262, 263
(*middle, bottom*), 298. Michal Heron: pages 1, 7, 9, 11, 53
(*top*), 60, 81, 93, 98, 104, 133 (*top, bottom*), 139, 156, 159,
164, 176, 183, 237 (*top*), 248, 263 (*top*), 280, 281, 299.
Courtesy Meadowlands Giants Stadium, New Jersey: page 210.

Library of Congress Cataloging-in-Publication Data

Zoubek, Charles E., date
   Gregg shorthand : basic principles / Charles E. Zoubek. --
Centennial ed.
    p. cm.
   Includes index.
   ISBN 0-07-073664-2 (v. 1)
   1. Shorthand--Gregg.   I. Title.
Z56.2.G7Z73 1990
653´.427--dc19   88-9348
                                     CIP

The manuscript for this book was processed electronically.

Gregg Shorthand: Basic Principles, Centennial Edition

  2 3 4 5 6 7 8 9 0 DOWDOW   9 5 4 3 2 1 0

ISBN 0-07-073664-2

CONTENTS

The Value of Shorthand

Gregg Shorthand is one of the most valuable subjects you will ever learn. There are several reasons why such a powerful statement is true.

First of all, shorthand is a lifelong personal skill which relieves one from the drudgery of writing longhand. Shorthand makes it possible for most people to write three or four times faster than their longhand writing speed. Over a lifetime this saves a tremendous amount of time.

All personal notes, such as shopping lists, telephone messages, reminders, and "to do" lists, can be written in shorthand. To the student, shorthand is particularly valuable. The shorthand writer takes notes completely and easily while the longhand writer struggles and often misses important information. In the library, the shorthand writer saves valuable time in making research notes.

Professionals in all occupations find their jobs made easier and more efficient if they know shorthand. News reporters use shorthand when listing facts for a news story. Lawyers use shorthand when listing facts for the presentation of a case. Managers in a wide variety of jobs use shorthand to record instructions given to them by their supervisors. Professionals in all occupations and citizens pursuing active roles in civic organizations use shorthand in order to make notes in meetings.

Most secretaries use shorthand. They use it for taking dictation of letters and for the personal and administrative uses already discussed. The best-paying secretarial jobs require shorthand. For those secretarial jobs which do not require shorthand, the person having shorthand skill is pre-ferred for employment. Once a person has a secretarial job, shorthand skill is most likely to be required for promotion to even better jobs. Shorthand skill pays too. Typically, people who know shorthand earn between $1,000 and $3,000 a year more than those who do not have this skill.

Another benefit derived from the study of Gregg Shorthand is that other skills grow as one learns shorthand. Many people who have never considered themselves particularly strong students of English are amazed at how much the study of shorthand improves their knowledge of punctuation, grammar, and word usage.

A familiar old saying tells us, "You can't get something for nothing." Shorthand is something of tremendous value, but it can only be acquired through reasonable, honest effort. That is another reason why employers prefer to hire people who know shorthand—they are most likely to be dependable and take pride in their work.

The Study of Shorthand

The speed with which you learn to read and write Gregg Shorthand will depend largely on two factors—the *time* you devote to practice and the *way* in which you practice. If you practice efficiently, you will be able to complete each lesson in the shortest possible time and derive the greatest possible benefit.

Before you begin, select a quiet place in which to practice. Do not try to practice while listening to music, watching television, or carrying on a conversation.

Here are some features of the materials along with learning suggestions that will help you get the maximum benefit from the time you invest in shorthand practice.

LINE PLACEMENT

Gregg Shorthand can, of course, be written on either ruled or unruled paper. The printed lines of a shorthand notebook lessen the hesitation in writing and provide a guide for the eyes to follow as the shorthand outlines are read.

With the Centennial Edition of *Gregg Shorthand*, a commonsense approach to line placement has been adopted. The line placement of each outline has been selected as that which is the most reasonable for speed of writing and maintenance of proportion.

Shorthand writers are encouraged to "throw" outlines upon the page as rapidly as possible. Therefore, the placement may vary slightly because it is difficult when writing to begin at, or touch, the same place every time.

READING WORD LISTS

With the presentation of each shorthand principle is a list of words that illustrates the principle. As part of your out-of-class practice, read these word lists in this way:

1. Using the typed word and shorthand outline, spell—aloud if possible—the shorthand symbol in each outline in the list, thus: *s-e, see; f-e, fee.* Reading aloud will help impress the shorthand outlines firmly on your mind. Read all the shorthand words in the list in this way—with the typed word exposed—until you feel you can read the shorthand outlines without referring to the typed word.
2. Cover the typed word with a piece of paper and read aloud from the shorthand, thus: *s-e, see; f-e, fee.*
3. If the spelling of a shorthand outline does not immediately give you the meaning, refer to the typed word and determine the meaning of any outline you cannot read. Do *not* spend more than a few seconds trying to decipher an outline.

4. After you have read all the words in the list, read them again if time permits.

Note: In reading brief forms for common words and phrases, which first occur in Lessons 4 and 5, respectively, do not spell the shorthand outlines.

READING SENTENCES, LETTERS, AND ARTICLES

The presentation of each shorthand principle is followed by connected practice material. Each lesson concludes with additional practice material in which sentences, letters, or articles are written in shorthand. Proper practice of all this material will help you develop your shorthand ability.

First, *read* the material. Using the transcript to the shorthand in the back of the textbook, you should follow this procedure:

1. Read the shorthand outlines aloud until you come to a word you cannot read. Spell the shorthand symbols in that outline. If this spelling does not *immediately* give you the meaning, refer to the transcript.
2. To find the shorthand outline in the transcript, look for items that precede or follow the outline, such as the salutation, closing, or a new paragraph.
3. After determining the outline that cannot be read, write it on a piece of paper.
4. Return to the shorthand from which you are reading and continue reading in this manner until you have completed the material.
5. If time permits, read the material a second time.

By following this procedure, you will lose no time in finding your place in the shorthand and in the transcript when you cannot read an outline.

Remember, during the early stages your shorthand reading may not be very rapid. That is only natural as you are, in a sense, learning a new language. If you practice regularly, however, you will find your reading rate increasing almost daily.

WRITING THE READING AND WRITING PRACTICE

Before you do any writing of shorthand, you should acquire an appropriate notebook and pen.

Your Notebook. The best notebook for shorthand writing is one that measures 6 by 9 inches and has a vertical rule down the center of each page. It should have a spiral binding so the pages lie flat at all times. The paper should take ink well.

Your Pen. A pen is a satisfactory instrument for writing Gregg Shorthand. A pencil is not recommended. Because writing with a pen requires little pressure, you can write for long periods of time without becoming fatigued. A fine ballpoint pen facilitates the fastest writing for most people. Pen-written notes remain legible almost indefinitely; pencil notes become blurred and hard to read.

Having selected your writing tools, follow these steps in writing the Reading and Writing Practice.

1. Read the material you are going to copy. Always read the Reading and Writing Practice before copying it. Make sure you can read the copy easily before attempting to write.

2. When you are ready to start writing, read a convenient group of words from the printed shorthand; then write the group, reading aloud as you write.

In the early stages your writing may not be very rapid, nor will your notes be as well written as those in the book. With regular practice, however, your notes will rapidly improve.

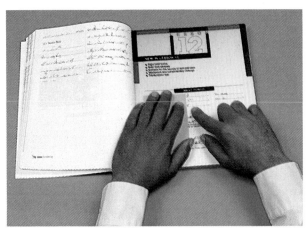

Study the word lists by placing a card or a piece of paper over the typed words and reading the shorthand words aloud.

Read a convenient group of words aloud and then write that group in a notebook. Notice how the student keeps the place in the shorthand notes.

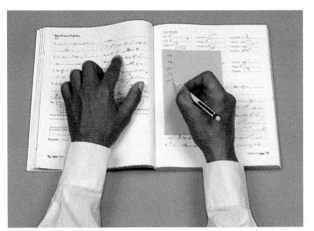

Read the practice material, using the transcript to determine any outlines that cannot be read. Write these outlines on a piece of paper for further study.

U N I T

I

L E S S O N

1

- Concept of *you write what you hear*
- Concept of symbols representing sounds
- Symbols for the sounds of *a*, *e*, *n*, *m*, *t*, and *d*
- Shorthand symbols for punctuation, paragraph, and capitalization

You Write What You Hear

In shorthand silent letters are omitted and other letters may have different sounds. Following are some English words with their shorthand spellings and an explanation of the sounds.

Word	Sounds	Explanation
name	nam	*e* is silent
right	rit	*gh* is silent
navy	nave	*y* sounds like *e*
stay	sta	*y* is silent
face	fas	*c* sounds like *s*
phone	fon	*ph* sounds like *f*
snow	sno	*w* is silent
safe	saf	*e* is silent
age	aj	*g* sounds like *j*
home	hom	*e* is silent
lead	led	*a* is not heard
large	larj	*g* sounds like *j*
cope	kop	*c* sounds like *k*

Can you determine the shorthand spellings for each of the following words?

may	aid	eat
aim	main	tea
day	date	team

SOUNDS OF A, E, N, M

The shorthand symbols for *a* and *e* are circles that are differentiated by size much the same as they are in longhand.

The *a* is a large circle. $\mathcal{O}$

The *e* is a small circle. o

The shorthand symbols for *n* and *m* are straight lines written forward along the line of writing.

The *n* is a short straight line. ‿

Example: knee ‿o

The *m* is a long straight line. ⎯

Example: may ‿o

A, E, N, M Words

The following words contain the long sounds of *a*, *e*, *n*, and *m*. The symbols for each sound in a word are joined together to form a word called an *outline*.

may ⎯⎯⎯⎯⎯⎯⎯⎯

main ⎯⎯⎯⎯⎯⎯⎯⎯

me ⎯⎯⎯⎯⎯⎯⎯⎯

mean ⎯⎯⎯⎯⎯⎯⎯⎯

knee ⎯⎯⎯⎯⎯⎯⎯⎯

name ⎯⎯⎯⎯⎯⎯⎯⎯

aim ⎯⎯⎯⎯⎯⎯⎯⎯

A, E, N, M Practice
1.1

1 I ⎯ to please.

2 She ⎯ go to the game.

3 My ⎯ hurts.

4 He did not meet ⎯ .

5 What is her ⎯ ?

6 Meet ⎯ at 3 o'clock.

7 The ⎯ gate is open.

8 His ⎯ is Jim.

9 He is not ⎯ .

10 I ⎯ ⎯ the dog.

Key: 1 I aim to please.   6 Meet me at 3 o'clock.
          2 She may go to the game.   7 The main gate is open.
          3 My knee hurts.   8 His name is Jim.
          4 He did not meet me.   9 He is not mean.
          5 What is her name?   10 I may name the dog.

SOUNDS OF T, D

The shorthand symbols for *t* and *d* are *upward* slanting straight lines differentiated by length.

The *t* is a short slanting straight line. ╱

Example: tea ╱°

The *d* is a long slanting straight line. ╱

Example: day ╱

T, D Words

tea ╱° _____   date ╱° _____   meet, meat ____╱°

team ╱° _____   deed ╱° _____   eat ╱°

tame ╱° _____   made ____╱° _____   ate ╱°

day ╱ _____   mate ____╱° _____   aid, aide ╱°

T, D Practice
1.2

1 The dog is ╱° .

2 The ╱° has been decided.

3 My sister ____╱° ╱° .

4 Jeff will ____╱° my father.

5 The ╱° is signed.

6 Check the ╱° on the calendar.

7 Our ╱° won!

8 When will you ╱° dinner?

9 Kathy is a nurse's ╱° .

10 We ╱° lunch late.

1 The dog is tame.
2 The date has been decided.
3 My sister made tea.
4 Jeff will meet my father.
5 The deed is signed.
6 Check the date on the calendar.
7 Our team won!
8 When will you eat dinner?
9 Kathy is a nurse's aide.
10 We ate lunch late.

PUNCTUATION, PARAGRAPH, AND CAPITALIZATION SYMBOLS

Since ordinary longhand marks of punctuation are similar to some of the shorthand symbols that will be presented in later lessons, special symbols are used to represent those punctuation marks. There are also special paragraph and capitalization symbols.

Punctuation and Paragraph Symbols

Special symbols are used to represent the period and question mark at the end of a sentence. Note that an ordinary comma is used within a circle.

A sentence ending with a period or question mark may also be the last sentence in a paragraph. In this case, if the last sentence in the paragraph ends with a period, the period is dropped and a paragraph symbol is used alone. If the last sentence ends with a question mark or an exclamation point, both the punctuation mark and the paragraph symbol are retained.

period ＼

question mark ✗

paragraph ⟩

comma ⊙

semicolon ⊙

colon ⊙

hyphen ＝

dash ＝

exclamation point ／

left parenthesis ⟨

right parenthesis ⟩

Capitalization

Shorthand capitalization is indicated with a pair of tiny upward slanting straight symbols. These capitalization marks are placed underneath the word to be capitalized at the end of the outline. While vertical placement is not critical, the capitalization marks should be close enough to the body of the outline to be unmistakably associated with it. In order to promote writing speed, the first word of each short-hand sentence does not contain capitalization marks. When shorthand notes are typed in English—which is called *transcribing*—the first word of each sentence is, of course, capitalized.

Salutations such as *William* or *Dear William* or sentences beginning with a proper noun will contain capitalization marks. However, when a letter begins with a salutation such as *Dear Mr. Franklin* or *Dear Ms. Harrington,* the proper noun will not contain capitalization marks. When the notes are transcribed, the names will be capitalized.

Capitalized Words

May _____

Amy _____

Dean _____

Nate _____

Punctuation and Capitalization Practice
1.3

1 _____ won the track _____ for his _____

2 Put your _____ on the _____ next to the _____

3 _____

4 _____ a _____ with _____

5 Our friend _____

6 _____ the _____

7 _____ for a _____ in _____

8 Can _____ too ✗

9 _____ is _____

10 What _____ ✗

Key:
1 Dean won the track meet for his team.
2 Put your name on the deed next to the date.
3 Amy ate meat.
4 Nate made a date with May.
5 Our friend, Amy Dean, made the team.
6 Dean made the team.
7 Meet me for a day in May.
8 Can Dean meet me too?
9 Amy is mean.
10 What made Amy mean?

Things can get hectic in a television newsroom. If a reporter uses shorthand, instructions from the news director can be jotted down quickly.

1.4

1 My ⟋ ⟋ stop ⟋ from going ⟍

2 ⟋ will ⟋ ⟋ any ⟋ ⟍

3 ⟋ ⟋ at 4 o'clock for ⟋ ⟍

4 ⟋ ⟋ ⟋ ⟋ ⟍

5 ⟋ ⟋ be on the ⟋ ⟍

6 ⟋ ⟋ sign the ⟋ in

7 He will ⟋ the ⟋ of the track

⟋ ⟍

8 ⟋ ⟋ ⟋ for the ⟋ ⟍

9 ⟋ ⟋ on East ⟋ to sign the

⟋ ⟍

10 Mark the ⟋ on the ⟋ ⟍

LESSON 2

- **Symbol for the sound of *h* at the beginning of words**
- **Word ending *-ing***
- **Symbol for the sound of *long i***
- **Efficient use of a steno pad**

SOUNDS OF H, -ING

The shorthand symbol for the sounds of *h* and *-ing* is a dot.

h, -ing ·

The letter *h*, which almost always occurs at the beginning of a word, is represented by a dot placed above the vowel.

Example: he ˙o

The sound of *-ing*, which almost always occurs at the end of a word, is represented by a dot placed close to the end of the body of the outline.

Example: meeting ——ⱷ ·

H, -ing Words

he ˙o	heeding ⱷ·	naming ⱷ.
heat ˙ⱷ	hate ˙ⱷ	taming ⱷ.
heating ˙ⱷ·	meeting ——ⱷ·	dating ⱷ.

H, -ing Practice

2.1

1　I ✍ missing the ——✍· with ⌀⌒⍀

2　A ✍ ——✍· was held in ——⌀⍀

3　⌀ ——⌀ be ——✍· ——⌀ that ✍⍀

4　✍ is ✍ ⌀⌒⍀

5　——✍ enjoys ✍· animals all ✍⍀

6　⌀ ——⌀ ✍ the ——✍· ⍀

7　——⌀ is not ✍· our warning about ✍⍀

8　The ✍ for the ——✍· is in ——⌀⍀

9　Who is ——⌀. the ✍ ×

10　⌀ ——⌀ repair the ✍· ⍀

Key:

1　I hate missing the meeting with Amy.
2　A team meeting was held in May.
3　He may be meeting me that day.
4　Dean is dating Amy.
5　Nate enjoys taming animals all day.

6　He may hate the meeting.
7　May is not heeding our warning about Dean.
8　The date for the meeting is in May.
9　Who is naming the team?
10　He may repair the heating.

A reporter uses shorthand to obtain a complete and accurate record of the interview.

SOUND OF LONG I

The shorthand symbol for *long i* is a broken *a* circle. ⟋

Example: high ⟋

Long I Words

high ⟋

my ⟋

might ⟋

mine ⟋

night ⟋

tie ⟋

tied ⟋

die, dye ⟋

dying ⟋

Long I Practice
2.2

1 ⟋ ended the game in a ⟋

2 The ⟋ is in ⟋

3 ⟋ go out at ⟋

4 ⟋ did not ⟋ ⟋ ⟋ before the ⟋

5 ⟋ learn to ⟋ his ⟋

6 The rate on ⟋ ⟋ ⟋ be ⟋

7 ⟋ write ⟋ at ⟋

8 ⟋ is in the safe at ⟋

9 ⟋ ⟋ ⟋ ⟋

10 The price of ⟋ ⟋ is too ⟋

Key:
1 My team ended the game in a tie.
2 The date is in May.
3 Amy might go out at night.
4 He did not dye my tie before the meeting.
5 He might learn to tie his tie.

6 The rate on my deed might be high.
7 He might write Dean at night.
8 My deed is in the safe at night.
9 Nate tied my tie.
10 The price of my deed is too high.

Notebook Management

Use a two-column steno pad and write in one column at a time. By writing your shorthand notes in one column at a time, you will minimize wasted *return* writing motions.

Use one side of paper. In order to avoid wasting time turning pages, you should write on one side of the page only. When you reach the end of the notebook, turn it around and proceed to write on the back of all the pages.

Use a rubber band. Group completed pages together with a rubber band so that the pad falls open at the first page available for writing.

Date the notes. Each day you use your steno pad, write the current date first.

Separate your notes. Draw a line across the column to clearly indicate the separation between the letters or other notes.

Maintain good posture. You will have the greatest writing speed when your arms are fully supported by the writing surface. Use your free hand to steady the notebook. Have your steno pad opened flat. When turning pages, do not waste time tucking the used pages underneath the pad.

Select the right pen. Pencils should definitely be avoided. The ideal pen allows the ink to flow freely. The ink should be dark enough to be clearly legible.

Shorthand can be used to keep up with the hectic pace that can arise in a newsroom.

2.3

1  her ⟋⟍

2 The ⟋ is not ⟍⟋⟍

3 ⟍⟋ will ⟍⟋ the ⟋⟍

4 ⟍⟋ ⟍⟋ be at the ⟋ ⟍⟋· ⟍

5 The ⟍⟋· will be held with ⟋⟍ ⟍

6 ⟍⟋ ⟋ ⟍⟋ ⟍⟋ ⟍⟋ at 10 at ⟍⟋⟍

7 We ⟍⟋ ·⟍⟋ in the room at ⟍⟋⟍

8 ⟋⟍ will ⟍⟋ the warning of ⟍⟋⟍

9 The rate ⟋⟍ gave ⟍⟋ is 𝒪⟍

10 The price of the ⟋ is too 𝒪⟍

LESSON 3

- **Symbols for the sounds of *o*, *r*, and *l***
- **Minor vowels omitted as an abbreviating principle**
- **Symbol for the sound of *short i***
- **Listening as a communication skill**

SOUNDS OF O, R, L

The symbols for *o*, *r*, and *l* are short forward "under" curves differentiated by length.

o ‿   r ‿   l ‿

Sound of O

The *o* is a tiny hook. ‿

Example: no ‿

O Words

no, know ‿	own ■ ‿	total ■ ‿
tow ‿	owning ■ ‿	note ■ ‿
dough ‿	known ■ ‿	noting ■ ‿
home ■ ‿	tone ■ ‿	mode ■ ‿

■ When the *o* is joined to the beginning of *t*, *d*, *n*, and *m*, it is written without an angle to make writing faster.

Sound of R

The *r* is a short forward curve.

Example: ray

R Words

ray	or	Mary
rate	more	dear
raid	row	road
trade	wrote	ride
rain	write	try
train	reading	tried

Sound of L

The *l* is a long forward curve.

Example: lay

L Words

lay	lane	line
late	lean	Dale
Lee	lie	mailing
leading	light	low

O, R, L Practice
3.1

1 _____ a _____

2 _____ the _____

3 _____ without a

_____

4 Do not ⟋ ⟋ · without a

⟋ ⟍

5 ⟋ ⟋ a ⟋ with

⟋ ⟍

6 ⟍ will ⟋ the ⟋ in

⟋ ⟍

7 ⟋ ⟋ a ⟋ about the

⟋ ⟍

8 At ⟋ ⟋ ⟋ the ⟋

to his ⟋ ⟍

9 ⟋ was ⟋ in ⟋ the ⟋ ⟍

10 ⟋ was ⟋ for the ⟋ ⟍

Key:

1 Lee wrote a note home.	**6** He will trade the team in May.
2 He may mail the note.	**7** Lee may write a note about the low rate.
3 Dale may read without a light.	**8** At night Dale rode the train to his home.
4 Do not try reading without a light.	**9** Nate was late in writing the note.
5 Dale made a deal with Ray.	**10** Leo was late for the meeting.

MINOR VOWELS OMITTED

Many words contain vowels that are barely pronounced in ordinary speech. Such vowels may be omitted from shorthand outlines if they do not contribute to speed or readability.

Example: later ⟋

later ⟋　　　　dealer ⟋　　　　total ⟋

leader ⟋　　　　trailer ⟋　　　　title ⟋

light ⟋　　　　meter ⟋　　　　delay ⟋

reader ⟋　　　　motor ⟋　　　　delight ⟋

Minor-Vowel-Omitted Practice
3.2

1  will ⟋ ⟋ ⟋ in

the ⟋ ⟍

2 Will ⟋ make a ⟋ with a car

⟋ ✕

3 ⟋ is ⟋ as a ⟋ ⟍

4 A ⟋ will make ⟋ even

⟋ ⟍

5 ⟋ set a ⟋ ⟍

6 Do you ⟋ the ⟋ of the

7 ⟋ ⟋ to speak to the

⟋ about the ⟋ ⟍

8 ⟋ ⟋ ⟋ in ⟋ · the

⟋ ⟍

9 ⟋ will ⟋ to ⟋ the car for a

⟋ ⟍

10 The ⟋ of the account is not

⟋ ⟍

Key:

1 Dale will write Amy later in the day.
2 Will Mary make a trade with a car dealer?
3 Lee is known as a leader.
4 A delay will make Amy even later.
5 Lee set a low rate.
6 Do you know the leader of the team?
7 Lee tried to speak to the dealer about the low rate.
8 Ray may delight in reading the title.
9 He will try to trade the car for a trailer.
10 The total of the account is not known.

SOUND OF SHORT I

The short sound of the vowel *i* is represented by the shorthand *e* symbol. Phonetically, they are the same family of sounds.

short i = ⟋

Example: did ⟋

Short I Words

did _____   hitting _____   little _____

him _____   Tim _____   knit _____

hit _____   litter _____

Short I Practice
3.3

1 _____ a sweater for

_____

2 The _____ is _____ a _____

better

3 The baseball _____ on the ankle

4 _____ better than _____

5 _____ pick up the _____ on

the _____

6 _____ the _____ choose _____

7 _____ not _____ to _____ the

_____

8 Is _____ at _____

9 _____ not _____ the _____

10 A _____ is needed to

_____

Key:

1 Lee did knit a sweater for Mary.
2 The team is hitting a little better.
3 The baseball hit him on the ankle.
4 Lee did better than Tim.
5 Did Tim pick up the litter on the train?

6 Did the team choose him?
7 He did not try to trade the trailer.
8 Is Ray eating at home?
9 Tim did not write the note.
10 A little light is needed to write.

Listening as a Communication Skill

Communication is a process whereby people are able to understand each other. One person may be very good at describing facts, ideas, or emotions. Other people will not *understand* these messages, though, unless they are effective listeners.

Effective communication is a two-way street, with listening skills being an essential part of the process. Good listening skills are among the many communications skills that you will refine through your study of Gregg Shorthand.

Reading Practice

3.4

1 ⟋ is ⟋. his ⟋ to ⟋ ⟋ ⟍

2 ⟋ will ⟋ the ⟋ at the ⟋ ⟍

3 We are deciding the ⟋ of the book in ⟋ ⟍

4 The ⟋ price is not ⟋ ⟍

5 We will ⟋ the ⟋ of the ⟋ ⟍

6 ⟋ ⟋ ⟋ a new ⟋ ⟍

7 Do you ⟋ who will ⟋ the ⟋ ×

8 The ⟋ will ⟋ the ⟋ ⟍

9 ⟋ ⟋ the ⟋ at ⟋ ⟍

10 ⟋ ⟋ ⟋ to ⟋ a report ⟍

LESSON 4

NEW IN LESSON 4

- **Nine abbreviated words called brief forms**
- **Short and soft vowel sounds of *a* and *e***

Note: Outlines for brief forms will be highlighted in the practice materials.

BRIEF FORMS

Some of the most common words have abbreviated shorthand spellings called *brief forms*. The nine brief forms in this lesson are all written with single shorthand symbols. Since these words occur often in our language, their brief forms are a major source of writing speed. They must be learned for instant recall and are highlighted in the *practice* material.

a, an ._____   I *O*_____   of *ʋ*_____

am _____   in, not _____   will, well _____

are, our, hour _____   it, at _____   would _____

Brief-Form Derivatives

Some brief forms can be used for longer words by making the brief forms plural or past tense, or by adding a common prefix or a common suffix such as *-ing*. One brief-form derivative is possible using the alphabetic characters presented so far.

Example: will + ing _____

Brief-Form Practice

4.1

1   ⌣ ⌣ ⌣ — . ⌣ ⟍

2   ⌣ ⌣ ⌣ ⌣ ⌣ ⌣

     ⌣ ✕

3   You and ⊘ ⌣ doing ⌣ ⁄

     ⌣ . ⟍

4   ⊘ — the ⌣ ⌣ ⌣ .

     — ⌣ . ⟍

5   ⊘ ⁄ — miss ⁄ ⟍

6   ⌣ is ⌣ . to ⌣ the

     — ⌣ . — . ⌣ ⟍

7   ⁄ ⌣ ⌣ ⌣ — . ⌣ ✕

8   ⌣ ⌣ ⌣ ⌣ ⌣ ⌣ ✕

9   ⌣ ⌣ ⌣ leave — . ⌣ ⟍

10   We ⌣ ⌣ . — ⌣ car ⟍

Key:
1   Lee will meet me in an hour.
2   Will Leo Dean lead our team?
3   You and I are doing well at reading.
4   I am the leader of a meeting.
5   I would not miss it.
6   Ray is willing to lead the meeting in an hour.
7   Would Leo meet me in an hour?
8   Will Lee read our note?
9   Our train will leave in an hour.
10   We are trading in our car.

SHORT AND SOFT SOUNDS OF A

The large *a* circle, which represents the long sound of *a* as in *made*, also represents the short sound of *a* as in *man* and the soft sound of *a* as in *arm*.

Example: man

Short A Words

man   dad   matter

had   hammer   ran

hat   Matt   ladder

Soft A Words

arm _[shorthand outline]_ harm _[shorthand outline]_ art _[shorthand outline]_

Army _[shorthand outline]_ heart _[shorthand outline]_ alarm _[shorthand outline]_

Short and Soft A Practice
4.2

1 _[shorthand outline]_ to get . _[shorthand outline]_

2 _[shorthand outline]_ bought . new _[shorthand outline]_ for _[shorthand outline]_

3 Is something the _[shorthand outline]_ with his _[shorthand outline]_ ×

4 _[shorthand outline]_ to strengthen his _[shorthand outline]_

5 She _[shorthand outline]_ . old _[shorthand outline]_ from the _[shorthand outline]_

6 _[shorthand outline]_ the story ＼

7 _[shorthand outline]_ _[shorthand outline]_

8 _[shorthand outline]_ go to the _[shorthand outline]_ ×

9 The _[shorthand outline]_ be settled _[shorthand outline]_

10 _[shorthand outline]_ . play ＼

Key:
1 Leo ran home to get a ladder.
2 My dad bought a new hammer for me.
3 Is something the matter with his arm?
4 Matt ran to strengthen his heart.
5 She had an old hat from the Army.

6 A man will write the story.
7 Matt had a low reading rate.
8 Will my dad go to the meeting at night?
9 The matter will be settled in May.
10 Dad had a leading role in a play.

SHORT AND SOFT SOUNDS OF E

The tiny *e* circle, which represents the long sound of *e* as in *Lee*, also represents the short sound of *e* as in *let* and the soft sound of *e* as in *her*.

Examples: let ⌣ℰ   her ℯ

Short and Soft E Words

let ⌣ℰ _____   letterhead ℯℯℯ _____   led ⌣ℰ _____

letter ⌣ℯ _____   net ℯ _____   her ℯ _____

head ℯ _____   met ℯ _____   hurt ℯ _____

heading ℯ _____   red ℯ _____   hurting ℯ _____

Short and Soft E Practice
4.3

1 ℯ ℯ   was — the ℯℯ

2 ⌣ℯ ℯℯ have the ℯ ℯ

3 ℯ ℯ his ℯ on the ℯ

4 ℯℯ ℯ ℯ ℯ

5 ℯ ℯ ℯ ℯ , ℯ ℯ

6 ⌣ℯ ℯ ℯ the ⌣ℯ

7 ℯ ⌣ ℯ ℯ to ℯ

8 ℯ ⌣ℯ was sent to ℯ ℯ

9 ℯ ℯ ℯ is missing

10 What ⌣ be the ℯ ℯ on the ⌣ℯ ✗

Key: **1**   Her dad was in the Army.
       2   Let Amy have the red ladder.
       3   Matt hurt his head on the ladder.
       4   Mary read her letter.
       5   He met her dad, Matt Dean.

       6   Let Tim meet the leader.
       7   He will mail a letter to Leo.
       8   A letter was sent to my home.
       9   My red tie is missing.
     10   What will be the net rate on the loan?

Reading Practice

4.4

1   *[shorthand]*

2   *[shorthand]*

3   *[shorthand]* the *[shorthand]*

4   Is the *[shorthand]* to hold . *[shorthand]*

5   *[shorthand]* and *[shorthand]* . story *[shorthand]*

6   We *[shorthand]* car — / the

sale — *[shorthand]*

7   *[shorthand]* arrive — the *[shorthand]*

8   *[shorthand]*

9   *[shorthand]* be *[shorthand]* to *[shorthand]* the *[shorthand]*

10   *[shorthand]* hold . *[shorthand]* — *[shorthand]*

U N I T

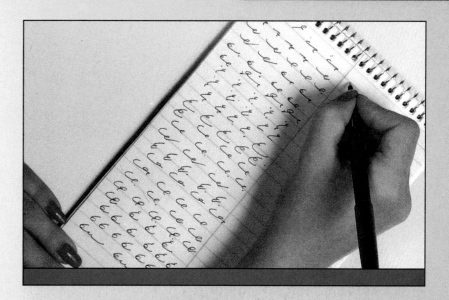

5

NEW IN LESSON 5

- **Shorthand phrases**
- **Symbols for the sounds of *s*, *f*, and *v***
- **Shorthand blends for *fr* and *fl***
- **Short and soft sounds of *o***
- **Differentiating between sound-alike words *sight*, *site*, and *cite***

Note: Beginning with Lesson 5, outlines for new words and phrases will be highlighted in the practice materials.

PHRASES

In Lesson 4 you learned special abbreviations, called brief forms, for some very common words. Very often these occur together. Much of the writing speed of shorthand comes from combining these brief forms into a single outline called a *phrase*.

Example: I ⟲ + will ⟍ = I will ⟲

I will ⟲	I would ⟋	are in, are not ⟍
will not ⟍	I would not ⟋	in it ⟋
I will not ⟲⟍	in our ⟏	it will ⟏
I am ⟋	of our ⟍	it will not ⟏

Phrase Practice

5.1

1 *[shorthand]*

2 *[shorthand]*

3 *[shorthand]*

[shorthand]

4 *[shorthand]*

[shorthand]

5 *[shorthand]*

[shorthand]

¶ **Paragraph**

[shorthand]

[shorthand]

[shorthand]

[shorthand]

[shorthand]

[23 words]

Key:
1 I am not well.
2 Meet me in our home.
3 I will not try writing in our trailer.
4 It will delay my meeting. It will not matter.
5 I would not try reading in low light.

You Write What You Hear

The *s* symbol represents the soft sound of *c* as in *face*.

sight = S I T	cite = S I T	nice = N I S
site = S I T	lace = L A S	face = F A S

The past-tense *d* has the sound of either *d* or *t*. In shorthand, remember, you write what you hear.

saved = S A V D   faced = F A S T   laughed = L A F T

SOUNDS OF S, F, V

The symbols for *s*, *f*, and *v* are *downward* right curves differentiated by length.

s)   f)   v)

Sound of S

The symbol for the sound of *s* as in *see* is a short downward curve. Because of its size, slope, and direction, it is often called the *comma s.*)

Example: see ∂

S Words

see ∂	say ∂	as 9
seem ⟋	same ⟋	has ▪ 9
seen, scene ⟋	sign ∂	stay ⟋
seat, set, sit ⟋	sight, site, cite ⟋	so 2

▪ The letter *s* often has the *z* sound in longhand. In shorthand the *s* is always used for the sound of *z*.

Sound of F

The symbol for the sound of *f* as in *fee* is a medium-size downward curve.)

Example: fee ∂

F Words

fee ∂	face ∂	safes 9
feet ⟋	fast, faced ⟋	laugh ⟍
feed ⟋	fame ⟋	if 9
Fay ∂⁻	safe 9	phone ∠

Sound of V

The symbol for the sound of *v* as in *vase* is a long downward curve. ⟩

Example: vase ⟩

V Words

vase	saved	Navy
vain, van	even	Dave
vote	evening	leaves
save	Steven	relieve

S, F, V Practice
5.2

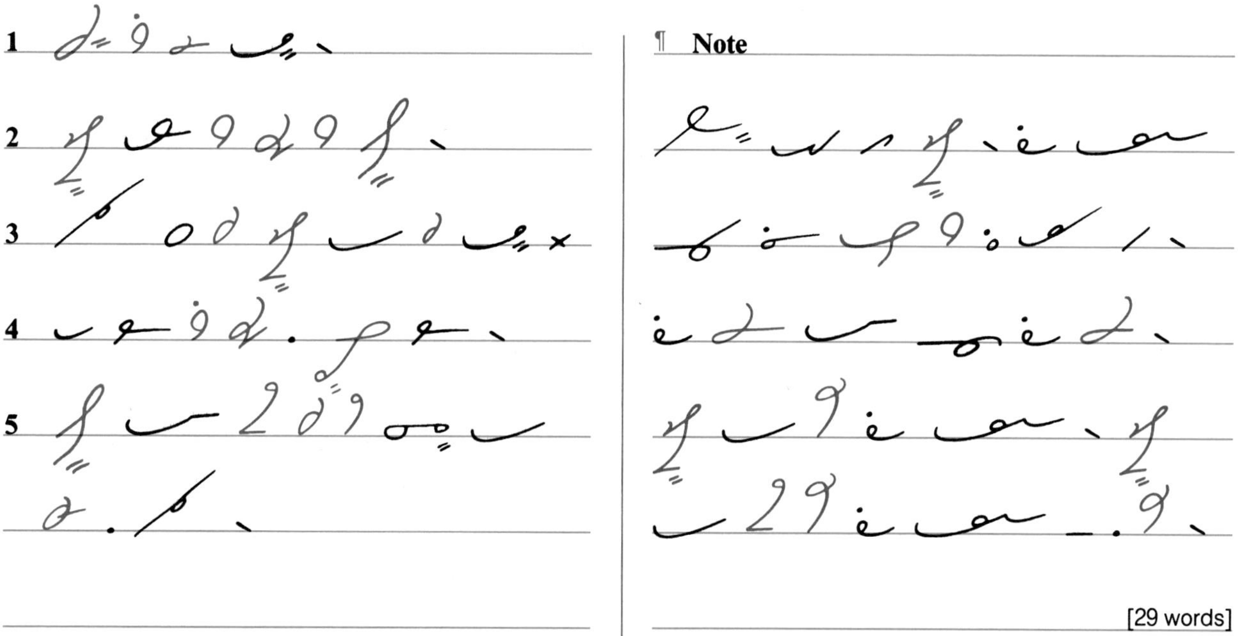

1

2

3

4

5

¶ **Note**

[29 words]

Key:
1 Fay has seen Lee.
2 Steven ran as fast as Dave.
3 Did I say Steven will see Lee?
4 Our team has faced a Navy team.
5 Dave will not even say if Amy will sign a deed.

Another way in which Gregg Shorthand provides writing speed is through several *blends* of symbols that frequently occur together. Writing speed is gained by eliminating the pen stop.

fr ∠ fl ∠

Examples: frame ∠ℯ fly ∠ℯ

Fr, Fl Words

frame ∠ℯ

free ∠

Fred ∠

fry ∠ℯ

afraid ℰℯ

fly ∠ℯ

flying ∠ℯ.

flight ∠ℯ

flown ∠

flame ∠ℯ

flat ∠ℯ

Fr, Fl Practice
5.3

1 (shorthand outlines)

2 (shorthand outlines)

(shorthand outlines)

3 (shorthand outlines)

4 (shorthand outlines)

5 (shorthand outlines)

¶ **Phone Message**

To: (shorthand outlines)

From: (shorthand outlines)

Date: (shorthand outlines)

Time: 12:15

(shorthand outlines)

(shorthand outlines)

(shorthand outlines)

(shorthand outlines)

(shorthand outlines)

[32 words]

You Write What You Hear

The *o* symbol that represents the long sound of *o* as in *home* also represents the short sound of *o* as in *Tom* and the soft sound of *o* as in *thought*.

own = O N	Ron = R O N	saw = S O
hot = H O T	brought = B R O T	stop = S T O P
taught = T O T	stone = S T O N	tall = T O L
home = H O M	job = J O B	Paul = P O L

SHORT AND SOFT SOUNDS OF O

The *o* symbol represents the short and soft sounds of *o*, no matter how the word is spelled in longhand.

Short and Soft O Words

on	hot	saw
law	Tom	taught
lot	small	all

Short and Soft O Practice
5.4

1

2

3

4

5 *[shorthand]*

¶ **Letter**

[shorthand lines]

[shorthand] [23 words]

Key:
1. I saw Tom at home.
2. He met Tom on a rainy day.
3. He saw a small tame deer.
4. I hear a lot of laughter in our home.
5. Tom taught in a small city.

Shorthand notebooks are divided into two columns to gain writing speed.

Communication Skill Builder

Similar Words: sight, site, cite

sight: having to do with seeing; vision
site: a place; a location
cite: (v.) to make reference to; to quote

More light may harm her *sight*.

Dale has a home on a small *site*.

I will *cite* a name in my farm deed.

Reading and Writing Practice

5.5 Agenda for Yearbook Staff Meeting

(shorthand outlines)

1 hurt   2 if   3 Decide

(shorthand outlines)   [28 words]

5.6 "To Do" List

(shorthand outlines)

[23 words]

4 I will   5 Reno   6 afraid

LESSON

NEW IN LESSON 6

- Word beginning *in-*
- Symbols for the sounds of *oo*, *k*, and *g*
- Symbols for the sounds of *w*, *sw*, and *wh* at the beginning of words
- Differentiating between sound-alike words *to*, *too*, *two* and *knew*, *new*

WORD BEGINNING IN-

The brief form *in* is also used as a word beginning, as in *indeed*.

Example: indeed

In- Words

indeed

investing

inviting

invest

invite

inside

In- Practice
6.1

1

2

3

4 [shorthand symbols]

5 [shorthand symbols]

¶ **Phone Message**

To: [shorthand symbols]

From: [shorthand symbols]

Date: [shorthand] _13_

Time: _11:30_

[shorthand symbols]

[shorthand symbols]

[shorthand symbols] [15 words]

Key: 1 I will invest in a motor home.
2 If Fred arrives, invite him in.
3 Rain has made our river high indeed.
4 Light a fire inside our stove.
5 Dave will invite him in an hour.

SOUNDS OF OO, K, G

The symbols for *oo*, *k*, and *g* are forward "over" curves differentiated by length.

oo ⌒ k ⌒ g ⌒

Sound of OO

The symbol for the sound of *oo* as in *who* is a tiny upward hook. ⌒

Example: who [shorthand]

OO Words

who [shorthand]	noon [shorthand]	suit [shorthand]
do [shorthand]	move [shorthand]	food [shorthand]
duty [shorthand]	moved [shorthand]	room [shorthand]
to, too, two [shorthand]	whom [shorthand]	fruit [shorthand]
knew, new [shorthand]	Sue [shorthand]	flew [shorthand]

Sound of K

The symbol for the sound of *k* as in *came* is a short over curve written from left to right across the writing line.

Example: came

K Words

came	make	take
car, care	making	crate ■
like	Mike	clearing ■
liked	cake	clean ■

■ Writing Tip: Curves of the same length, like *kr*, are written as somewhat flat reverse curves. Curves of unequal length, like *kl*, have an exaggerated joining to ensure readability.

kr   kl

Sound of G

The symbol for the sound of *g* as in *go* is a long over curve written from left to right across the writing line.

Example: go

G Words

go	guide	again
goal	gray ■	eager ■
gain	great ■	regret ■
game	grade ■	legal ■
gave	green ■	Gary
give	greet ■	Greg ■

■ Writing Tip: Curves of the same length, like *gl*, are written as somewhat flat reverse curves. Curves of unequal length, like *gr*, have an exaggerated joining to ensure readability.

gl   gr

OO, K, G Practice

6.2

1 *(shorthand outline)*

2 *(shorthand outline)*

3 *(shorthand outline)*

4 *(shorthand outline)*

5 *(shorthand outline)*

¶ **Note**

(shorthand outlines)

[33 words]

Key:
1 Gary will move to Reno.
2 Sue will clean her car.
3 I may move to a new room.
4 Mike may make a cake.
5 Greg will take care of our legal file.

Learning shorthand is an opportunity to acquire a personal and professional life skill.

At the beginning of words, the sound of *w* is represented by the *oo hook*, as in the word *we*. The sound of *sw* at the beginning of a word is written *s oo*, as in *sweet*. The *wh* sound at the beginning of words, such as in *why*, is represented by the *oo hook*. ⌒

Examples: we ∂   sweet ⅔   why ∂

W, Sw, Wh Words

we	∂	white	⅄	waiting	⅄˙
week	∂⌐	while	⊋	waste	⅄
weeks	∂⌐⌐	way	∂	sweet	⅄
why	∂	wait	⅄	swell	⅛

W, Sw, Wh Practice
6.3

[32 words]

¶ **Note**

Communication Skill Builder

Similar Words: to, too, two

to: (prep.) toward

too: (adv.) excessive; also

two: a number

Give my letter *to* Fay.

The room stayed *too* cool.

Lee gave me a gift *too*.

Fred has *two* free airline flights.

Similar Words: knew, new

knew: had prior knowledge

new: not having existed before

We *knew* our trailer tire might go flat.

I will need a *new* trailer tire.

6.4   List of Points for Phone Call

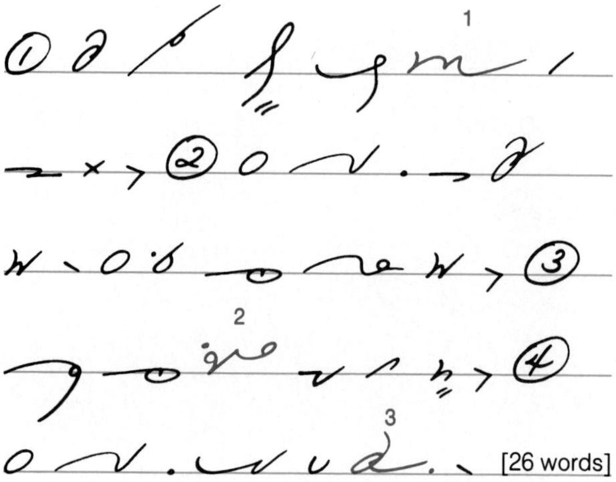

[shorthand outlines] [26 words]

6.5   Army-Navy Game

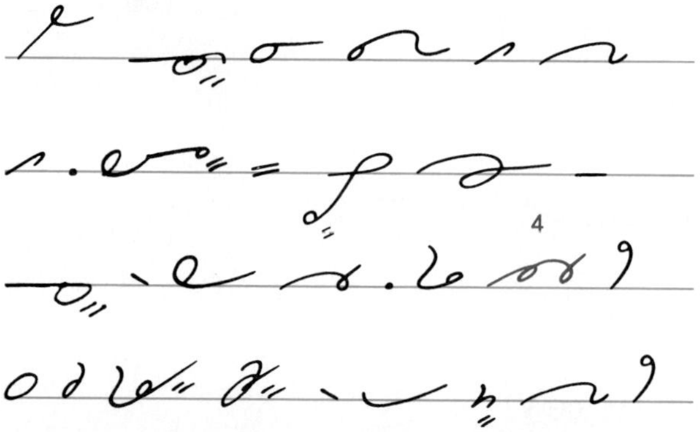

[shorthand outlines]

1 school   2 history   3 filing   4 ticket

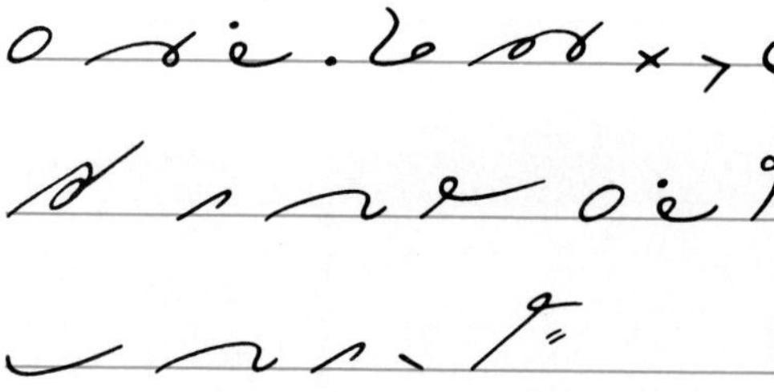

[shorthand outlines] [40 words]

6.6   Memo

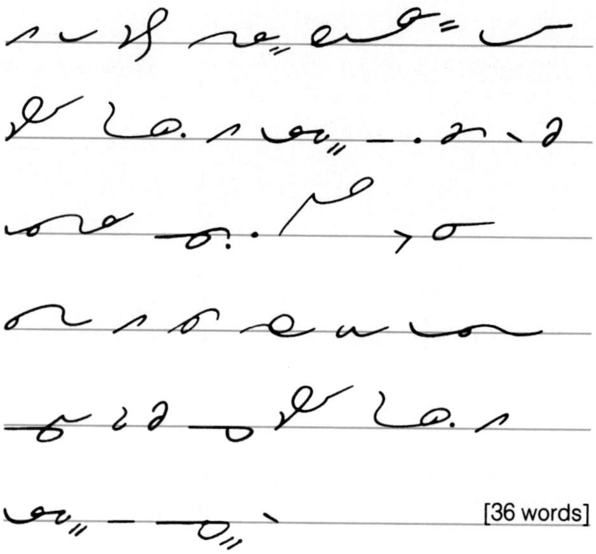

[shorthand outlines] [36 words]

LESSON 7

NEW IN LESSON 7

- **Another way of writing *s***
- **Symbols for the sounds of *p* and *b***
- **Symbol *oo* for the short and soft sounds of *oo***
- **Intelligent notetaking**

SOUNDS OF S, P, B

The symbols for *left s* and for *p* and *b* are *downward* left curves differentiated by length.

left s   *p*   b

Left S

The *left s* is a mirror image of the *comma s*. There are two symbols for *s* so that this frequent letter may always join curves in the same direction as the curve and so that it may join straight strokes with a sharp angle. Joining patterns will become clear through reading practice.

Example: needs

Left S Words

needs	writes	names
sales	nice	seems
leads	days	desk, disk

leasing _____   raised _____   increase _____

list, least _____   readers _____   most _____

Sound of P

The symbol for the sound of *p* as in *pay* is a medium-size downward left curve.

Example: pay

P Words

pay _____   piece _____   hope _____

pays, pass _____   paper ■ _____   opens _____

please ■ _____   people ■ _____   despite _____

place ■ _____   price, prize ■ _____   Paul _____

space _____   post _____   April _____

■ Writing Tip: The *p* symbol joins to the *l* and *r* symbols in a single curve.

Example: purple

Sound of B

The symbol for the sound of *b* as in *base* is a long downward left curve.

Example: base

B Words

base _____   beats _____   blame ■ _____

based _____   beds _____   bright ■ _____

best _____   better _____   brief ■ _____

buy _____   big _____   bought, boat _____

bay _____   label ■ _____   neighbor ■ _____

■ Writing Tip: The *b* symbol joins to the *l* and *r* symbols in a single curve.

Example: bright label

Left S, P, B Practice

7.1

1 [shorthand outline]

2 [shorthand outline]

3 [shorthand outline]

4 [shorthand outline]

5 [shorthand outline]

¶ **Note to a Sales Manager**

[shorthand outlines]

[49 words]

Key:
1 My neighbor may buy my boat.
2 Most people hope to please.
3 Please place a piece of paper on my desk.

4 It pays most of our readers to lease floor space.
5 Our sale price beats our best list price.

SHORT AND SOFT SOUNDS OF OO

The *oo* hook that represents the sound of *oo* as in *too* also represents the short sound of *u* as in *up* and the soft sound of *oo* as in *book*. [shorthand]

Examples: up [shorthand] book [shorthand]

Short and Soft OO Words

up [shorthand] does [shorthand] must [shorthand]

number [shorthand] enough [shorthand] us ■ [shorthand]

■ *Us* is written *oo s* in a single pen motion.

book 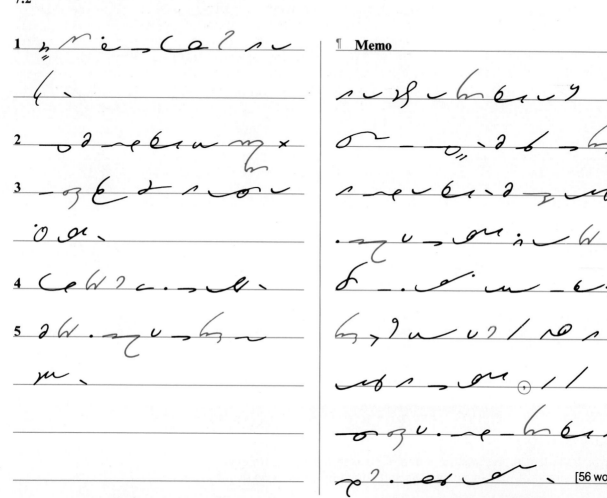   cookbook   pull

books   foot   took

cook   put

Short and Soft OO Practice
7.2

¶ **Memo**

[56 words]

Key:
1. Sue took her new plan up to our boss.
2. May we increase sales of our cookbook?
3. Not enough people seem to like our high rates.
4. Please put us on a new list.
5. We put a number of new books in our store.

Intelligent Notetaking

One of the most valuable uses for shorthand is the taking of intelligent notes. The person who knows shorthand and has good listening habits has a tremendous advantage in terms of personal efficiency. To the student, taking notes in shorthand means that all the key points of a lecture will be recorded in class notes for later study. To the secretary, taking notes in shorthand means that all the elements of a list of instructions will be retained the first time the executive gives those instructions, which in turn will avoid mistakes and embarrassment later on. To the executive, taking notes in shorthand means that once a business meeting has been concluded, details of agreements will be remembered and commitments met.

Whether you are taking notes as a student, a secretary, or an executive, shorthand enables you to record all the pertinent information.

Reading and Writing Practice

7.3 Sales Letter

[39 words]

1 copy   2 book

7.4 Notes From a Meeting

[51 words]

3 Dallas

LESSON 8

NEW IN LESSON 8

- **Eight brief forms**
- **Brief-form phrases**
- **Differentiating between similar words *it is* and *its***

BRIEF FORMS

be, by   good   Mr.

can   have   you, your

for   is, his

Brief-Form Derivatives

form   forgive   because

forms   afford   beside

inform   being   before

force   believe   having

forced   became   goods

forget   began   cannot

Brief-Form Practice

8.1

1 *[shorthand outlines]*

2 *[shorthand outlines]*

3 *[shorthand outlines]*

4 *[shorthand outlines]*

5 *[shorthand outlines]*

¶ **Travel Plans**

[shorthand outlines]

[38 words]

Key:
1 Mr. Lee believes he can sell his goods for a good price.
2 Mr. Lee cannot forget his trip.
3 Tom can go to Dallas before May.
4 Mr. Baker believes in having a good sales force.
5 Please call me before 10 if Dave cannot afford to buy goods.

BRIEF-FORM PHRASES

The new brief forms in this lesson, together with those in Lesson 4, make possible a large number of high-speed phrases—so many that they cannot all be used in this lesson. The phrases presented here, along with additional similar phrases, will be used in the following lessons.

You, Your Phrases

of you, of your	you are	you have
for you, for your	you are not	you have not

Will Phrases

I will be	you will not	he will ■
I will not be	you will be	he will be ■
I will have	you will not be	we will ■
you will	you will have	we will be ■

Would Phrases

I would be	you would be	you would not have
I would not be	you would not be	we would ■
you would	you would have	we would not ■

■ Contains a theory word and brief form(s).

Can Phrases

I can	can have	you can be
I can be	you can have	can you
I cannot	you can	we can
I cannot be	you cannot	we cannot

Additional Phrases

it is	by you, by your	have not
for our	I have	I have not

Phrase Practice
8.2

[shorthand characters]

1

2

3

4

5

¶ **Note**

[shorthand characters]

[52 words]

Communication Skill Builder

Similar Words: it is, its

it is: shorthand outline for this phrase is identical with outline for the word *its*

its: possessive meaning "belonging to it"

It is a nice, bright day.

Our plane is flying off *its* course.

Students learning shorthand can be bilingual secretaries and assistants.

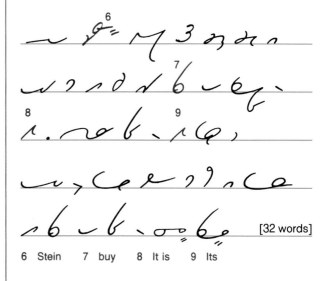

8.3 Changing Jobs

[57 words]

8.4 Personal Note

[32 words]

1 Carol   2 White   3 salary   4 believe
5 smaller

6 Stein   7 buy   8 It is   9 Its

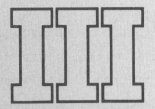

U N I T

III

LESSON 9

NEW IN LESSON 9

- Phrases containing theory words and brief forms
- Symbol for the sound of *th*
- Symbols for the sounds of *sh*, *ch*, and *j*
- Transcribing dates within sentences

THEORY AND BRIEF-FORM PHRASES

A large number of high-speed phrases are possible by combining a few simple theory words with the brief forms already learned.

I know	if you can	do not
we know ■	if you cannot	I do not
as you, as your	I need	we do ■
as you know	we need ■	do you
on our	we are	do you know
if you, if your	we are not	to you, to your
if you have	we have	to take ■
if you are	we have not	for me
if you will	I do	for my

■ This phrase does not contain a brief form.

54 ■■■ LESSON 9

Will and Would Phrases

we will have _(shorthand outline)_   we will not be _(shorthand outline)_   we would not have _(shorthand outline)_

we will not _(shorthand outline)_   we would have _(shorthand outline)_   would not be _(shorthand outline)_

we will not have _(shorthand outline)_   we would be _(shorthand outline)_   we would not be _(shorthand outline)_

May, Might Phrases

I may _(shorthand outline)_   we may be _(shorthand outline)_   we might have _(shorthand outline)_

we may _(shorthand outline)_   I might _(shorthand outline)_   we might be _(shorthand outline)_

I may have _(shorthand outline)_   I might be _(shorthand outline)_   you might be _(shorthand outline)_

I may be _(shorthand outline)_   we might _(shorthand outline)_   you might have _(shorthand outline)_

Phrase Practice
9.1

1 _(shorthand outline)_

2 _(shorthand outline)_

3 _(shorthand outline)_

4 _(shorthand outline)_

5 _(shorthand outline)_

¶ **List of Points to Discuss With the Boss**

① _(shorthand outline)_

② _(shorthand outline)_

③ _(shorthand outline)_

[16 words]

Key: 1 We will be flying to Reno in May.
2 We cannot see people in our rooms.
3 Do you have a legal problem for our staff?

4 We will not be in our home, so we will have our heat off.
5 We are afraid we cannot be of help to you.

SOUND OF TH

The sound of *th* as in *booth* is written with an *upward* sloping short curve, much like a curved *t* symbol. This symbol is called *ith*.

Example: booth

Th Words

booth   math   Ruth

these   Smith   smooth

then, thin   Beth   truth

thick   Keith   faith

Th Practice
9.2

1

2

3

4

5

¶ **Personal Note**

(shorthand outlines) [29 words]

Key: 1 Beth took these notes in her math class.
2 Our sales staff has faith in our math book.
3 Keith has Mr. Smith for math.
4 Ruth will read her book, then go to class.
5 Mr. Smith writes in thin, smooth lines.

SOUNDS OF SH, CH, J

The symbols for *sh*, *ch*, and *j* are *downward* straight symbols differentiated by length.

sh / ch / j /

Sound of Sh

The sound of *sh* as in *share* is represented by a short downward straight symbol called *ish*. /

Example: share *(outline)*

Sh Words

share *(outline)*	show *(outline)*	issued *(outline)*
shape *(outline)*	showed *(outline)*	sure *(outline)*
she *(outline)*	issue *(outline)*	assure *(outline)*

Sound of Ch

The sound of *ch* as in *chair* is represented by a medium-size downward straight symbol called *chay*.

chay /

Example: chair *(outline)*

Ch Words

chair	chapter	search
check	each	French
checked	teach	March
church	reach	attach

You Write What You Hear

The letter *g* has two sounds in English. For the hard sound of *g* as in *go*, you write the *g* symbol in shorthand. For the soft sound of *g* as in *age*, you write the *j* symbol. Here are a few more examples of the *j* symbol for the soft sound of *g*.

page = P A J
change = ch A N J

changed = ch A N J D
large = L A R J

charge = ch A R J
college = K O L E J

Sound of J

The sound of *j* as in *age* is represented by a long downward straight symbol called *j*.

j

Example: age

J Words

age	job	urge
page	jobs	James
charge	large	June
charged	George	July
change	major	college

Sh, Ch, J Practice
9.3

1 *[shorthand]*

2 *[shorthand]*

¶ **Evening Class**

[shorthand]

[27 words]

Key:
1 Janet showed me her new chair.
2 James changed jobs in search of higher pay.
3 She teaches in a large college.
4 Check each page of our math papers.
5 June showed up late each day for her college class.

Dates Within Sentences

In business communications it is common practice for the month to precede the day. In expressing dates this way, it is not appropriate to use *th*, *st*, or *d*, and no punctuation is required.

[shorthand]

Call me on *July 8* if you can.

If for some reason the day precedes the month, then it is appropriate to use *th*, *st*, or *d* in the transcript. For the sake of writing speed, the *th*, *st*, or *d* is not written in shorthand.

[shorthand]

Our *17th of March* due date will be met.

9.4 French Teacher

[shorthand text]

[51 words]

1 urge   2 Page   3 practice   4 Briggs

9.5 Personal Note

[shorthand text]

[45 words]

5 Ruth   6 Great Falls   7 Beth

An attorney with shorthand skills can save valuable time by writing research notes in shorthand.

LESSON 10

NEW IN LESSON 10

- **Eight brief forms**
- **Phrases containing theory words and brief forms**
- **Word ending *-ly***
- **Tips on taking dictation**

BRIEF FORMS

but _____   that _____   this _____

could _____   the _____   which _____

should _____   them _____

Brief-Form Practice
10.1

(shorthand outlines)

Key: 1 I had a delay in writing this paper.
2 Ann forgot which book is mine.
3 The school is small, but the class is good.
4 Our team should beat them in football.
5 Did you know that Jean could fly a plane?

[53 words]

THEORY AND BRIEF-FORM PHRASES

The and This Phrases

in the	by the	is this
on the	to the	this is
is the	for the	this is the
in this	as the	this will
on this	if the	this will be
of the	for this	

Could and Should Phrases

I could	I could not	should not be
could not	should be	should have

Additional Phrases

of these _____ is in, is not _____ that are _____

of them _____ in which _____ that will _____

for that _____ which is _____ did not _____

Phrase Practice
10.2

1

2

3

4

5

¶ **Business Letter**

[45 words]

Key:

1 By the way, this will be the first test of our new factory.

2 You have the same chance as the best member of the class.

3 This is the first day of our new French course.

4 Will the airline increase the number of flights to the East?

5 Is this the paper that you will give to the teacher?

The word ending -ly (which sounds like "lee") as in *only* is written with the *e* circle. ρ

Example: only $\sim_o$

-ly Words

only $\sim_o$	sincerely	highly
likely	weekly	mostly
early	clearly	greatly
properly	daily	

But: When the *l* is double, both the *l* and the *ly* are written.

finally   really   totally

-ly Practice
10.3

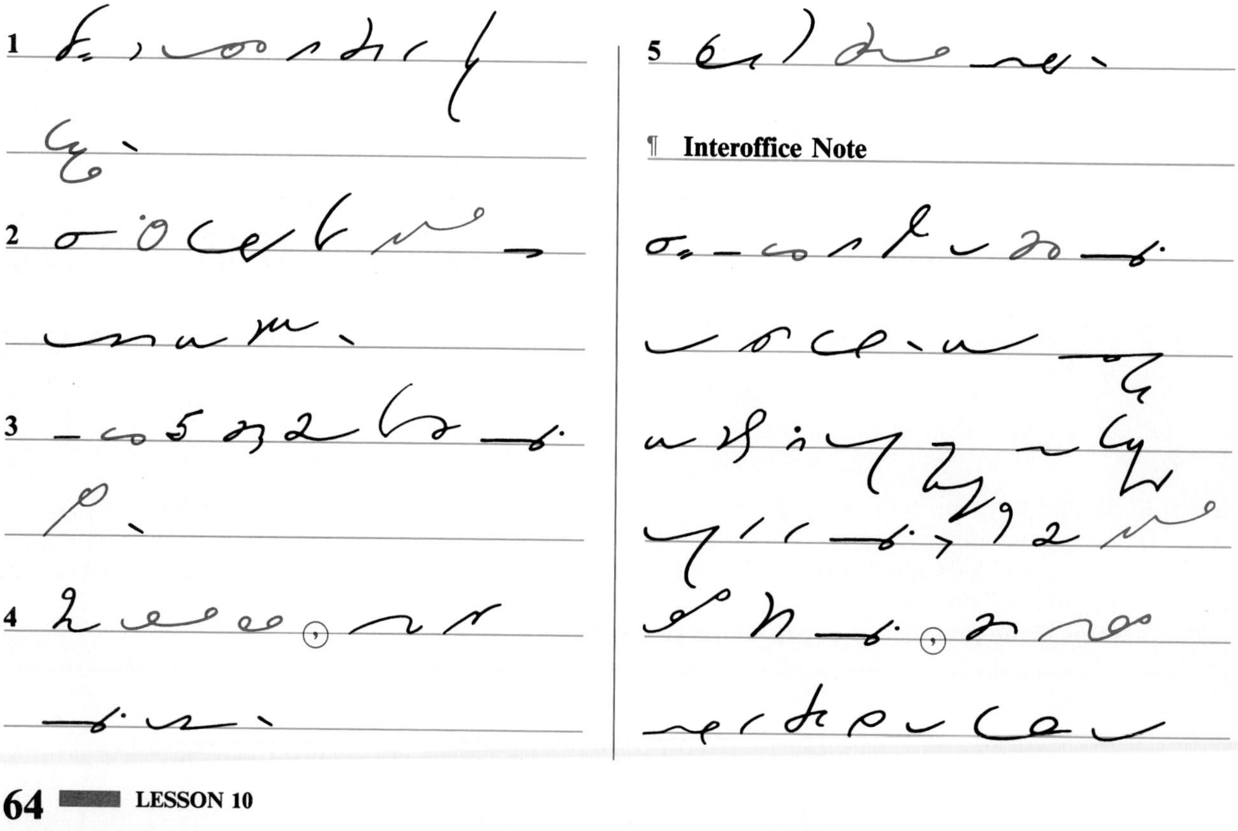

1

2

3

4

5

¶ **Interoffice Note**

[61 words]

Key:
1 Beth is likely to finish the job properly.
2 I am highly pleased by the totally new look of our store.
3 In only five weeks we will begin meeting daily.
4 If you are really early, go to the meeting room.
5 Sales have finally increased.

Taking Dictation

While shorthand has many personal and professional uses, taking dictation is what comes to mind when most people think of shorthand. Shorthand dictation is one of four basic ways executives may *input* to the information cycle.

Here are a few tips in taking dictation:

Write fluently. Shorthand must be practiced to the point where outlines can be "thrown" on the paper. Theoretical accuracy and proper writing proportions are important, but it is more important to get the work *done*.

Write something. When you do not know the outline for a word that is being dictated, write something. You may write the first sound of the word, the most distinctive sound of the word, or an outline that you consider to be a good guess.

Do not give up. If the dictation is so fast that you get too far behind, you should leave a gap in the notes and pick up what the dictator is currently saying. As soon as the dictation is completed, you should fill in the gap on the basis of memory and context clues.

Watch proportion. From the very start, you should concentrate on keeping the tiny characters tiny—specifically *e*, *n*, *t*, *s*, and *ish*. At very high speeds straight strokes tend to curve a bit. Therefore, it is very important that the symbols which are supposed to be curved are curved deeply.

10.4 Travel Note

[shorthand outlines] [28 words]

10.5 Notes About Accident

[shorthand outlines]

[shorthand outlines] [58 words]

1 travel   2 members   3 of them   4 airline
5 easy   6 of our

7 owns   8 ticket   9 too   10 limit
11 wrecked

LESSON

11

NEW IN LESSON 11

- **Word endings *-tion*, *cient*, and *ciency***
- **Shorthand symbols for numbers**
- **Phrases containing *been*, *able*, and *to***
- **Transcription of numbers**

WORD ENDINGS -TION, -CIENT, -CIENCY

The word ending *-tion*, pronounced *shun* as in *nation*, is represented by the *ish* symbol.

The word ending *-cient*, pronounced *-shunt* as in *proficient*, is written *ish, t*.

The word ending *-ciency*, pronounced *shun see* as in *proficiency*, is written *ish, s, e*.

Examples: nation _ proficient _ proficiency _

-tion Words

nation _

national _

occasion _

occasionally ■ _

operation _

cooperation _

corporation _

promotion _

section _

collection _

selection _

location _

decision _

vacation _

possession, position _

■ The sounds of *l* and *ly* are heard in the word *occasionally*.

-cient and -ciency Words

proficient _(shorthand)_   efficiently _(shorthand)_   patiently _(shorthand)_

proficiency _(shorthand)_   efficiency _(shorthand)_   sufficient _(shorthand)_

efficient _(shorthand)_   patient _(shorthand)_   sufficiently _(shorthand)_

-tion, -cient, -ciency Practice
11.1

1 _(shorthand outlines)_

2 _(shorthand outlines)_

3 _(shorthand outlines)_

4 _(shorthand outlines)_

5 _(shorthand outlines)_

¶ **Vacation Photos**

(shorthand outlines)

[76 words]

Key:
1 I made the decision to accept the position.
2 Occasionally, we do receive promotion on the art collection.
3 The National Corporation will move to a new location.
4 Can the patient have the operation?
5 Typing proficiency makes her an efficient staff member.

NUMBER EXPRESSIONS

The numerical expressions *hundred*, *thousand*, *million*, and *dollars* are given special shorthand abbreviations which greatly increase writing speed.

Hundred is written with the *n* symbol.

Thousand is written with the *over th* symbol.

Hundred thousand is written with the *n* and *th* symbols.

Million is written with the *m* symbol.

Dollars is written with the *d* symbol.

Hundred dollars is written with the *n* and *d* symbols.

Thousand dollars is written with the *th* and *d* symbols.

Hundred thousand dollars is written with the *n*, *th*, and *d* symbols.

Million dollars is written with the *m* and *d* symbols.

An amount of money containing both dollars and cents is represented by writing the dollar figure in normal-size handwriting and the cents as smaller raised figures.

$2.50

Number Examples

These expressions often occur in combinations.

200 ■

5,000 ■

200,000 ■

5 million ■

$8

$600 ■

$7,000 ■

$800,000 ■

$10 million ■

$4.50

a dollar

a million ■

■ The *n* for *hundred* and the *over th* for *thousand* are placed underneath the figure. The *m* for *million* is written beside the figure.

Number Practice
11.2

1 *[shorthand notation with 5]*

2 *[shorthand notation with 8]*

3 *[shorthand notation]*

4 *[shorthand notation with 9]*

5 *[shorthand notation]*

7^{50}

¶ **Art Collection**

[shorthand notation]

[shorthand notation with 10]

[shorthand notation]

[shorthand notation with 3]

[shorthand notation with 30]

[shorthand notation] [59 words]

Key: 1 Only 500 people bought a ticket.
2 Fred paid a dollar for my book.
3 The check is for $7,000.

4 His nation has only 900,000 people.
5 Beth will sell a book for $7.50.

Legal secretaries are often called upon to witness legal documents.

BEEN, ABLE, TO PHRASES

In phrases the *b* symbol may represent *been*, while the *a* symbol may represent *able*. Twenty-four such phrases are possible. A representative sample follows.

has been

you have been

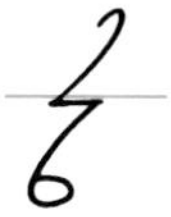

we have not been able

has been able

you have not been able

I have not been able

it has been

we have not been

you will be able

In two very common phrases the *t* symbol represents the word *to*.

to have

to be

Phrase Practice
11.3

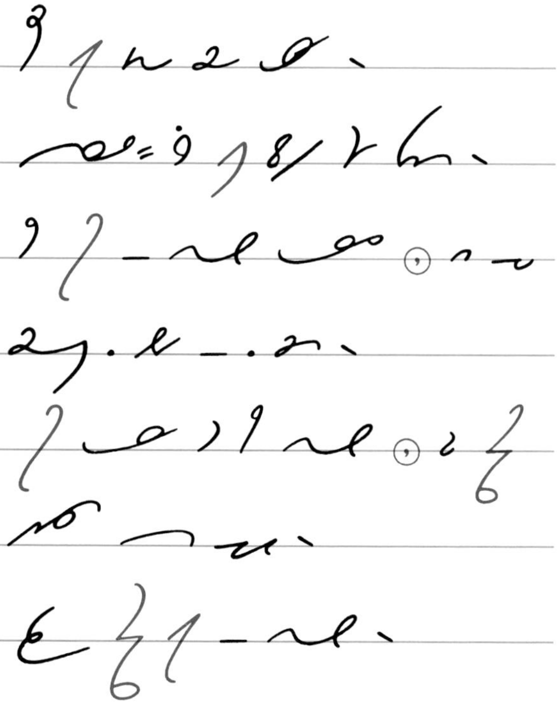

¶ **French Grade**

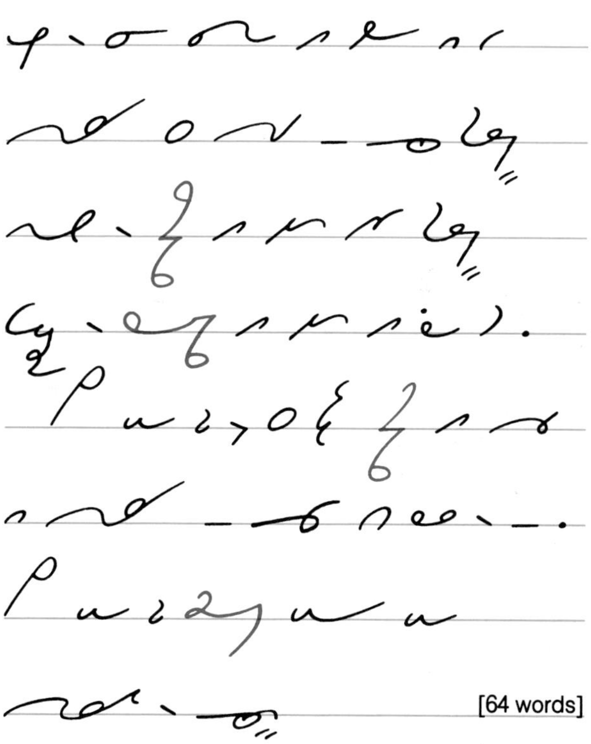

[64 words]

Key: 1 We have to be sure we are right.
2 Gary has to have $8 for the book.
3 If you have been in class lately, you know we will have a test in a week.
4 You have been late for each class, so you have not been able to take good notes.
5 People have not been able to be in class.

Transcription of Numbers

The basic rule of number expression is to spell out the numbers *one* through *ten* and to use numerals for numbers above *ten*.

Only *five* days of the vacation remain.

We need *17* books for class.

Numerals are used to express exact amounts of money. A decimal point and zeroes are not used with whole-dollar amounts.

Jean gave me *$10* for the tickets.

The sale price is only *$4.95*.

When transcribing, use a comma to express *thousand* and *thousand dollars*.

We need *3,000* books.

The price of the collection is *$12,000*.

When transcribing *million* and *million dollars*, replace the commas and ciphers with the word *million*.

[shorthand outline]

Our company has *5 million* people across the nation.

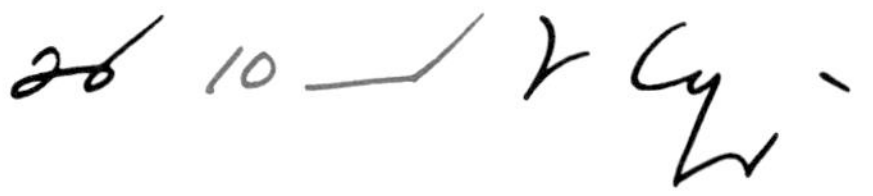

[shorthand outline]

We need *$10 million* for the project.

11.4 Collection Letter

[shorthand outline]

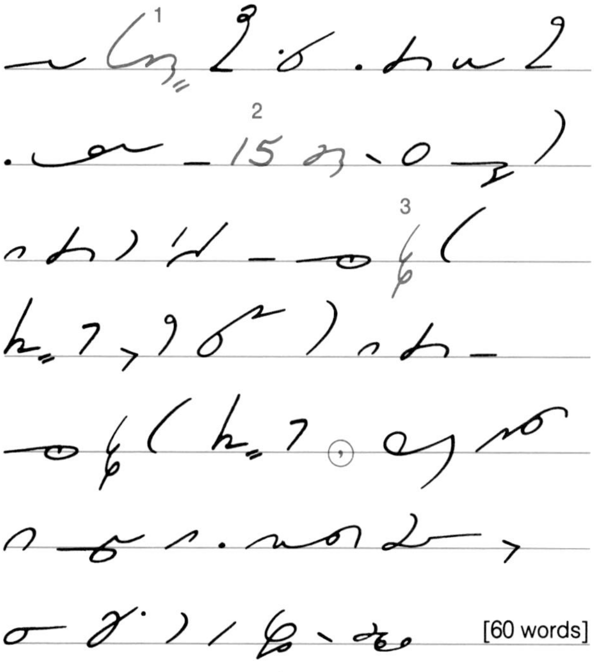

[60 words]

1 Brooks 2 15 weeks 3 possession

11.5 News Reporter's Notes

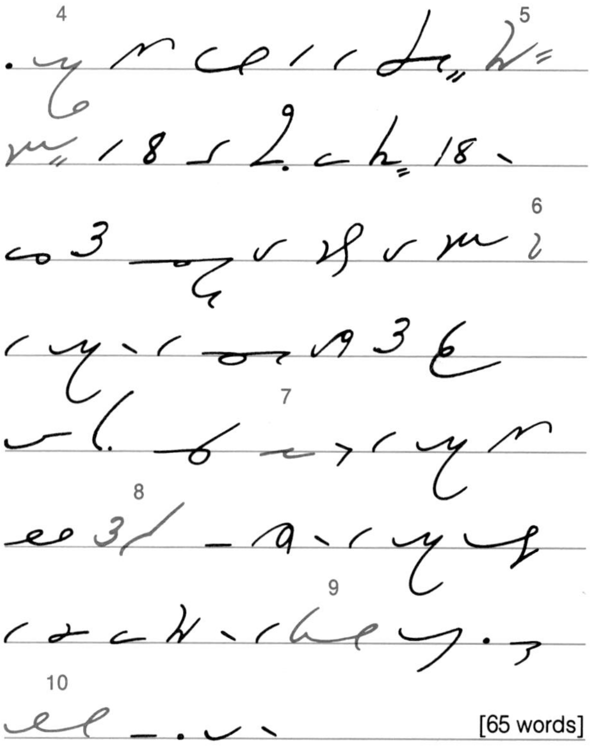

[shorthand outline]

[65 words]

4 robbery 5 Food Store 6 saw 7 known
8 $3,000 9 police 10 release

L E S S O N
12

NEW IN LESSON 12

- **Eight brief forms**
- **Brief-form phrases**
- **Symbols for the sounds of *tem* and *dem***
- **Salutations and complimentary closings**
- **Transcription tips**

BRIEF FORMS

about _____   glad _____   when _____

after _____   Mrs. _____   with _____

from _____   street _____

Brief-Form Derivatives

afternoon _____   within ■ _____   gladly _____

■ Combining the brief form *with* and *in* would produce an outline that would be difficult to read; therefore an extra *e* is added for readability.

Brief-Form Phrases

I am glad _____   about you, about your _____   with our _____

be glad _____   about this _____   from our _____

I will be glad _____   about them _____   from the _____

after the _____   with you, with your _____   from you, from your _____

about the _____   with the _____   when the _____

Brief-Form Practice

12.1

1 [shorthand outlines]

2 [shorthand outlines]

3 [shorthand outlines]

4 [shorthand outlines]

5 [shorthand outlines]

¶ **Staff Meeting**

[shorthand outlines]

[shorthand outlines] = 14.

[shorthand outlines]

[shorthand outlines]

[shorthand outlines]

[shorthand outlines]

[shorthand outlines]

[57 words]

Key:
1 I am glad to have a letter from Mrs. Bates.
2 After all these weeks, it is good to hear from Mr. Jones.
3 I will not be able to talk with you about the answers to the test.
4 Please get the facts about the game from the team.
5 I have not had a call from you.

SOUNDS OF TEM, DEM

The sounds of *tem* as in *item* and *dem* as in *seldom* are represented by a blend of *d* and *m*.

d ╱ + m ── = tem, dem ╭

Examples: item [shorthand]   seldom [shorthand]

Tem Words

item

items

temper

temporary

tomorrow

attempt

attempting

estimate

automobile

customer

customers

accustom

Dem Words

seldom

medium

freedom

Adams

Dempsey

damage

damages

demonstrate

demonstration

Tem, Dem Practice
12.2

1

2

3

4

5

¶ **Damage Estimate**

350

[60 words]

Key: 1 Dean lost his temper because of the damage to his car.

2 Our customers seldom arrive at our store by automobile.

3 Ann will attempt to have a cost estimate for us tomorrow.

4 Each item for sale in our store is in the medium price range.

5 We need an estimate for the items.

SALUTATIONS AND COMPLIMENTARY CLOSINGS

Dear Mr. _____

Dear Mrs. _____

Dear Miss _____

Dear Sir _____

Dear Madam _____

Very truly yours _____

Yours very truly _____

Cordially yours _____

Shorthand skill is a valuable asset to paralegal assistants and secretaries in the legal office.

Salutation and Complimentary Closing Practice
12.3

Key:
1. Dear Mr. Jones I will mail you the estimate for the damage. Very truly yours
2. Dear Mrs. Black We are glad to learn about the new items. Cordially yours
3. Dear Madam The demonstration will be on April 15. Yours very truly
4. Dear Sir We have two new staff members. Very truly yours
5. Dear Miss Dempsey We are pleased to have you as a customer. Cordially yours

Transcription Tips

When writing shorthand outlines for the names of places, such as streets and avenues, you should include capitalization marks below the outlines.

Therefore, when transcribing the names of places, you will remember to capitalize them.

When transcribing salutations such as *Dear Sir* and *Dear Madam*, capitalize the first letter of each word. When transcribing salutations such as *Dear Mr.* and *Dear Mrs.,* the words *Dear, Mr.,* and *Mrs.* are capitalized. A period follows *Mr., Mrs.,* and *Ms.* When transcribing *Dear Miss, Miss* is capitalized but not followed by a period.

When transcribing a letter, it is customary to place a colon at the end of the salutation and to place a comma at the end of the complimentary closing. In order to promote writing speed, omit these marks of punctuation in your shorthand notes.

12.4 A Student's "To Do" List

[shorthand outlines] 10

① *[shorthand]* ② *[shorthand]* ③ *[shorthand]* ④ *[shorthand]* ⑤ *[shorthand]*

[45 words]

12.5 Store Opening

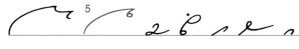

1 physics 2 news 3 helper 4 library
5 Dempsey

[shorthand outlines]

[75 words]

6 Mason City

U N I T

IV

LESSON 13

NEW IN LESSON 13

- **Word beginnings *con-* and *com-***
- **Second symbol for the sound of *th***
- **Word beginning *re-***
- **Using shorthand to compose rough drafts**

WORD BEGINNINGS CON-, COM-

The word beginnings *con-* as in *control* and *com-* as in *compare* are represented by the *k* symbol.

Examples: control   compare

Con- Words

control   conduct   concern

contract   consider   conference ■

contracts   consideration   conversation ■

■ When *k* is followed by an *f* or *v*, the outline is blended.

Com- Words

compare   complete   compile

comparing   completely   combine

complain   completion   combines

But: When *n* or *m* is double in *con-* or *com-* words, these word beginnings are represented by *kn* or *km*.

connect ⟿   committee ⟿   ac**comm**odate ■ ⟿

connection ⟿   commerce ⟿   ac**comm**odation ⟿

■ Transcription Alert.

Con-, Com- Practice
13.1

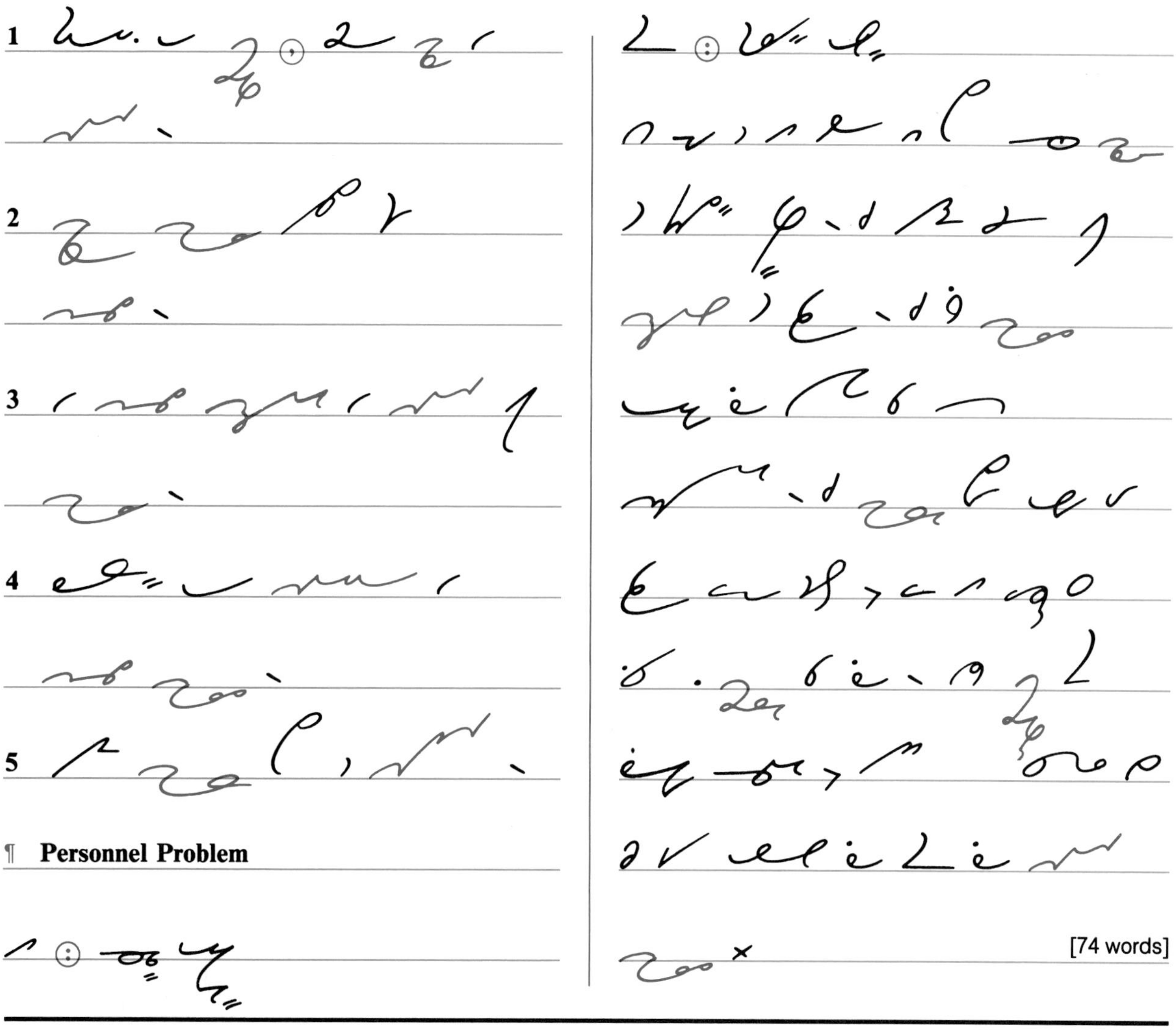

1

2

3

4

5

¶ **Personnel Problem**

[74 words]

Just as we have two *s* symbols to facilitate fluent joinings to other symbols, we have two *th* symbols for the same reason. The *th* you learned in Lesson 9 is called the *over ith*. The *under ith* is the mirror image of the *over ith*.

under ith ╱

Example: though ⟋

Under Ith Words

though	health	thorough
thought	healthy	both
those	clothes	growth
threw, through	clothing	wealth ∎

∎ Brief-form derivative.

Under Ith Practice
13.2

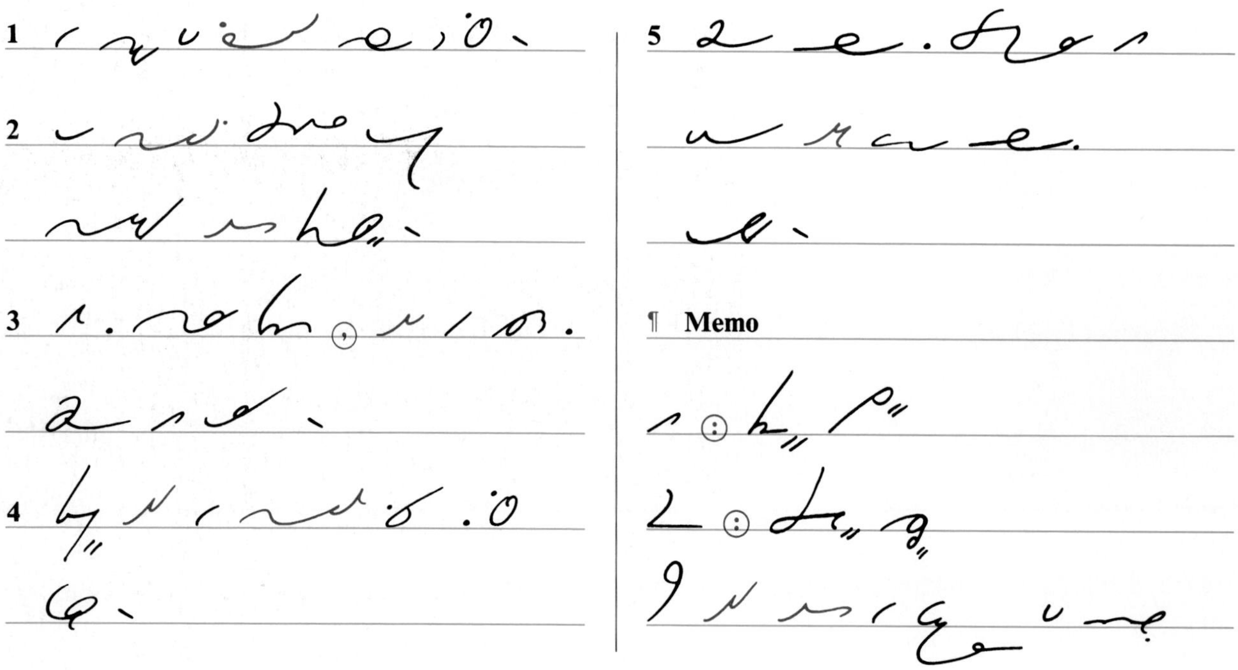

1

2

3

4

5

¶ **Memo**

(shorthand outlines) [49 words]

WORD BEGINNING RE-

The word beginning *re-* as in *receive* is represented by the *r* symbol. ⌣

Example: receive *(outline)*

Re- Words

receive *(outline)*	replies *(outline)*	refer *(outline)*
received *(outline)*	repair *(outline)*	referring *(outline)*
reason *(outline)*	replace *(outline)*	reference *(outline)*
reply *(outline)*	research *(outline)*	reject *(outline)*

But: Before a forward or upward stroke, *re-* is written *re.*

relate *(outline)*	remain *(outline)*	retire *(outline)*

Re- Practice
13.3

1 *(shorthand outline)*

2 *(shorthand outline)*

3 *(shorthand outline)*

4 *(shorthand outline)*

[Shorthand outlines]

5 [shorthand] ×

¶ **Reference Letter**

[shorthand outlines]

[53 words]

Using Shorthand to Compose Rough Drafts

Anyone who has ever completed a writing assignment knows that writing can be a difficult job. Much thought is required to formulate clear sentences and paragraphs. All too often those thoughts are fleeting. You might spend several minutes trying to mentally compose a smooth sentence, only to have the thoughts disappear during the slow, laborious process of writing them down in longhand. You could compose a rough draft by dictating to a tape recorder, but tape recorded thoughts are very difficult to review when you are trying to compose one sentence after another with grammatical precision, a certain progression of ideas, and a smooth style.

Shorthand, then, is the perfect medium for capturing those fleeting thoughts—those bursts of genius that you may never be able to create verbatim again. The rough draft in shorthand also provides the hard copy that you need for continual review in those instances when elements of grammar, logic, and style are critical.

13.4 Dictation Speed Letter

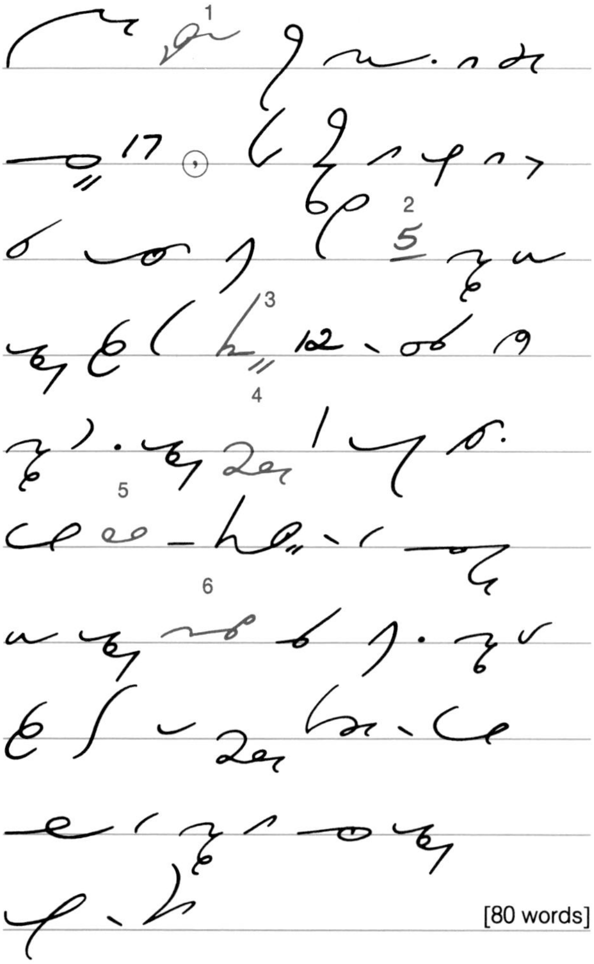

[80 words]

13.5 Car Leasing

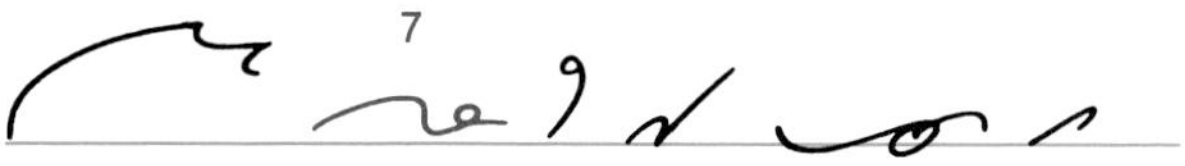

[93 words]

1 Steiner   2 500   3 June 12   4 conference
5 early   6 committee   7 Green

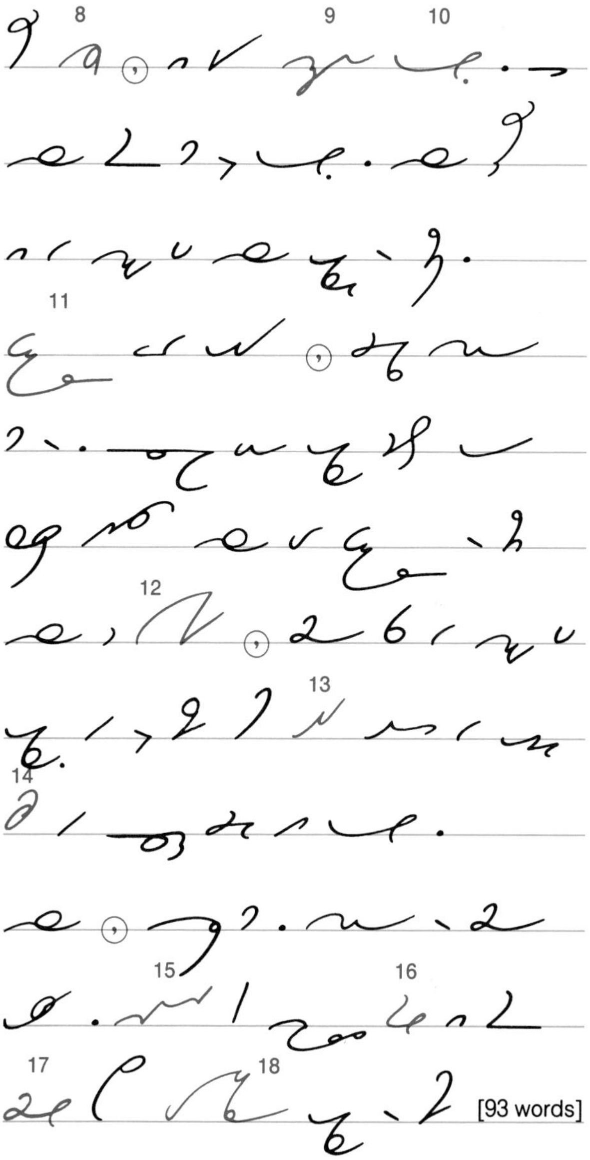

8 cash   9 consider   10 leasing   11 problem
12 damaged   13 thought   14 why   15 contract
16 frees   17 worries   18 automobile

LESSON

14

NEW IN LESSON 14

- **Eight brief forms**
- **Eliminated-word phrases**
- **Blend symbol for the sounds of *ted*, *ded*, and *dit***
- **Differentiating between *there* and *their***

BRIEF FORMS

doctor, Dr., during _⟋_

office _⟍_

one, won ■ _⟋_

there, their _⟋_

they _⌒_

was _ɤ_

where _Q_

yesterday _ɣ_

■ In shorthand, only the numbers *one* and *two* are written with shorthand symbols. All other numbers are written with arabic numerals.

Brief-Form Derivatives

doctors _⟋_

offices _⟍_

once _⟋_

Brief-Form Phrases

I was _ɡ_

it was _M_

there was _ᴌ_

there is _⟋_

there are _⟋_

there will _⟋_

they will _⌒_

they will be _⌒_

they are _⌒_

here is ■ _ė⟋_

here are ■ _ė⟍_

is there _⟍_

■ Contains theory word and brief form.

Brief-Form Practice
14.1

1 *(shorthand outline)*

2 *(shorthand outline)*

3 *(shorthand outline)*

4 *(shorthand outline)*

5 *(shorthand outline)*

¶ **Research Project**

(shorthand outlines)

15 × 8

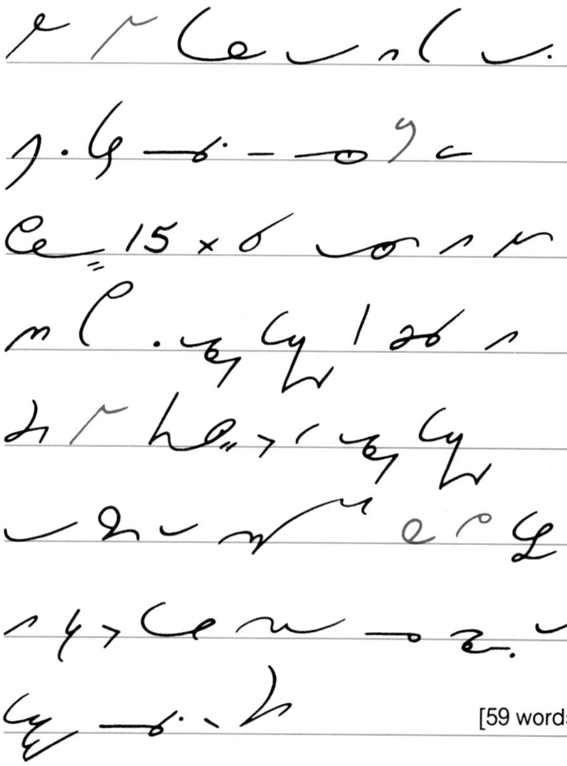

[59 words]

ELIMINATED-WORD PHRASES

In several common phrases the middle word is eliminated.

one of the *(shorthand outline)*

one of them *(shorthand outline)*

one of our *(shorthand outline)*

up to date *(shorthand outline)*

will you please *(shorthand outline)*

Phrase Practice
14.2

1 [shorthand outline]

2 [shorthand outline]

3 [shorthand outline]

[shorthand outline]

4 [shorthand outline]

5 [shorthand outline]

¶ **Memo**

[shorthand outlines]

[45 words]

SOUNDS OF TED, DED, DIT

The sounds of *ted* as in *drafted*, *ded* as in *needed*, and *dit* as in *credit* are represented by a blend of the *t* and *d* symbols.

t ∕ d ∕ ted ∕

Examples: drafted [outline] needed [outline] credit [outline]

Ted Words

drafted [outline]	listed [outline]	tested [outline]
started [outline]	rested [outline]	acted [outline]

accepted _(shorthand)_   today _(shorthand)_   studied _(shorthand)_

omitted ■ _(shorthand)_   steady, study _(shorthand)_

■ Transcription Alert.

Ded Words

needed _(shorthand)_   graded _(shorthand)_   deduct _(shorthand)_

added _(shorthand)_   dead _(shorthand)_   deduction _(shorthand)_

guided _(shorthand)_   deadline _(shorthand)_   provided _(shorthand)_

Dit Words

credit _(shorthand)_   audited ■ _(shorthand)_   editor _(shorthand)_

credited ■ _(shorthand)_   auditor _(shorthand)_   detail _(shorthand)_

audit _(shorthand)_   edit _(shorthand)_   debt _(shorthand)_

■ Note that the past tense _d_ joins the _dit_ with a jog.

Ted, Ded, Dit Practice
14.3

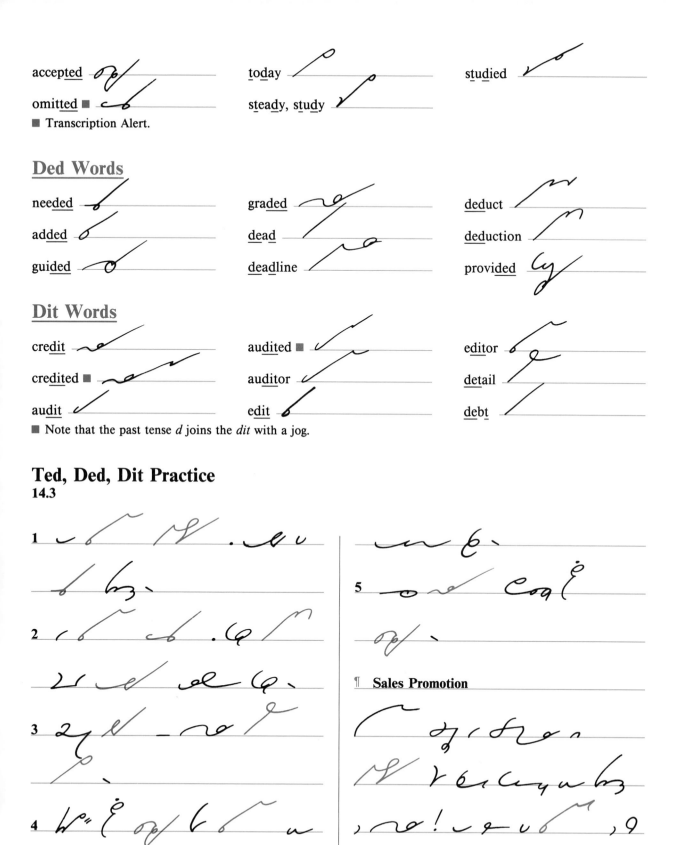

1 _(shorthand)_

2 _(shorthand)_

3 _(shorthand)_

4 _(shorthand)_

5 _(shorthand)_

¶ **Sales Promotion**

(shorthand)

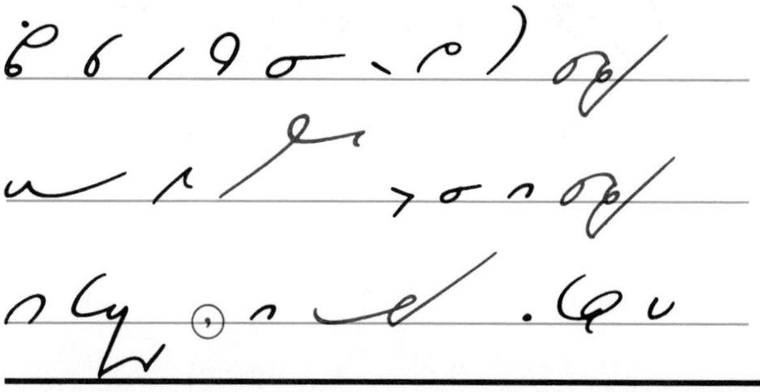

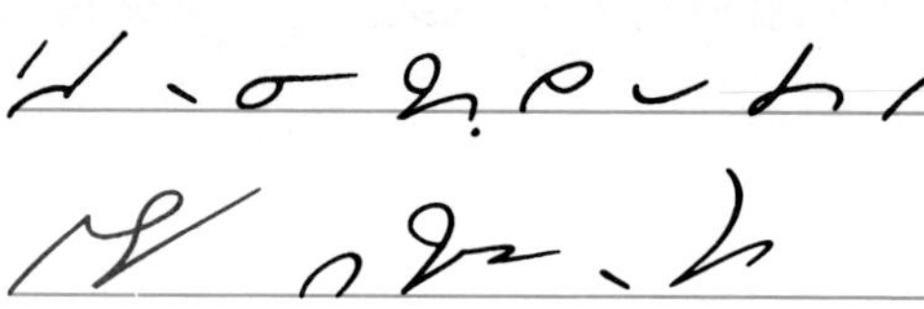

[shorthand outlines]　[60 words]

Communication Skill Builder

Similar Words: there, their

there:　function word used to introduce a thought; (adv.) at that place

their:　possessive pronoun meaning belonging to them

[shorthand outlines]

There should be a place listed for the meeting.

[shorthand outlines]

Place the book *there*.

[shorthand outlines]

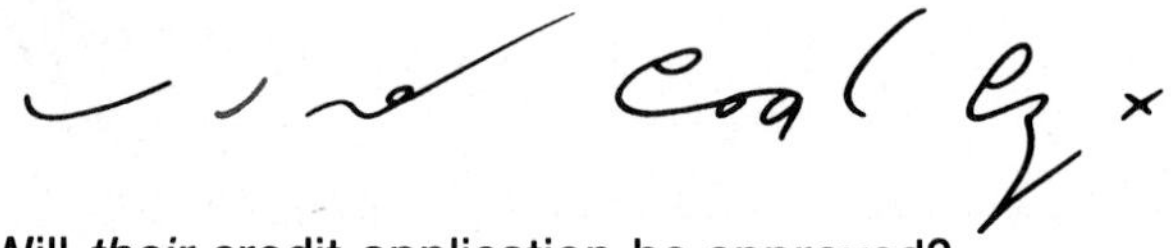

Will *their* credit application be approved?

Reading and Writing Practice

14.4　Dictation Speed Letter

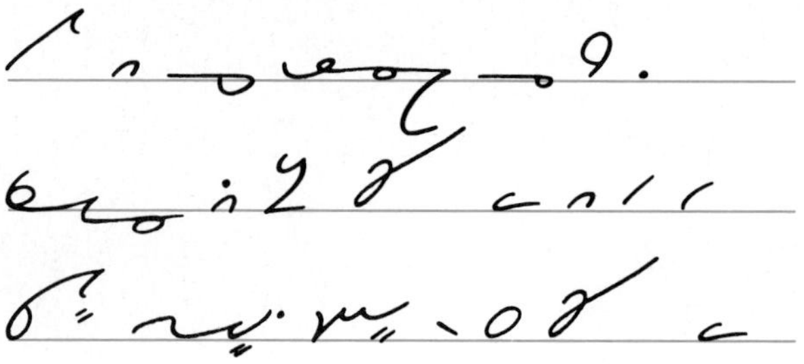

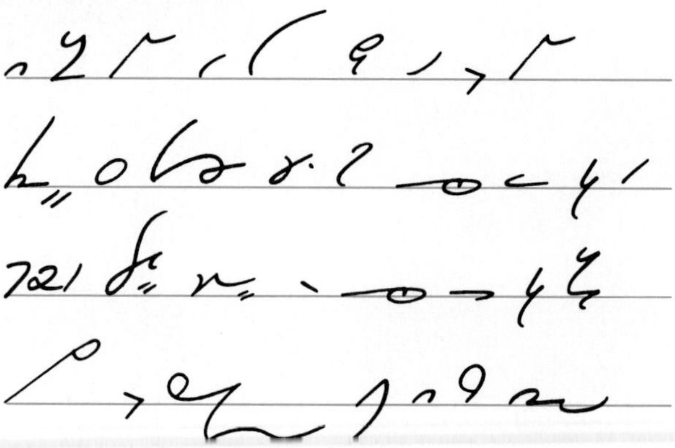

[shorthand outlines]

[shorthand outline]

[64 words]

14.5 A Page From a Real Estate Agent's Notebook

[shorthand outlines]

1 James Lake   2 offer

[shorthand outlines]

[73 words]

3 Stone   4 original   5 accepted

The use of shorthand can be beneficial as a study skill.

LESSON

NEW IN LESSON 15

- Word ending *-ther*
- Word beginning *fur-*
- Symbol for the sound of *ow*
- Differentiating between *weather* and *whether*

WORD ENDING -THER

The word ending *-ther* as in *either* and *father* is represented by both the *under ith* and the *over ith* symbols.

-ther ╱ or ╭

Examples: either ◌ʎ   father ⌀

-ther Words

either ◌ʎ	bothers ⌀	weather, whether ⌀
father ⌀	rather ◌ʎ	brother ⌀
author ⌀	other ⌀	another ⌀
authors ⌀	gather ⌀	together ⌀
bother ⌀	neither ⌀	mother ⌀

-ther Practice

15.1

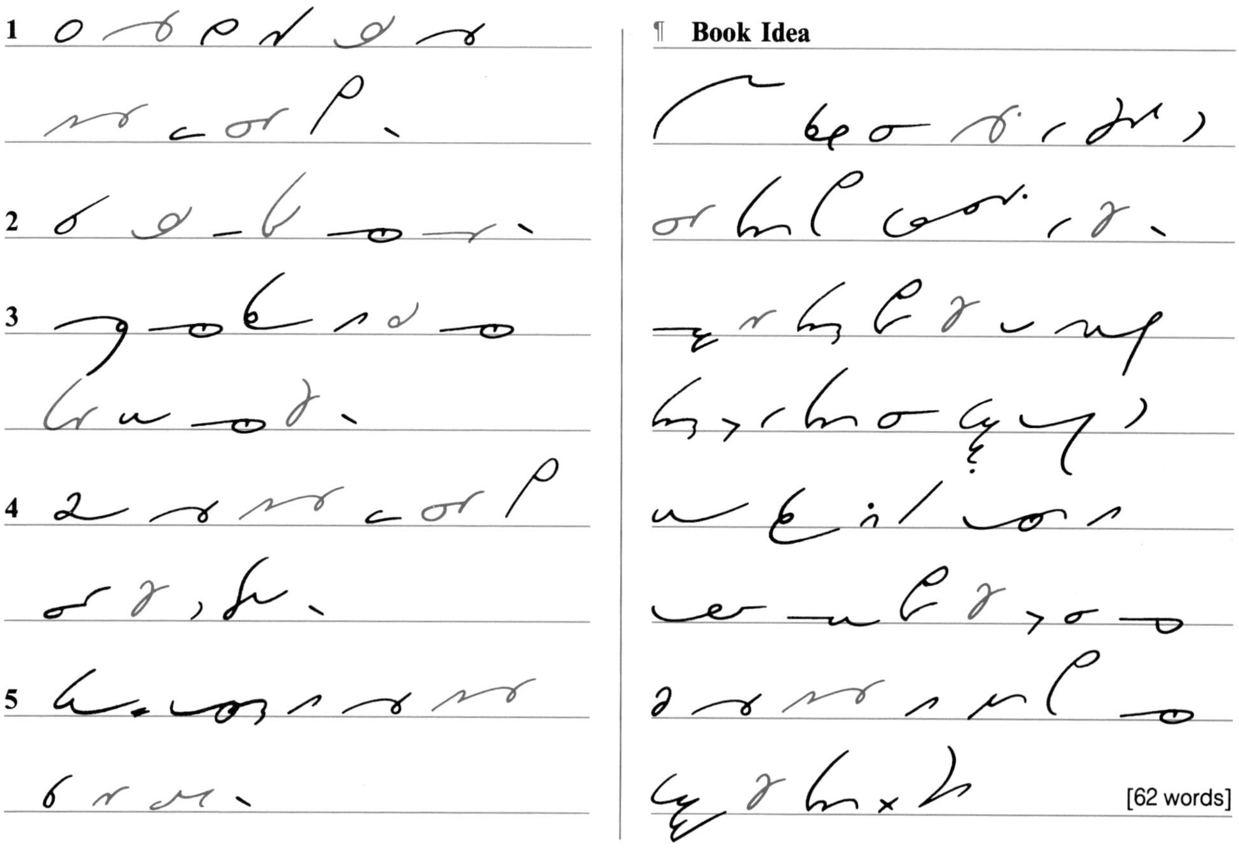

1 [shorthand outline]

2 [shorthand outline]

3 [shorthand outline]

4 [shorthand outline]

5 [shorthand outline]

6 [shorthand outline]

¶ **Book Idea**

[shorthand outlines]

[62 words]

WORD BEGINNING FUR-

The word beginning *fur-* as in *further* is written with the *f* symbol, which you have already been using as an abbreviation for the similar sound *for*.

fur- [shorthand symbol]

Example: further [shorthand symbol]

Fur- Words

further *(shorthand)*   furnace *(shorthand)*   furnishes *(shorthand)*

furthermore *(shorthand)*   furnish *(shorthand)*   refurnish *(shorthand)*

Fur- Practice
15.2

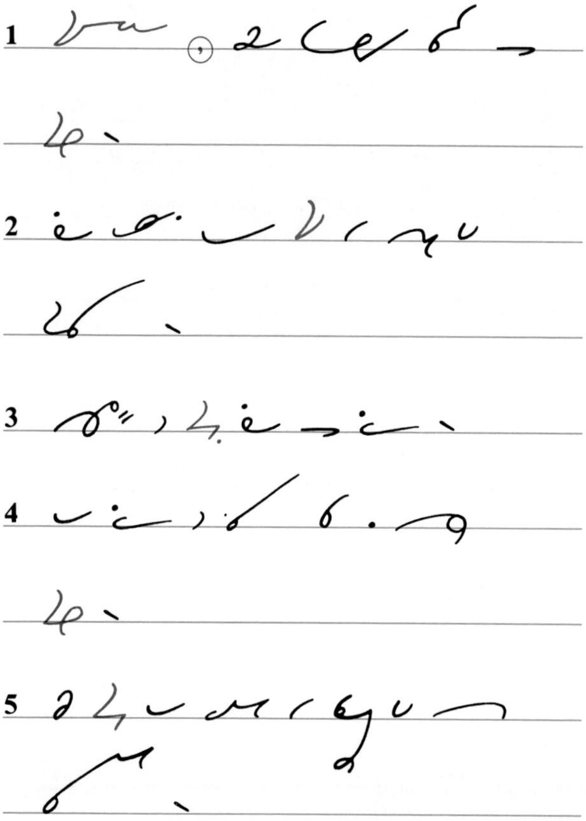

1 *(shorthand outlines)*

2 *(shorthand outlines)*

3 *(shorthand outlines)*

4 *(shorthand outlines)*

5 *(shorthand outlines)*

¶ **Service Contract**

(shorthand outlines)

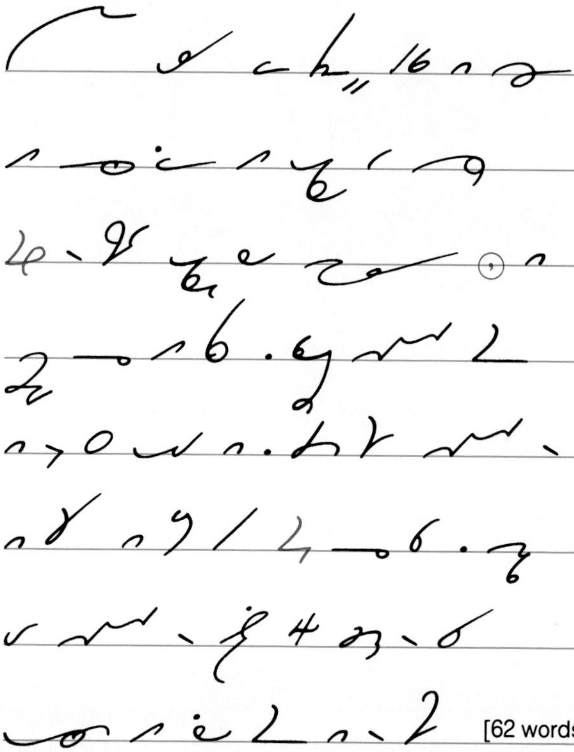

[62 words]

The sound of *ow* as in *how* is written with the *a* and *oo* symbols.

a ⟂ + oo ∧ = ow 𝒪

Example: how *⟋⟍*

Ow Words

how *𝒪*

now *ᓚ*

south *𝒩*

house *ℬ*

announce *ᓍᓍ*

announced *ᓍᓍ*

town *𝒪*

down *𝒪*

doubt *𝒪*

doubts *𝒪*

crowd *𝒪*

brown *𝒞𝒪*

Ow Practice
15.3

1 *[shorthand outlines]* ×

2 *[shorthand outlines]* ,

[shorthand outline] ˙

3 *[shorthand outlines]* ,

[shorthand outline] ˴

4 *[shorthand outlines]* —

[shorthand outlines] ˙

5 *[shorthand outlines]*

[shorthand outlines] ˴

¶ **Rough Draft for a School News Release**

[shorthand outlines]

[shorthand outlines]

[shorthand outlines]

[shorthand outlines]

[shorthand outlines]

[shorthand outlines] ˛

[shorthand outlines] ˛

[shorthand outlines] "*[shorthand outlines]*!"   [60 words]

[shorthand outlines]

Communication Skill Builder

Similar Words: weather, whether

weather: state of the atmosphere

whether: if

[shorthand outline]

The *weather* is cloudy.

[shorthand outline]

Lee cannot decide *whether* he should buy a new camera.

Taking lecture notes in shorthand has two prime benefits: it is faster than long-hand and, unlike recording devices, it enables the student to edit so that only the key points are recorded.

15.4 Dictation Speed Letter

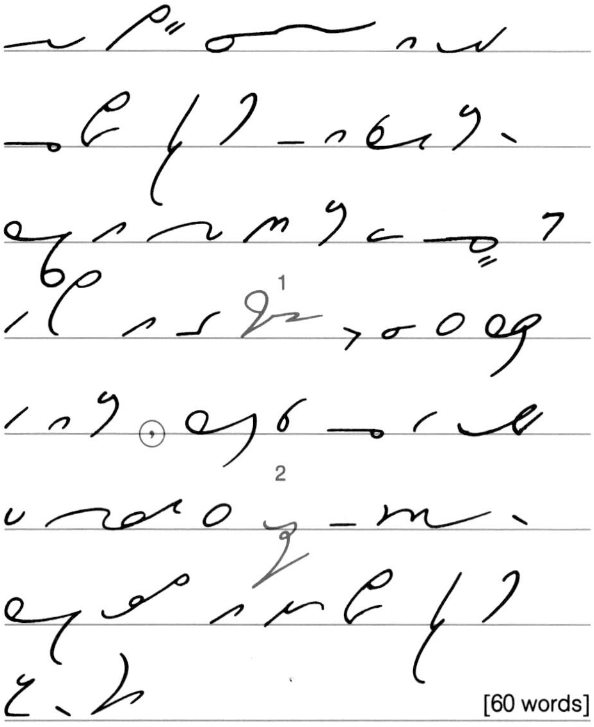

[shorthand]

[60 words]

1 afternoon   2 received

15.5 Letter of Application

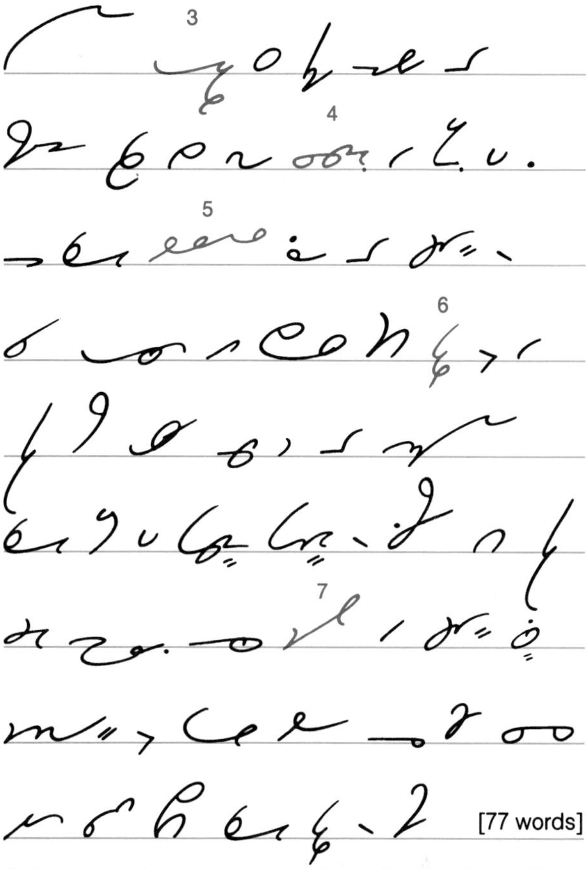

[shorthand]

[77 words]

3 Lopez   4 announcing   5 territory   6 position
7 studies

LESSON 16

NEW IN LESSON 16

- **Eight brief forms**
- **Special phrases**
- **Word endings *-ure* and *-ual***
- **Transcription tips**

BRIEF FORMS

communicate _____   ever, every _____   state _____

company _____   recommend _____   work _____

direct _____   soon _____

Brief-Form Derivatives

communication _____   director _____   recommends _____

communicated _____   directly _____   recommended _____

communications _____   direction _____   recommendation _____

companies _____   everywhere _____   recommendations _____

accompany _____   whenever _____   sooner _____

directed _____   stated ■ _____   worker _____

■ Note the jog which distinguishes the *t* and *d*.

Brief-Form Practice
16.1

(shorthand outlines)

1 *(shorthand outlines)*

2 *(shorthand outlines)*

3 *(shorthand outlines)*

4 *(shorthand outlines)*

5 *(shorthand outlines)*

¶ **Notes for a News Story**

(shorthand outlines)

[65 words]

SPECIAL PHRASES

The following phrases contain shorthand symbols representing one or two sounds from each word.

| to us *(outline)* | as soon as *(outline)* | let us *(outline)* |
| of course *(outline)* | as soon as possible *(outline)* | let me *(outline)* |

A phrase beginning with *to* followed by the sound of *m* is written with the *tem* blend. A phrase beginning with *to* followed by the sound of *d* as in *do* is written with the *ted* blend.

to me *(outline)*   to make *(outline)*   to do *(outline)*

Phrase Practice
16.2

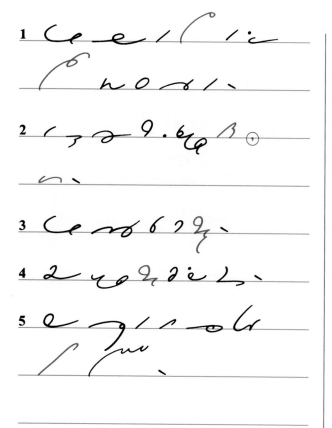

1

2

3

4

5

¶ **Note to Secretary**

[58 words]

WORD ENDINGS -URE, -UAL

The word ending *-ure* as in *procedure* is written with an *r;* the word ending *-ual* as in *annual* is written with an *l.*

-ure ⌣ -ual ⌣

Examples: procedure annual

-ure Words

procedure *(shorthand)* picture *(shorthand)* natural *(shorthand)*

failure *(shorthand)* nature *(shorthand)* feature *(shorthand)*

-ual Words

annual *(shorthand)* actually *(shorthand)* gradual *(shorthand)*

annually *(shorthand)* factual *(shorthand)* gradually *(shorthand)*

actual *(shorthand)* equal *(shorthand)* contractual *(shorthand)*

But: After a downstroke, the *oo* is written.

pleasure *(shorthand)* pressure *(shorthand)* visual *(shorthand)*

-ure, -ual Practice
16.3

1 *(shorthand outlines)*

2 *(shorthand outlines)*

¶ **Class Notes From a Marketing Course**

(shorthand outlines)

3 *(shorthand outlines)*

4 *(shorthand outlines)*

5 *(shorthand outlines)*

[shorthand outlines] [70 words]

③ *[shorthand outlines]*

Transcription Tips

Transcription is the process of "translating" shorthand notes into standard English. The ultimate measure of transcription skill is called *mailable-letter production*. This term is broadly defined since not everything that is transcribed at a keyboard is a letter and not every transcript is mailed.

Many of the personal and administrative uses of shorthand do not require that shorthand be transcribed at a keyboard. But all short-hand notes are written with the intention that they will at least be read at some later time. Reading shorthand is the most basic component of transcription skill. In order to make your shorthand skill as useful as possible, you should practice reading your own shorthand notes until you can read them fluently.

If any outlines are difficult to read, or if they are missing from the notes entirely, the context of the sentence should serve as a clue in helping you to fill in the missing words.

If an outline in your notes does not make sense, you may have made an error in writing proportion. Failure to curve the *ith* will make it appear as a *t*, turning *father* into *fat*, for example.

One of the best ways to learn the meanings of the shorthand symbols is through reading. Practice reading. It will make you a faster shorthand writer in the next few weeks and a better transcriber later on.

As a student, you can use your shorthand skill while drafting a report for a class assignment.

16.4 Phone Message

To: *[shorthand]* [1]

From: *[shorthand]*

Date: *[shorthand]* 18

Time: 12:15

[shorthand outlines] [2]

[shorthand outlines] [3]

[53 words]

[shorthand outlines] [5] [6]

[7]

[8]

[shorthand outlines] 12

[85 words]

16.5 Hotel Reservation

[shorthand outlines] [4]

1 Brown   2 communications   3 directing
4 Carson

5 confirming   6 reservation   7 recall
8 schedule

UNIT

V

NEW IN LESSON 17

- ■ Symbol for the sounds of *nd* and *nt*
- ■ Sound of short *u* omitted
- ■ More minor vowels omitted
- ■ Differentiating between *personal* and *personnel*

SOUNDS OF ND, NT

The sound of *nd* (end) as in *signed* and the sound of *nt* (ent) as in *sent* are both written with a blend of *n* and *t*.

n ⌒ + t ╱ = nt ⌣

Examples: signed ⟋ sent ⟋

Nd Words

signed ⟋ _____

assigned ⟋ _____

sound ⟋ _____

found ⟋ _____

find ⟋ _____

friend ⟋ _____

friendly ⟋ _____

kind ⟋ _____

kindly ⟋ _____

planned ⟋ _____

trained ⟋ _____

mind ⟋ _____

remind ⟋ _____

reminder ⟋ _____

spend ⟋ _____

Nt Words

sent *(shorthand outline)*

agent *(shorthand outline)*

account *(shorthand outline)*

accountant *(shorthand outline)*

amount *(shorthand outline)*

print *(shorthand outline)*

printer *(shorthand outline)*

rental *(shorthand outline)*

current *(shorthand outline)*

currently *(shorthand outline)*

apparent *(shorthand outline)*

spent *(shorthand outline)*

into *(shorthand outline)*

entire *(shorthand outline)*

entirely *(shorthand outline)*

Nd, Nt Practice

17.1

1 *(shorthand outlines)*

2 *(shorthand outlines)*

3 *(shorthand outlines)*

4 *(shorthand outlines)*

5 *(shorthand outlines)*

¶ **Memo**

(shorthand outlines) = 25

(shorthand outlines)

(shorthand outlines)

[49 words]

The short sound of *u* as in *some* is omitted before *n*, *m*, and straight downstrokes (*ish, chay, j*).

Examples: some ⟋⟍   much ⟋

Short U Omitted Before N and M

some	become	lunch
summer	welcome	run
come	done	begun
income	fun	refund

But: *Number* retains the *oo* to facilitate the joining of *n* and *m*.

number	numbers	numbering

Short U Omitted Before a Straight Downward Symbol

much	touch	judge
such	rush	budget

Short-U-Omitted Practice
17.2

[shorthand outlines]

[69 words]

MINOR VOWELS OMITTED

In Lesson 3 you were taught to omit minor vowels. Here is a brief review of minor-vowel-omitted words you have been reading and writing:

fin<u>a</u>l *[shorthand]*   read<u>er</u> *[shorthand]*   del<u>a</u>y *[shorthand]*

tot<u>a</u>l *[shorthand]*   writ<u>er</u> *[shorthand]*   reas<u>on</u> *[shorthand]*

Here are some more minor-vowel-omitted words:

court<u>e</u>sy *[shorthand]*   p<u>er</u>son *[shorthand]*   dist<u>u</u>rb *[shorthand]*

secr<u>e</u>tary *[shorthand]*   p<u>er</u>sonal *[shorthand]*   d<u>e</u>scribe *[shorthand]*

displ<u>a</u>y *[shorthand]*   p<u>er</u>sonnel *[shorthand]*   d<u>e</u>scription *[shorthand]*

p<u>ur</u>chase *[shorthand]*   p<u>ur</u>sue *[shorthand]*   ag<u>en</u>cy *[shorthand]*

Minor-Vowel-Omitted Practice
17.3

1 *[shorthand]*

2 *[shorthand]*

3 [shorthand outline]

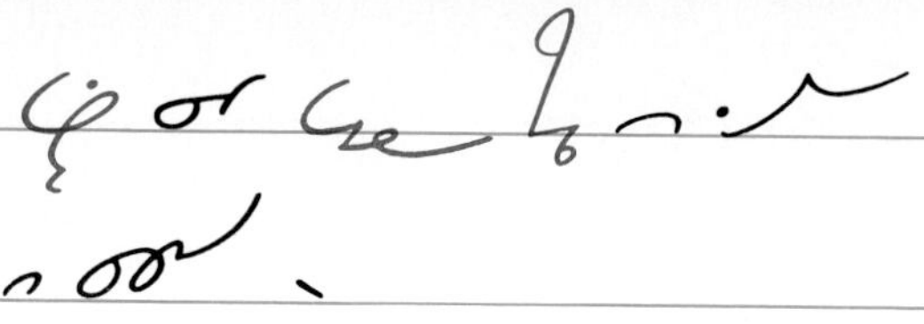

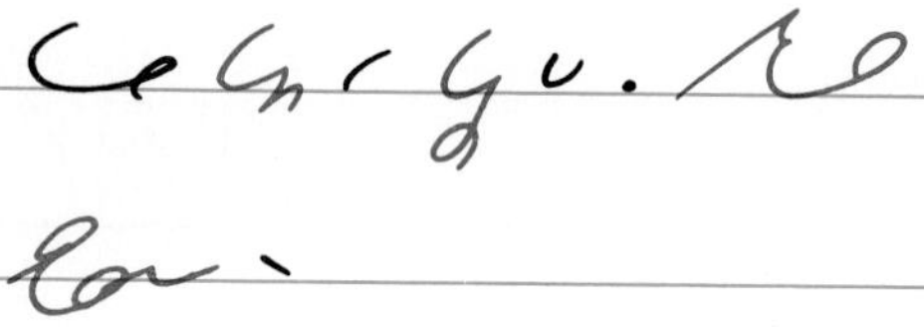

4 [shorthand outline]

5 [shorthand outline]

[right column shorthand outlines]

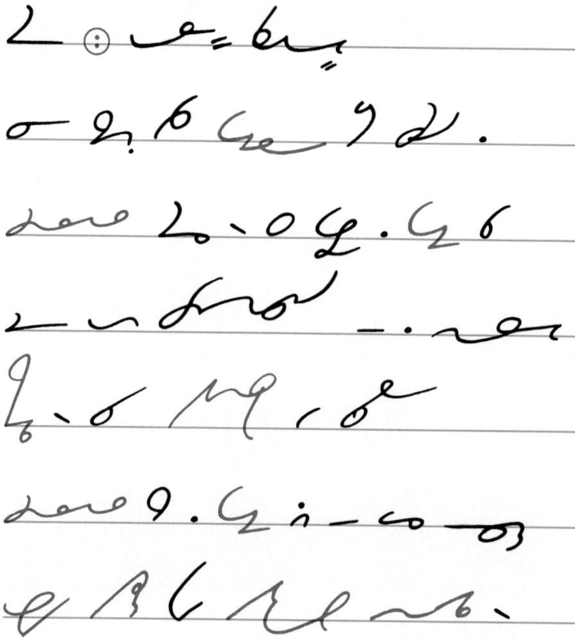

[56 words]

¶ **Memo**

[shorthand outline]

Communication Skill Builder

Similar Words: personal, personnel

personal: belonging to a person; private

personnel: people who make up an organization, such as military personnel; the staff

[shorthand outline]

Do not leave *personal* items in your office.

[shorthand outline]

All office *personnel* should attend the meeting.

17.4   Dictation Speed Memo

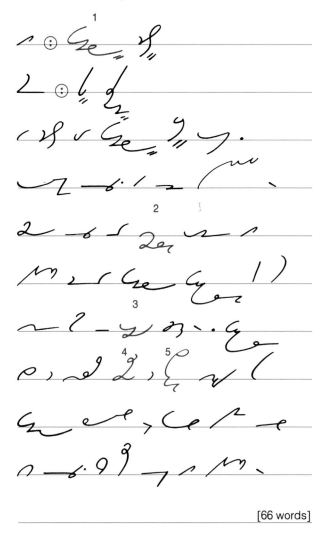

[66 words]

1 Personnel   2 conference   3 recent   4 severe
5 absence

17.5   Sales Letter

[91 words]

6 Kennedy   7 perhaps   8 such   9 2,000

NEW IN LESSON 18

- Eight brief forms
- Word ending *-ble*
- Word ending *-ment*
- Using number as first word of sentence

BRIEF FORMS

advantage _____

advertise _____

and _____

immediate _____

part _____

several _____

value _____

were _____

Brief-Form Derivatives

advantages _____

disadvantage _____

advertising _____

■ Transcription Alert.

advertises _____

immediately ■ _____

partly, party _____

partner _____

depart _____

values _____

Brief-Form Practice
18.1

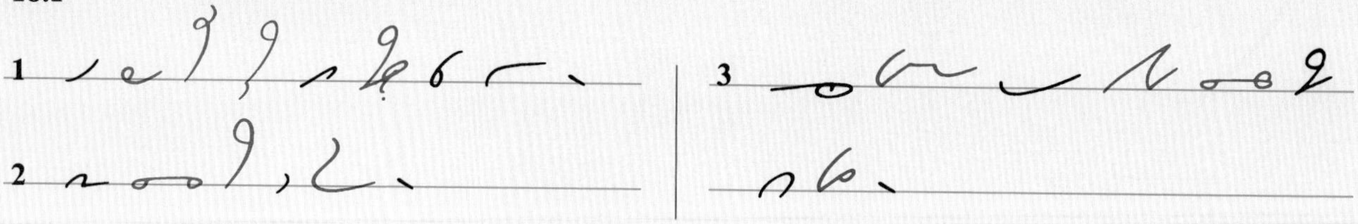

1 _____

2 _____

3 _____

4 *[shorthand]*

5 *[shorthand]*

[shorthand]

¶ **Rough Draft of an Idea for a Term Paper**

[shorthand]

[shorthand]

[shorthand]

[shorthand]

[shorthand]

[shorthand]

[47 words]

WORD ENDING -BLE

The word ending -*ble* as in *possible* is written with the *b* symbol.

-ble *[shorthand outline]*

Example: possible *[shorthand outline]*

-ble Words

possible *[shorthand]*	considerable *[shorthand]*	sensible *[shorthand]*
available *[shorthand]*	considerably *[shorthand]*	table *[shorthand]*
trouble *[shorthand]*	capable *[shorthand]*	suitable *[shorthand]*
troubled *[shorthand]*	reliable *[shorthand]*	valuable ■ *[shorthand]*
reasonable *[shorthand]*	favorable *[shorthand]*	desirable *[shorthand]*

■ Brief-form derivative.

-ble Practice

18.2

1 [shorthand outline]

2 [shorthand outline]

3 [shorthand outline]

4 [shorthand outline]

5 [shorthand outline]

¶ **Car Sale**

[shorthand outline]

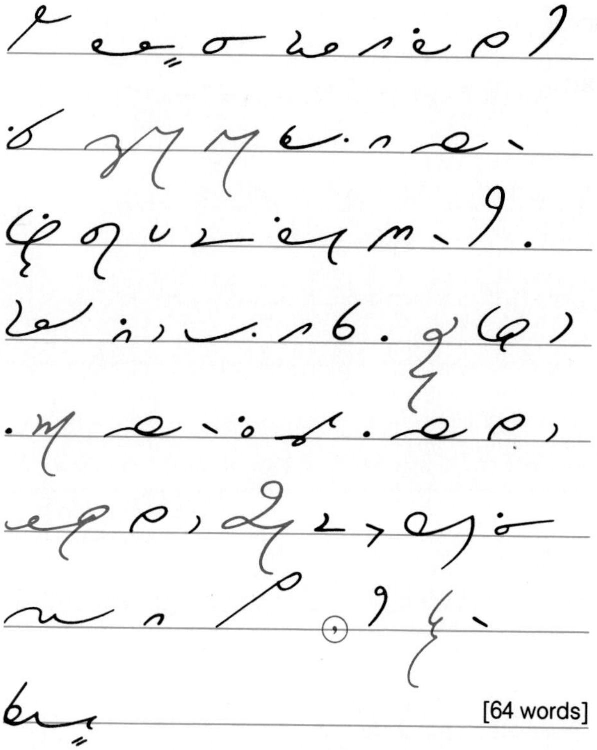

[64 words]

WORD ENDING -MENT

The word ending *-ment* as in *agreement* is represented by the *m* symbol.

-ment ——

Example: agreement [shorthand outline]

-ment Words

agree<u>ment</u>	pay<u>ments</u>	install<u>ment</u>
ship<u>ment</u>	retire<u>ment</u>	settle<u>ment</u>
commit<u>ment</u> ■	replace<u>ment</u>	state<u>ment</u>
attach<u>ment</u>	invest<u>ment</u>	advertise<u>ment</u>
base<u>ment</u>	assign<u>ment</u>	depart<u>ment</u>
pay<u>ment</u>	arrange<u>ment</u>	judg<u>ment</u> ■

■ Transcription Alert.

-ment Practice
18.3

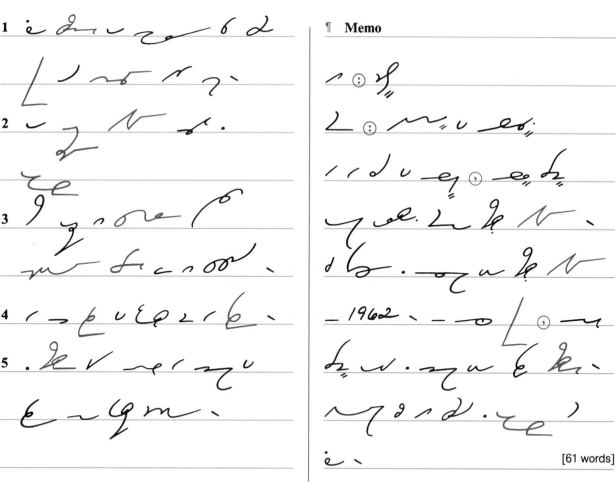

¶ **Memo**

[61 words]

Number as First Word of Sentence

One exception to the basic number rule is a number at the beginning of a sentence. When a number is the first word of a sentence, it is spelled out.

Five years have gone by since her retirement.

Seventeen members signed up for the meeting.

Twenty-four books need to be put back on the shelves.

Anyone can use shorthand to record notes quickly and easily.

18.4 Dictation Speed Letter

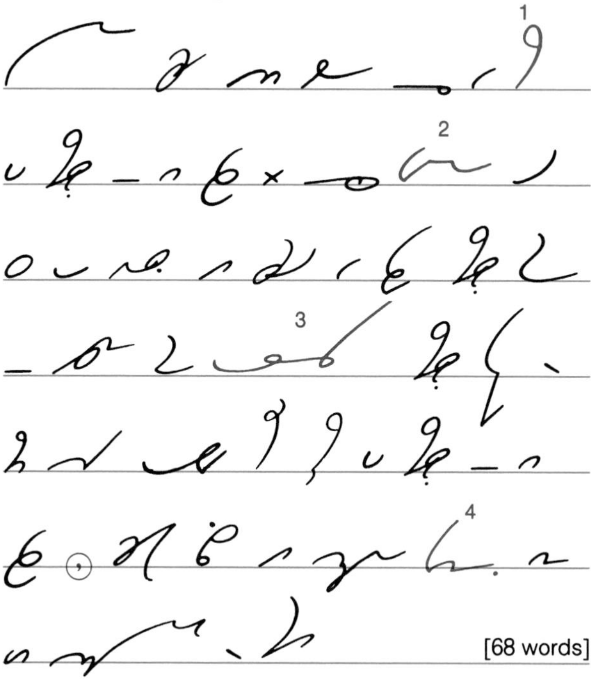

[shorthand outlines]

[68 words]

1 advantage   2 partner   3 limited   4 becoming

18.5 Urgent Request

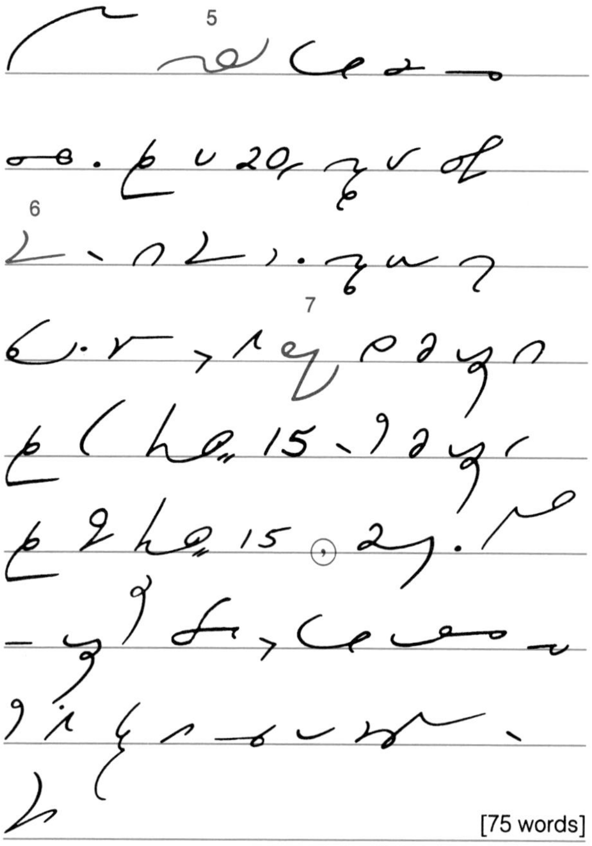

[shorthand outlines]

[75 words]

5 Grant   6 form   7 urgent

LESSON 19

NEW IN LESSON 19

- Nine new phrases
- Blends for the sounds of *rd* and *ld*
- *Sez* blend for the sounds of *ses*, *sis*, and *sus*

PHRASES

Writing speed is gained by representing the word *hope* with the *p* symbol in the following phrases.

I hope _____ I hope that the _____ we hope that _____

I hope the _____ we hope _____ we hope that the _____

I hope that _____ we hope the _____ we hope you will _____

The middle word is eliminated in the following phrases to gain writing speed.

some of the _____ some of our _____ some of them _____

Phrase Practice
19.1

1 _____ 5 _____

2 _____ _____

3 _____ ¶ **Office Note**

4 _____ _____

[shorthand notation]

[59 words]

SOUNDS OF RD, LD

The sound of *rd* as in *heard* and the sound of *ld* as in *old* are written with blends in which the end of the *r* and *l* curl upward to represent the *d*.

rd ⌣   ld ⌣

Examples: heard *[shorthand]*   old *[shorthand]*

Rd Words

heard *[sh]*	ignored *[sh]*	tired *[sh]*
hard *[sh]*	assured *[sh]*	word *[sh]*
stored *[sh]*	toward *[sh]*	record *[sh]*
answered *[sh]*	prepared *[sh]*	recorded *[sh]*

Ld Words

old *[sh]*	older *[sh]*	held *[sh]*
told *[sh]*	folder *[sh]*	child *[sh]*
sold *[sh]*	folded *[sh]*	children *[sh]*
build, billed *[sh]*	failed *[sh]*	called, cold *[sh]*

1 *[shorthand]*

2 *[shorthand]*

3 *[shorthand]*

4 *[shorthand]*

5 *[shorthand]*

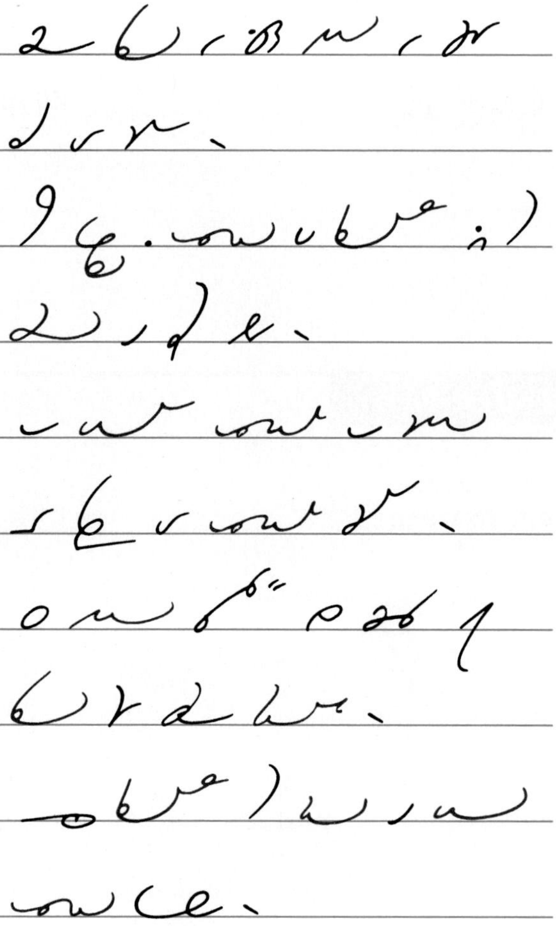

¶ **Lost Luggage**

[shorthand]

[shorthand] [77 words]

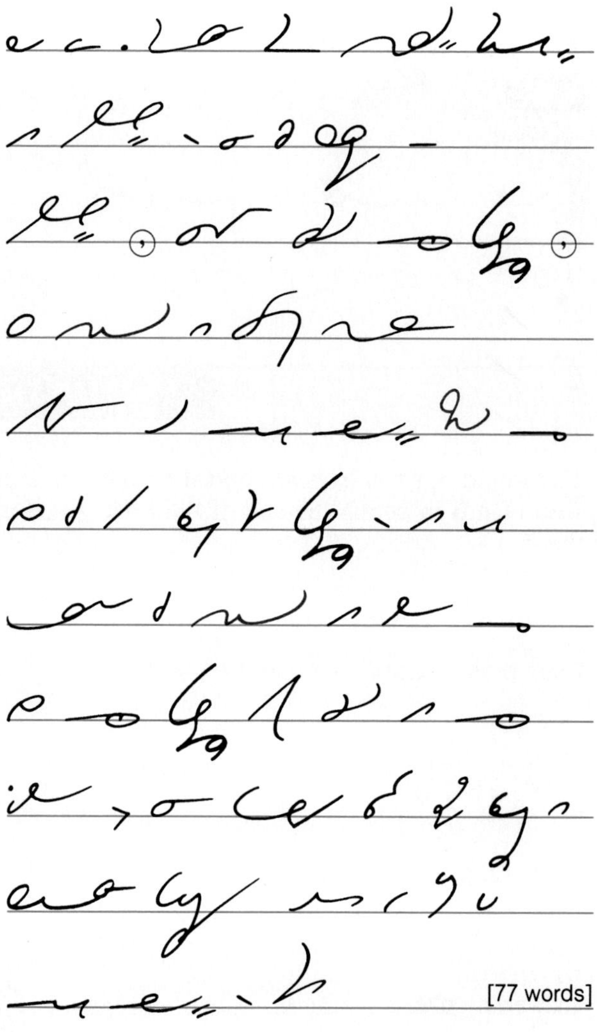

SOUNDS OF SES, SIS, AND SUS

The two forms of *s* are joined—and called the *sez* blend—in order to represent the sounds of *ses*, *sis*, and *sus* as in *senses*, *basis*, and *versus*. Notice the *right sez* begins with the *right s* and ends with the *left s*. The *left sez* begins with the *left s* and ends with the *right s*.

right sez ⟨ left sez ⟩

Examples: services *(outline)* spaces *(outline)*

Right Sez Words

services	*(outline)*	faces	*(outline)*	suspend	*(outline)*
advises	*(outline)*	suspect	*(outline)*	cases	*(outline)*

Left Sez Words

spaces	*(outline)*	insist	*(outline)*	basis, bases	*(outline)*
says	*(outline)*	system	*(outline)*	assist	*(outline)*
senses	*(outline)*	versus	*(outline)*	assisted	*(outline)*
process	*(outline)*	promises	*(outline)*	losses	*(outline)*
processes	*(outline)*	necessary	*(outline)*	Moses	*(outline)*
sister	*(outline)*	analysis	*(outline)*	crisis	*(outline)*

Sez Practice
19.3

(shorthand practice lines 1–4)

(shorthand outlines)

5

¶ **Note**

[78 words]

Shorthand can be used to record information from foreign dignitaries visiting the United States.

19.4 Dictation Speed Letter

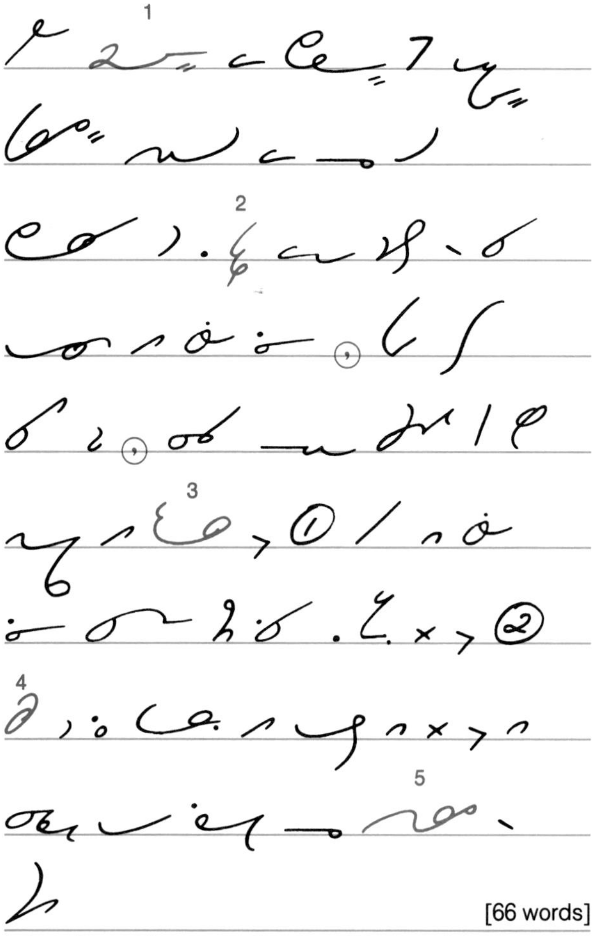

[shorthand outlines]

[66 words]

19.5 Memo

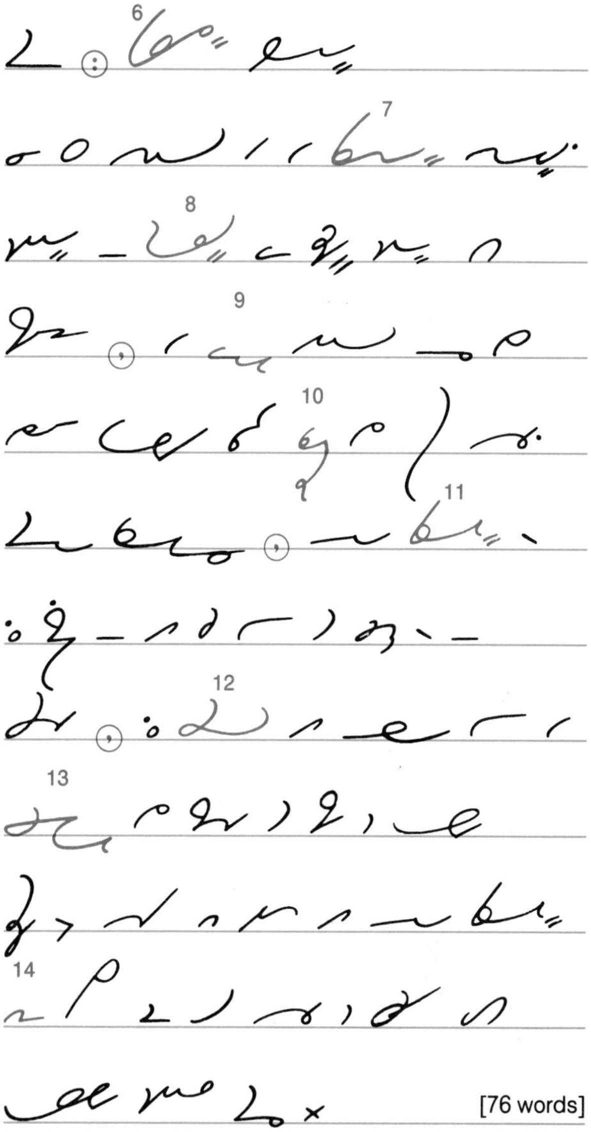

[shorthand outlines]

1 William   2 position   3 supply   4 why
5 greatly

[76 words]

6 Brady   7 Barker   8 Flint   9 owners
10 services   11 Childs   12 failed   13 samples
14 one

LESSON 20

NEW IN LESSON 20

- Seven brief forms
- Symbol for the sounds of *dev*, *div*, *def*, and *dif*
- Symbol for the sound of *u* (pronounced *you*) as in *use*
- Using shorthand to record instructions

BRIEF FORMS

acknowledge ■ _____   however _____   present _____

general _____   opportunity ■ _____   organize _____

govern _____   organize _____

■ Transcription Alert.

Brief-Form Derivatives

acknowledged _____   government _____   presently _____

acknowledges _____   opportunities _____   presented _____

acknowledgment _____   organization _____   represented _____

generally _____   organized _____   representative _____

Brief-Form Practice
20.1

1 _____

2 _____   3 _____

4. *[shorthand]*

5. *[shorthand]*

¶ **Good Government**

[shorthand]

[shorthand] [64 words]

SOUNDS OF DEV, DIV, DEF, DIF

The sounds of *dev*, *div*, *def*, and *dif* as in *devote*, *divide*, *definite*, and *differ* are all expressed with a blend which represents a rounded *d v* joining. It is called the *dev* blend.

d ╱ + v ╱ = dev ⌒

Examples: devote *[shorthand]*   divide *[shorthand]*   definite *[shorthand]*   differ *[shorthand]*

Dev, Div Words

devote	*[shorthand]*	develop	*[shorthand]*	divided	*[shorthand]*
devoted	*[shorthand]*	development	*[shorthand]*	division	*[shorthand]*
devise, device	*[shorthand]*	developing	*[shorthand]*	divisions	*[shorthand]*
devised	*[shorthand]*	divide	*[shorthand]*	divorce	*[shorthand]*

Def, Dif Words

| definite ■ | *[shorthand]* | defeat | *[shorthand]* | defend | *[shorthand]* |
| definitely | *[shorthand]* | defeated | *[shorthand]* | differ | *[shorthand]* |

■ Transcription Alert.

different _(shorthand)_   difference _(shorthand)_   differences _(shorthand)_

Dev, Div, Def, Dif Practice
20.2

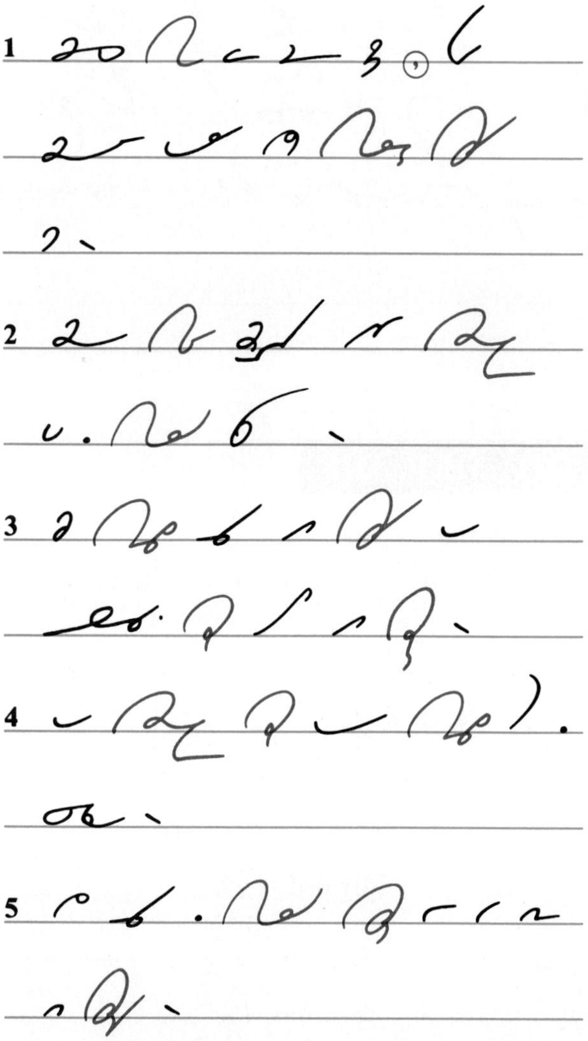

1 _(shorthand outlines)_

2 _(shorthand outlines)_

3 _(shorthand outlines)_

4 _(shorthand outlines)_

5 _(shorthand outlines)_

¶ **Product Development**

(shorthand outlines)

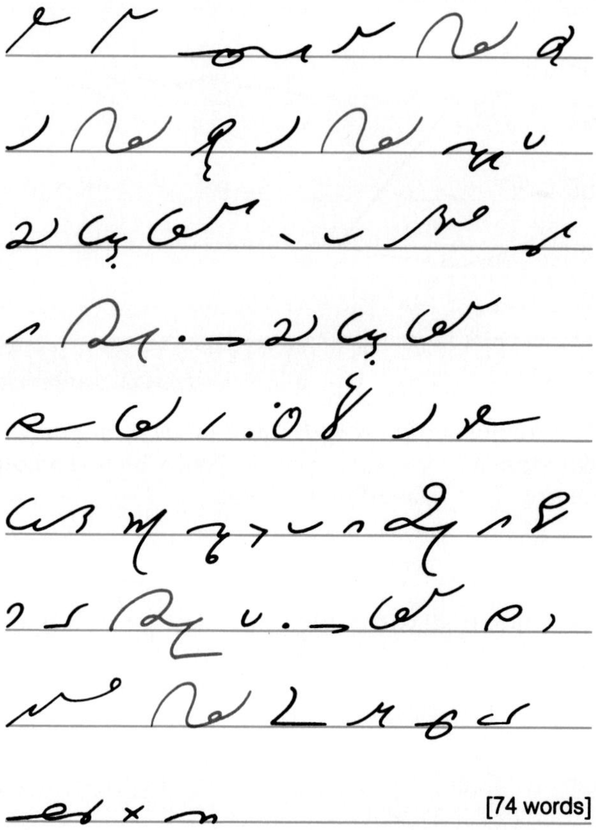

[74 words]

The sound of *u* as in *use* is written with a combination of the *e* and *oo* symbols. This *e oo* combination is called *u* (pronounced *you*).

Example: use

U Words

use	unite	refuse
used	unique	review
unit	few	Hughes

U Practice
20.3

1

2

3

4

5

¶ **History Book**

[67 words]

Using Shorthand to Record Instructions

One of the most valuable uses for shorthand is the recording of instructions on the job. This skill is equally useful for people at all levels of the organization.

Shorthand enables you to record your supervisor's instructions without having to ask the speaker to slow down or repeat major points. You will also know that the instructions are accurate and much more likely to be complete. You will thus avoid the embarrassment of having to go back to the supervisor to ask for the instructions a second time.

Finally, recording instructions in shorthand is a mark of professionalism. The supervisor who sees you recording instructions in shorthand knows that you are well prepared for the job, conscientious, and competent.

Shorthand-writing secretaries find the international department an exciting work environment to utilize their shorthand skill.

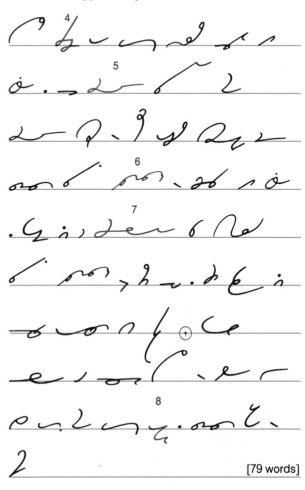

Reading and Writing Practice

20.4   Dictation Speed Letter

[72 words]

1   office   2   first   3   then

20.5   Job Opportunity

[79 words]

4   Jensen   5   film   6   techniques   7   familiar
8   represents

U N I T
VI

LESSON

NEW IN LESSON 21

- **Blends for the sounds of *ten*, *den*, and *tain***
- **Word ending *-ical***
- **Special phrase *to know***
- **Using shorthand to record information**

SOUNDS OF TEN, DEN, TAIN

The sounds of *ten* as in *attend, cotton, stand,* and *bulletin* and *den* as in *sudden* are represented by the same blend—a blend of the *t* and *n* symbols. The *ten* blend is also used for the word ending *-tain* as in *attain.* The curved *ten* blend symbol represents a rounding of the angle of the *t* and *n* joining.

t ╱   n ╾   ten ╭

Examples: attend *6*   sudden *⋎*   attain *6*

Ten Words

attend	stand ▪	assistant
attention	standard	maintenance
written	intend	Fenton
tonight	intention	Trenton
bulletin	assistance	Fulton

▪ Although an *a* is heard in the word *stand* and its derivatives, for ease of writing it is written with the *ten* blend.

Den Words

sudden _(shorthand)_

suddenly _(shorthand)_

deny _(shorthand)_

denies _(shorthand)_

dentist _(shorthand)_

dinner _(shorthand)_

danger ■ _(shorthand)_

evident _(shorthand)_

evidently _(shorthand)_

evidence _(shorthand)_

student _(shorthand)_

students _(shorthand)_

confident _(shorthand)_

president _(shorthand)_

presidency _(shorthand)_

■ Although an *a* is heard in the word *danger*, for ease of writing it is written with the *den* blend.

Tain Words

attain _(shorthand)_

attained _(shorthand)_

contain _(shorthand)_

contains _(shorthand)_

container _(shorthand)_

certain _(shorthand)_

certainly _(shorthand)_

maintain _(shorthand)_

retain _(shorthand)_

pertain _(shorthand)_

obtain _(shorthand)_

obtainable _(shorthand)_

Ten, Den, Tain Practice
21.1

1 _(shorthand)_

2 _(shorthand)_

3 _(shorthand)_

4 _(shorthand)_

5 _(shorthand)_

¶ **Visitor to the Office**

(shorthand)

[shorthand outlines]

[49 words]

WORD ENDING -ICAL

The word ending *-ical* as in *article* and *medical* is written with a *disjoined k*. A disjoined word ending such as *-ing* or *-ical* should be written close to its root word so that it is not mistaken for a separate outline.

-ical   [shorthand]

Example: article [shorthand]

-ical Words

article [shorthand]

articles [shorthand]

chemical [shorthand]

logical [shorthand]

logically [shorthand]

medical [shorthand]

physical [shorthand]

political [shorthand]

radical [shorthand]

technical [shorthand]

typical [shorthand]

typically [shorthand]

-ical Practice
21.2

1 [shorthand]

2 [shorthand]

3 [shorthand]

4 [shorthand]

5

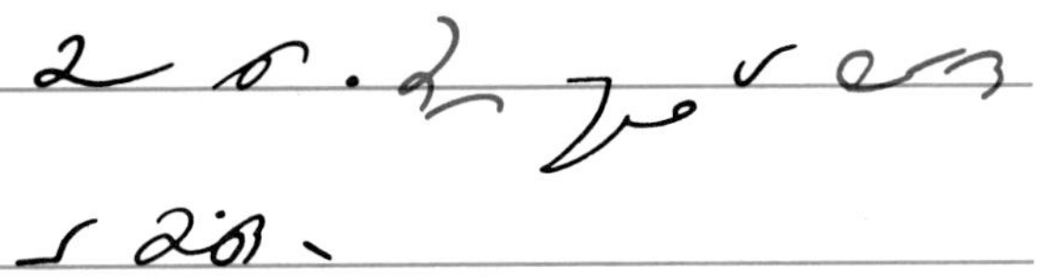

¶ **Library Orientation**

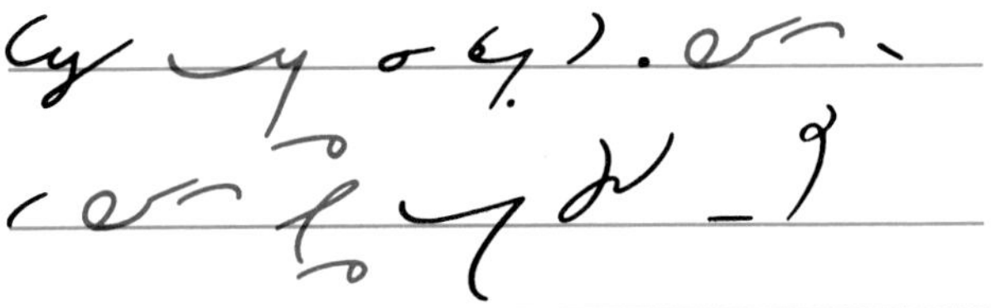

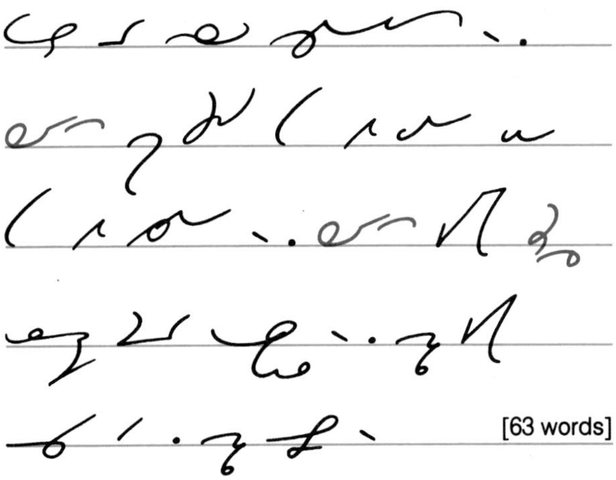

¶ **Library Orientation**

[63 words]

SPECIAL PHRASE

The *ten* blend is used in the frequent phrase *to know*.

to know

Phrase Practice
21.3

1

2

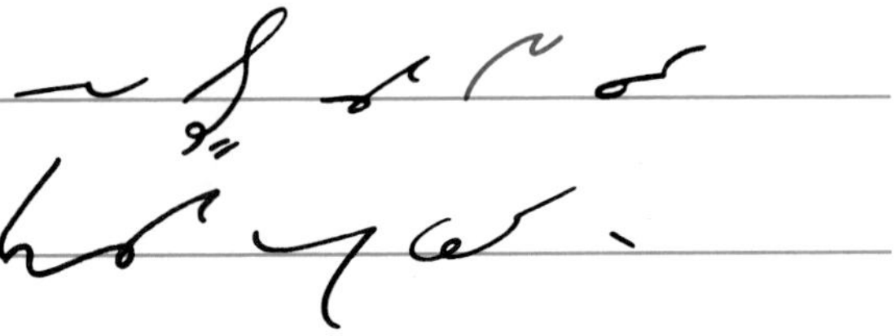

3

4

5

¶ **Holiday Schedule**

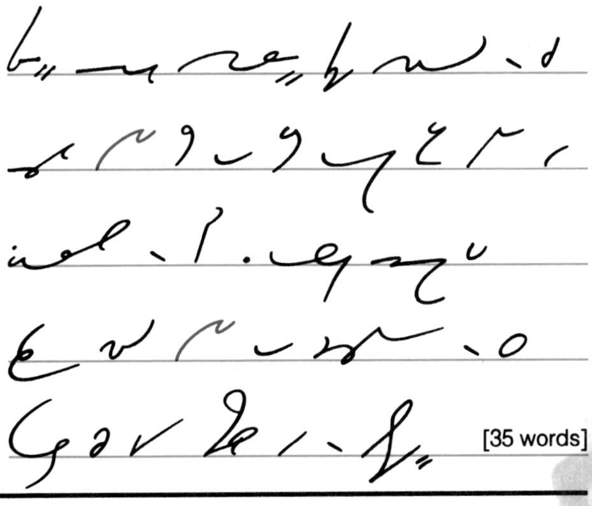

[35 words]

Using Shorthand to Record Information

One of the very valuable uses for shorthand skill is the recording of information from visitors to the office or from people who call on the telephone. People talk several times faster than you are able to write in longhand. Without shorthand skill, you would be forced to ask visitors and callers to repeat information where you failed to make complete notes.

By combining shorthand skill with good listening habits, you can write down all of the important facts that visitors and telephone callers give you. In this way information is complete, facts are accurate, and commitments may be kept. Moreover, using shorthand is evidence of being a competent professional and creates the best possible image for the company.

Reading and Writing Practice

21.4 Dictation Speed Letter

[67 words]

1 remittance   2 standing   3 $2,200

21.5 Dictation Speed Letter

4 Brandon   5 bulletin   6 Tennis   7 loan
8 duplicate

A secretary can use shorthand for more than just taking dictation — shorthand can be used to record telephone messages.

LESSON 22

NEW IN LESSON 22

- **Seven brief forms**
- **Word ending** *-tial*
- **Symbol for the sound of** *oi*

BRIEF FORMS

business _____

difficult _____

Ms. _____

out _____

over _____

than _____

what _____

Brief-Form Derivatives

businesses _____

businesslike _____

difficulty _____

difficulties _____

outstanding _____

outside _____

outcome _____

without _____

overhead _____

overlook _____

overnight _____

whatever _____

Brief-Form Practice
22.1

1 _____

2 _____

140 ▬ LESSON 22

3 *[shorthand outlines]*

4 *[shorthand outlines]*

5 *[shorthand outlines]*

¶ **Thank-You Letter**

[shorthand outlines]

[shorthand outlines]

[57 words]

WORD ENDING -TIAL

The word ending -tial (pronounced *shul*) as in *essential* is represented by the *ish* symbol. The context of the sentence tells the reader whether the *ish* represents -tial or whether it represents -tion, which was presented in Lesson 11.

-tial *[shorthand]*

Example: essential *[shorthand]*

-tial Words

essential *[shorthand]*	officially *[shorthand]*	initial *[shorthand]*
financial *[shorthand]*	social *[shorthand]*	initialed *[shorthand]*
financially *[shorthand]*	special *[shorthand]*	partial *[shorthand]*
official *[shorthand]*	especially *[shorthand]*	partially *[shorthand]*

1 *[shorthand outline]*

2 *[shorthand outline]*

3 *[shorthand outline]*

4 *[shorthand outline]*

5 *[shorthand outline]*

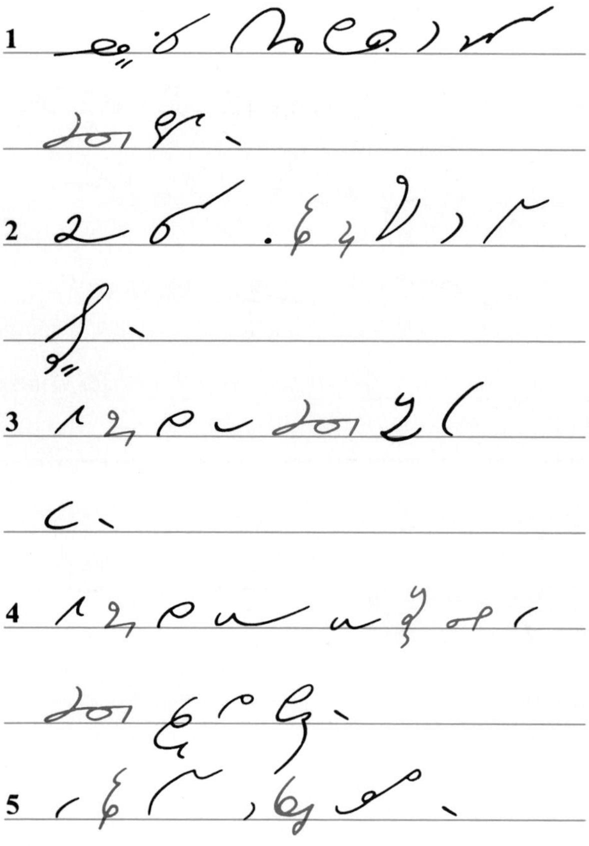

¶ **Business Letter**

[shorthand outlines]

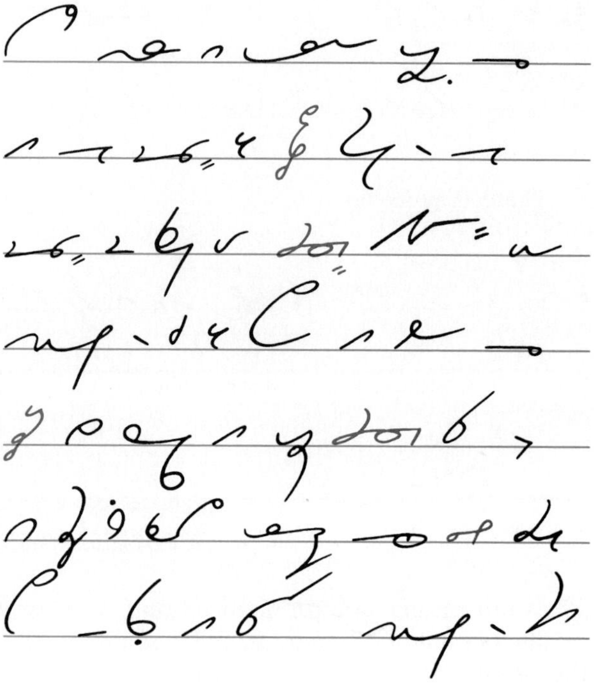

[66 words]

SOUND OF OI

The sound of *oi* as in *toy* is written with a joining of the *o* and *e* symbols. *[shorthand symbol]*

Example: toy *[shorthand symbol]*

Oi Words

toy _[shorthand]_

boy _[shorthand]_

join _[shorthand]_

oil _[shorthand]_

soil _[shorthand]_

Roy _[shorthand]_

royal _[shorthand]_

noise _[shorthand]_

point _[shorthand]_

appointed _[shorthand]_

appointment _[shorthand]_

invoice _[shorthand]_

invoices _[shorthand]_

void _[shorthand]_

avoid _[shorthand]_

Oi Practice
22.3

1 _[shorthand outline]_

2 _[shorthand outline]_

3 _[shorthand outline]_

4 _[shorthand outline]_

5 _[shorthand outline]_

¶ **Insurance**

[shorthand outlines]

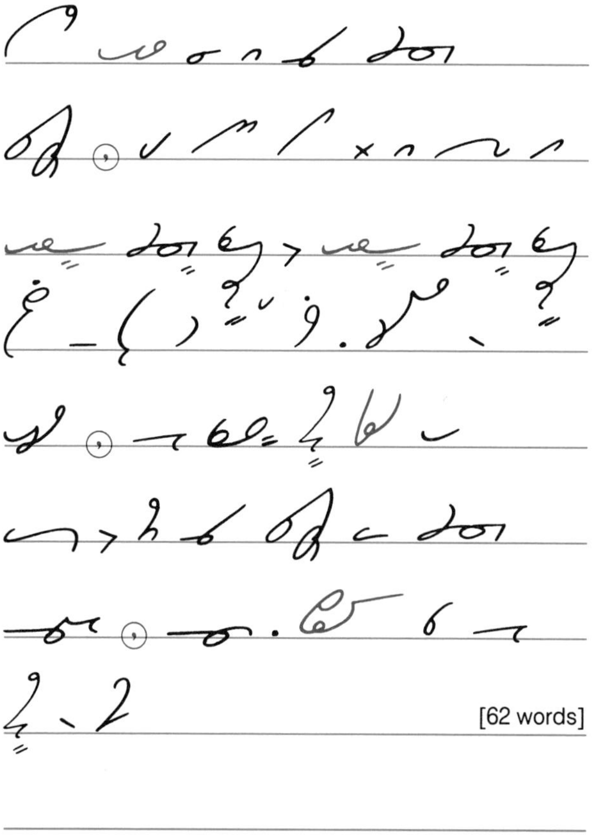

[62 words]

Reading and Writing Practice

22.4 Dictation Speed Letter

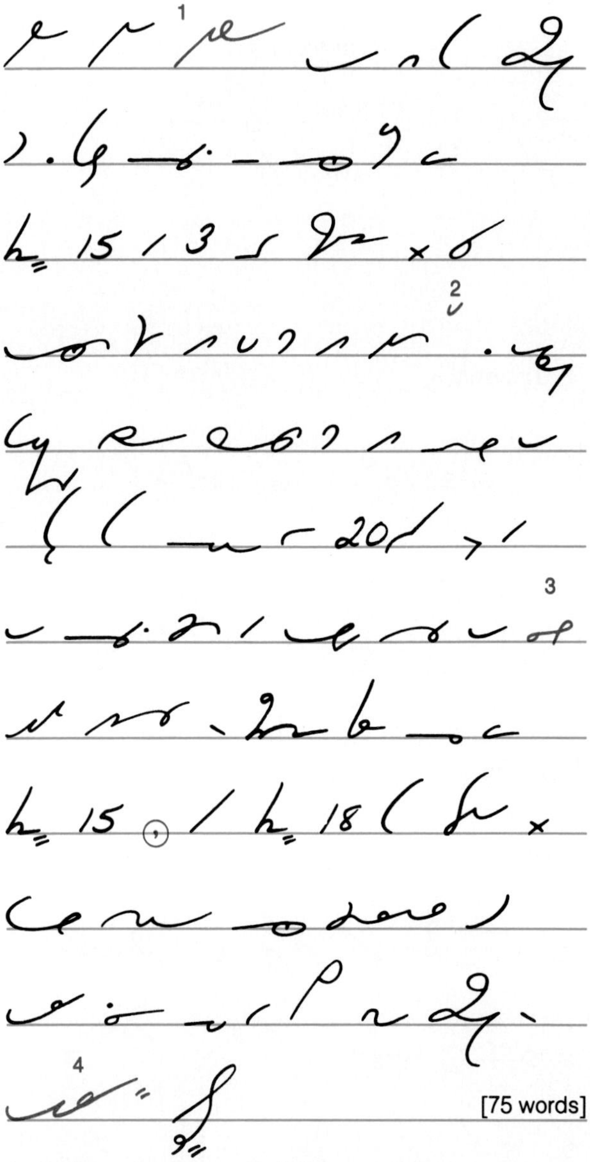

[shorthand]

[75 words]

1 Doyle 2 over 3 initial 4 Lloyd

22.5 Minutes Taken During a Meeting

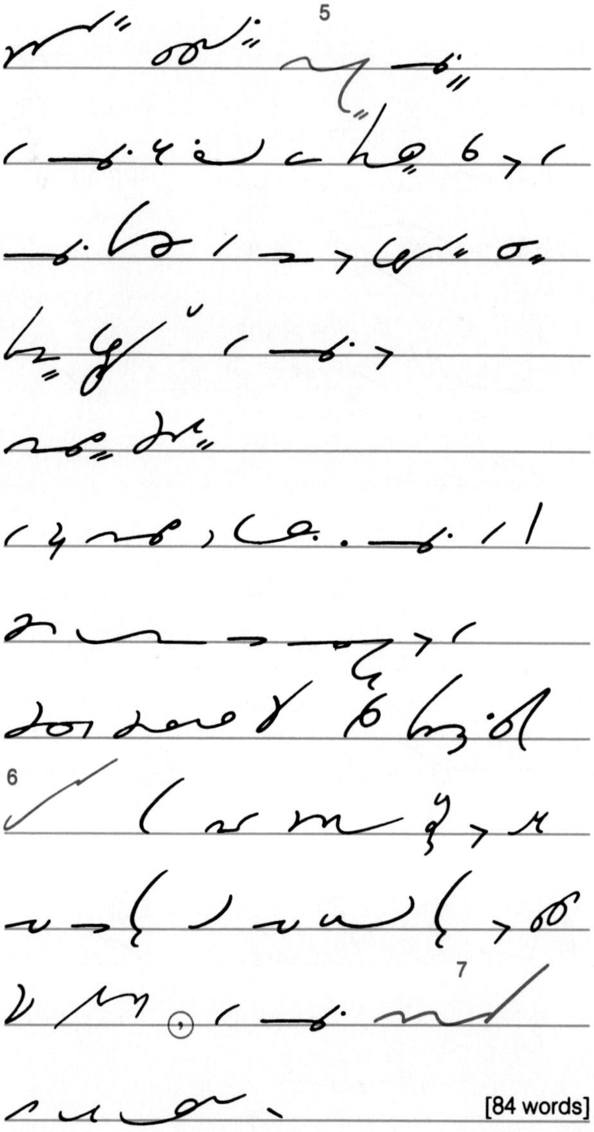

[shorthand]

[84 words]

5 Club 6 audited 7 concluded

LESSON 23

NEW IN LESSON 23

- **Expressing measures of time, percent, feet, and pounds**
- **Symbol for the sound of *men***
- **Word ending *-ward***
- **Transcribing expressions of time and amounts**

MEASURES

Special shorthand abbreviations are used for expressing time, percent, feet, and pounds.

Time

Hours and minutes are expressed in normal-size figures. Shorthand symbols are used for *a.m.*, *p.m.*, and *o'clock*.

The shorthand outline for *a.m.* is *a* with an intersected *m*. *θ*

The shorthand outline for *p.m.* is *p* with an intersected *m*. *ϯ*

The *o* is used for *o'clock* and is placed above the number.

11 a.m. *11 θ*   5 p.m. *5ϯ*   5 o'clock *5ᵒ*

Feet

The word *feet* is represented by the *f* symbol and is placed at the base of the number.

5 feet *5ᶨ*   200 feet *2ᶨ*

Percent

The word *percent* is represented by the *comma s.* It is placed at the base of the number and should intersect the line. The *comma s* is not used when writing the entire outline for percent.

75 percent    100 percent ■ 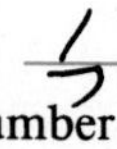

■ In *100 percent* the *n* for *hundred* is placed below the number and followed by the *commas s.*

Pounds

The word *pounds* is represented by the *p* symbol and is placed at the base of the number.

3 pounds 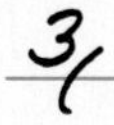   500 pounds 

Measures Practice

23.1

1–5

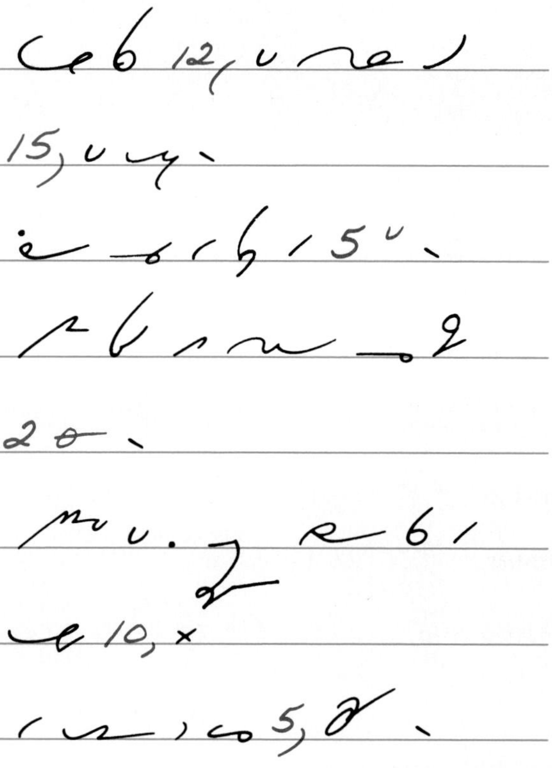

¶ **Notes for Placing a Phone Call**

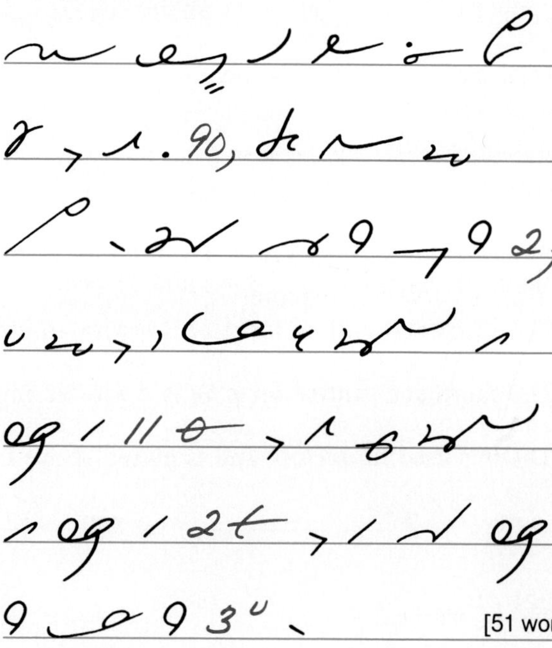

[51 words]

Telephone messages recorded in shorthand are transcribed onto a telephone message form at the conclusion of the call.

MEN BLEND

The sounds of *men*, *min*, *man*, and *mon* as in *mention*, *minute*, *manner*, and *month* are represented by a blend of the *m* and *n* symbols called the *men* blend.

m ——— + n ‿ = men ———

Examples: mention ———7 minute ——6 manner ———⌣ month ———

Men Words

men ———

mention ———7

mentioned ——⌄

mentions ——7

many ——o

meant ——/

mental ——∧

mentally ——∧o

women ⌐——

Min, Man, Mon Words

minute — manager — monthly

manner — woman — money

manage — month

Men, Min, Man, Mon Practice

23.2

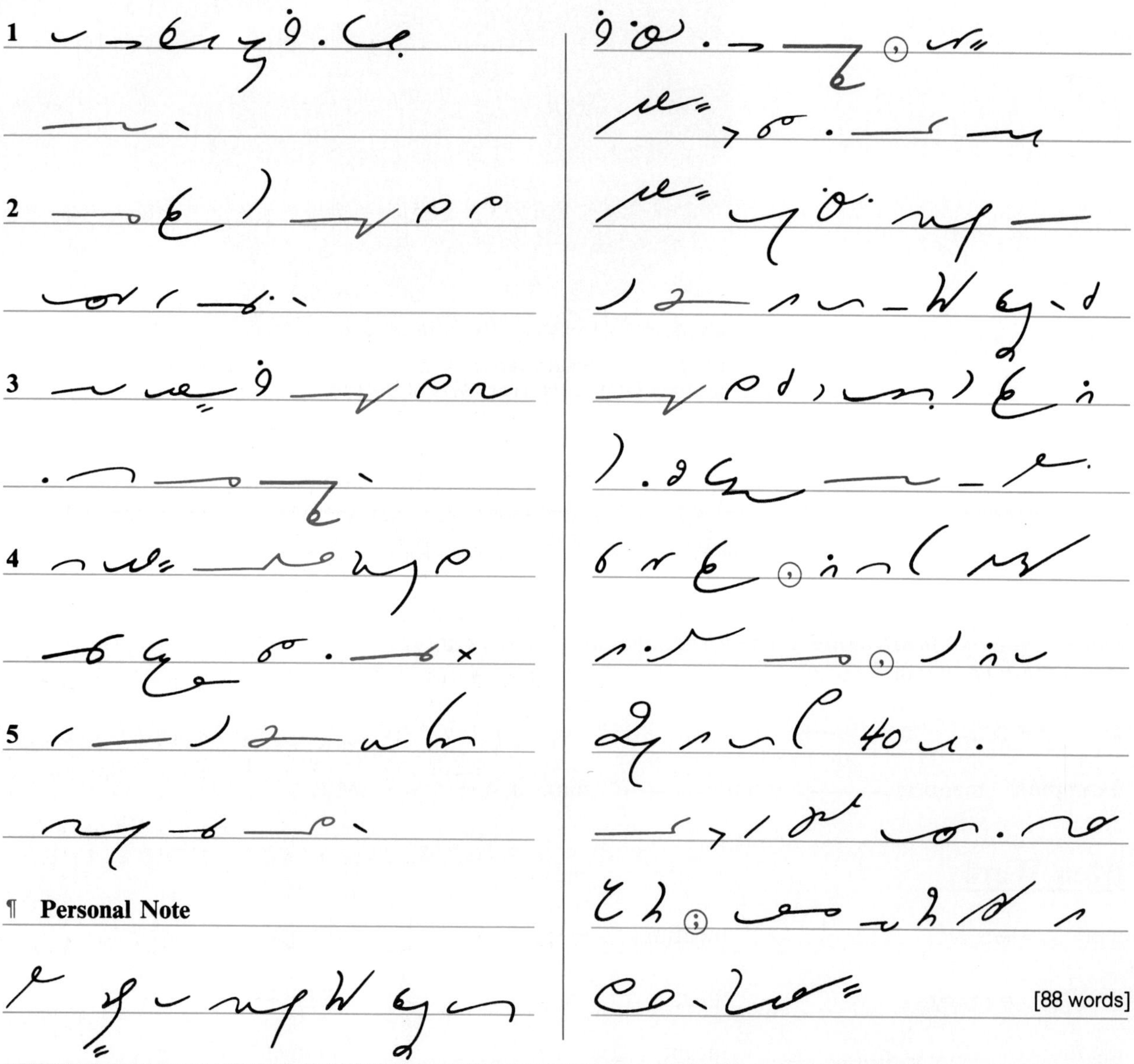
1
2
3
4
5
¶ Personal Note
[88 words]

WORD ENDING -WARD

The word ending -*ward* as in *afterward* is written with a disjoined *d*.

-ward ╱

Example: afterward ⟋

-ward Words

after<u>ward</u>	for<u>ward</u>ed	in<u>ward</u>
back<u>ward</u>	on<u>ward</u>	Edward
down<u>ward</u>	up<u>ward</u>	Wood<u>ward</u>
for<u>ward</u>	re<u>ward</u>	awk<u>ward</u>

-ward Practice
23.3

1 *[shorthand outlines]*

2 *[shorthand outlines]*

3 *[shorthand outlines]*

4 *[shorthand outlines]*

5 *[shorthand outlines]*

¶ **Retirement**

[shorthand outlines]

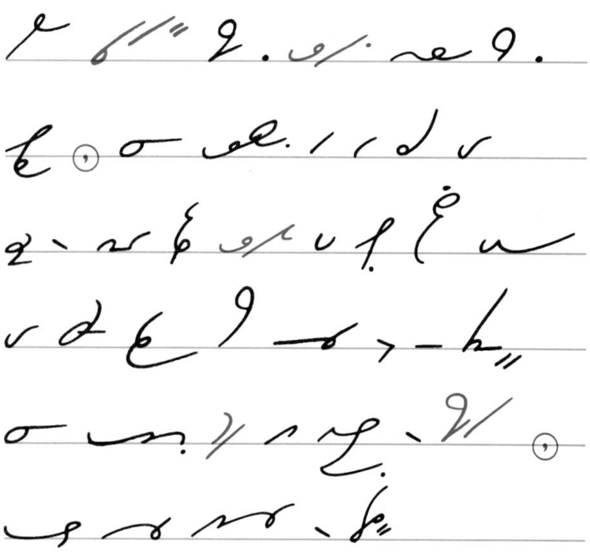

[53 words]

The basic number rule presented in Lesson 11 specifies that the numbers from one through ten are to be spelled out, while numbers higher than ten are to be written in figures. In Lesson 18 you learned that one exception to this basic number rule is that a number must be spelled out if it is the first word of a sentence.

Another exception to the basic rule is that expressions of time with *a.m.*, *p.m.*, or *o'clock* and percents and distances all may be written in figures for quick comprehension. The words *percent* and *feet* are spelled in full. Note that *a.m.* and *p.m.* appear in lowercase.

7:30 a.m.	7 o'clock	6 feet
6:17 p.m.	8 percent	23 feet
5 p.m.	17 percent	100 feet

Meet me at *11:30 a.m.* or *2 p.m.*

The price has been reduced by *20 percent.*

The cost of *5 feet* of nylon rope is $5.25.

Reading and Writing Practice

23.4 Dictation Speed Letter

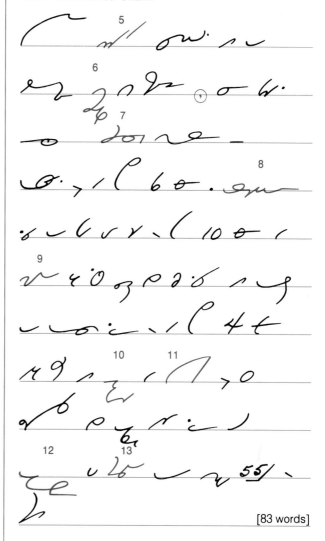

[66 words]

1 Lloyd   2 Edwards   3 While   4 selling

23.5 Insurance Claim

[83 words]

5 Woodward   6 conversation   7 financial
8 rainstorm   9 water   10 inspect   11 damage
12 replacement   13 furniture

L E S S O N

24

NEW IN LESSON 24

- Seven brief forms
- Word ending *-ings*
- Word endings *-rity*, *-lity*, and *-lty*

BRIEF FORMS

between _____   responsible _____   thing, think _____

regard _____   send _____

request _____   success _____

Brief-Form Derivatives

regarding _____   requested _____   thinking _____

regarded _____   requesting _____   things, thinks _____

regardless _____   sends _____   nothing _____

requests _____   sending _____   successes _____

Brief-Form Phrases

I think _____   send you _____   send the _____

we think _____   sending you _____   send us _____

Brief-Form Practice

24.1

(shorthand outlines, numbered 1–5)

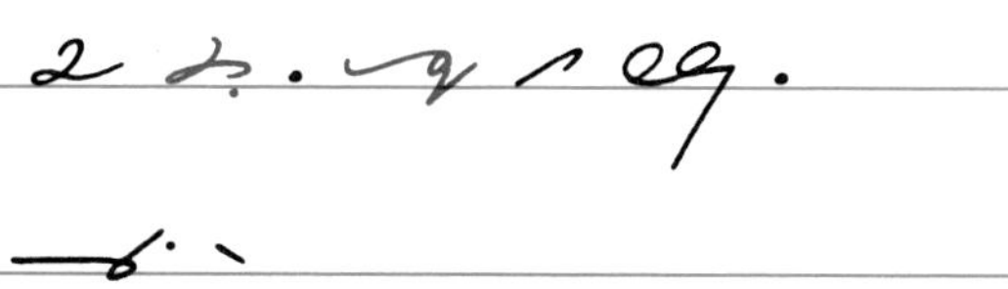

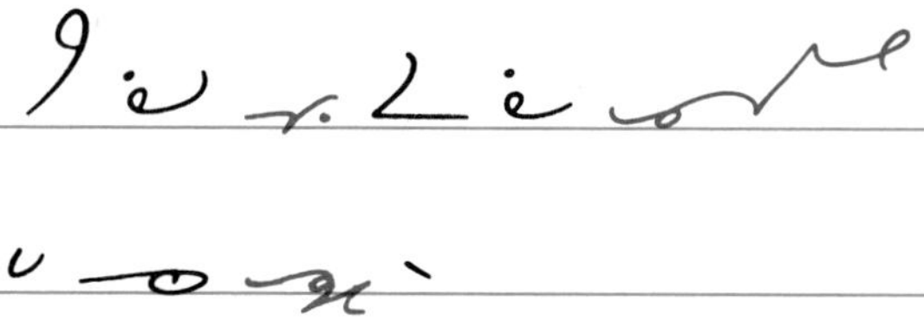

¶ **Business Letter**

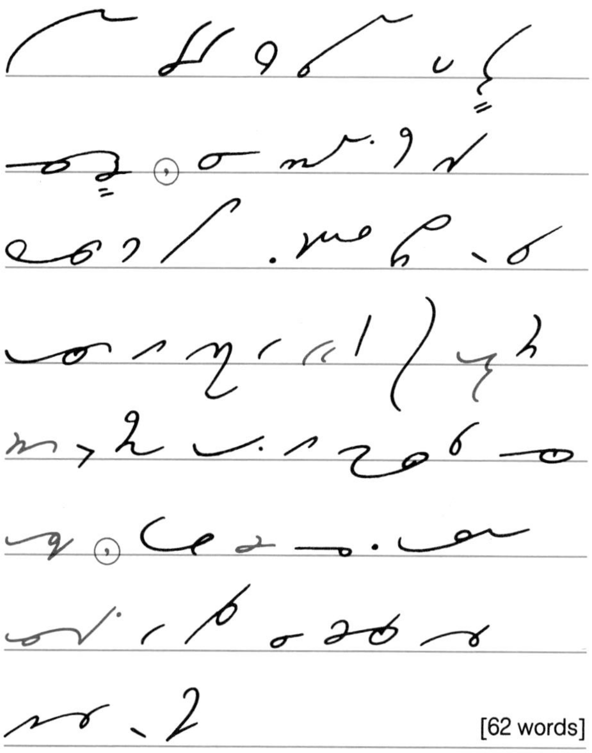

(shorthand outlines)

[62 words]

The word ending *-ings* as in *meetings* is represented by a disjoined *left*
s and is written close to the last symbol in the root word. *(shorthand)*

Example: meetings *(shorthand)*

-ings Words

meetings *(shorthand)*	openings *(shorthand)*	buildings *(shorthand)*
findings *(shorthand)*	savings *(shorthand)*	listings *(shorthand)*

proceedings ■ *[shorthand]*   feelings *[shorthand]*   drawings *[shorthand]*

earnings *[shorthand]*   sayings *[shorthand]*   Jennings *[shorthand]*

■ Transcription Alert.

-ings Practice
24.2

1 *[shorthand outline]*

[shorthand outline]

2 *[shorthand outline]*

3 *[shorthand outline]*

[shorthand outline]

4 *[shorthand outline]*

[shorthand outline] ×

5 *[shorthand outline]*

¶ **Cost Savings**

[shorthand outline]

[shorthand outline]

[shorthand outline]

[shorthand outline]

[shorthand outline]

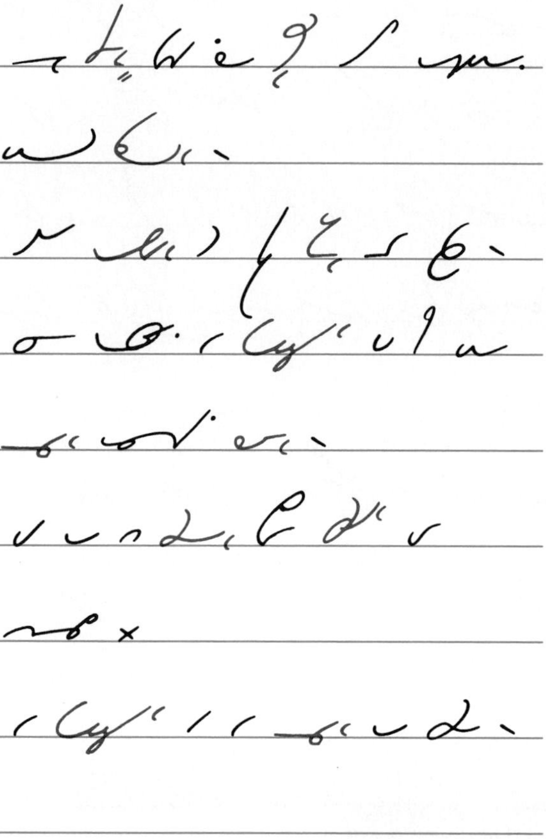

[shorthand outline]

[shorthand outline]

[shorthand outline] ×   [85 words]

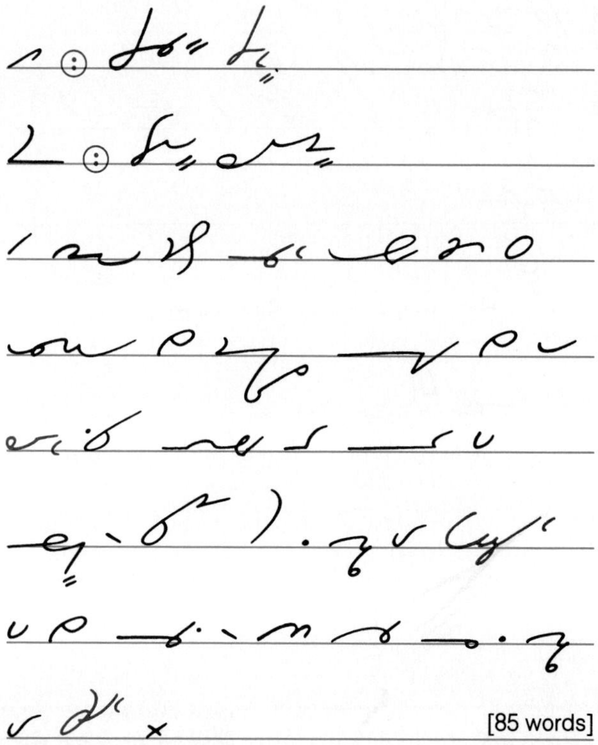

WORD ENDINGS -RITY, -LITY, -LTY

The word ending *-rity* as in *majority* is written with a disjoined *r*. The word endings *-lity* as in *ability* and *-lty* as in *faculty* are written with a disjoined *l*. The disjoined *r* and *l* are written close to the last symbol.

-rity ⌣   -lity, -lty ⌣

Examples: majority _⟋_   ability _(⌣_   faculty _⟍_

-rity Words

majority _⟋_   sincerity _⟍⌣_   authority _⌣_

security _⟍⌣_   charity _/⌣_   prosperity _⟍_

-lity Words

ability _(⌣_   dependability _⟍_   utility _⌣_

facility _⟍_   locality _⌣_   quality _⌣_

possibility _⟋_   personality _⟍_   responsibility ■ _⟍_

■ Brief-form derivative.

-lty Words

faculty _⟍_   penalty _⟍_   royalty _⌣_

-rity, -lity, -lty Practice
24.3

4 [shorthand outlines]

5 [shorthand outlines]

¶ **Memo**

[shorthand outlines]

[shorthand outlines]

[46 words]

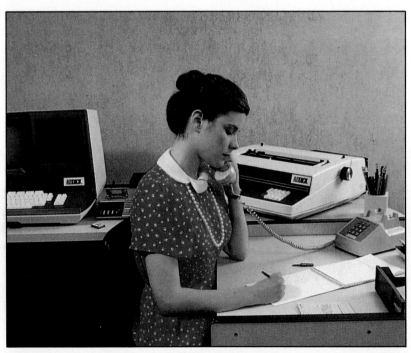

When away on a business trip, the manager may mail in recorded dictation or may call and dictate to the secretary over the phone.

24.4 Dictation Speed Letter

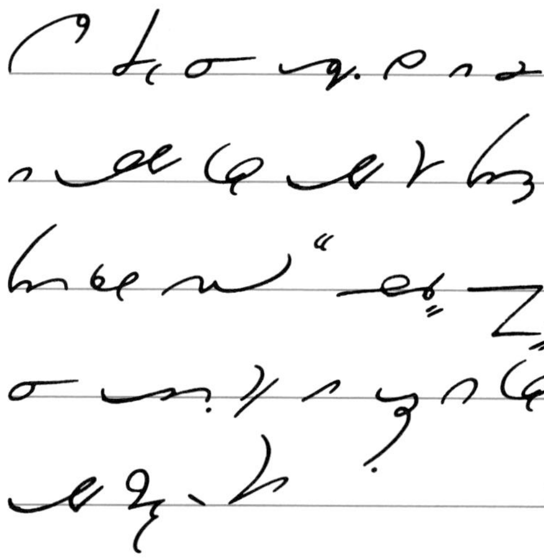

[shorthand outlines]

[40 words]

24.5 Business Memo

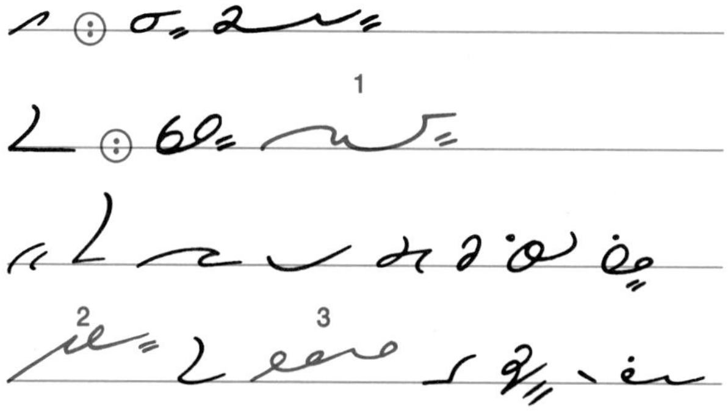

[shorthand outlines]

1 Golden 2 Doyle 3 territory

[shorthand outlines]

[97 words]

4 concerned 5 personality 6 dependability
7 items 8 performance

VII

NEW IN LESSON 25

- Sound of *ort*
- Symbol for the sound of *ea*
- Outlines for days and months

SOUND OF ORT

The sound of *ort* as in *port* is written with the *o* and *t* symbols. For ease of writing, the *r* is not written. Notice that all the words contain either the word *port* or *sort*.

Examples: port sort

Ort Words

port	reporter	sort
portable	support, sport	resort
deport	supports, sports	assort
report	airport	assorted
reported	airports	assortment

1 *[shorthand outline]*

2 *[shorthand outline]*

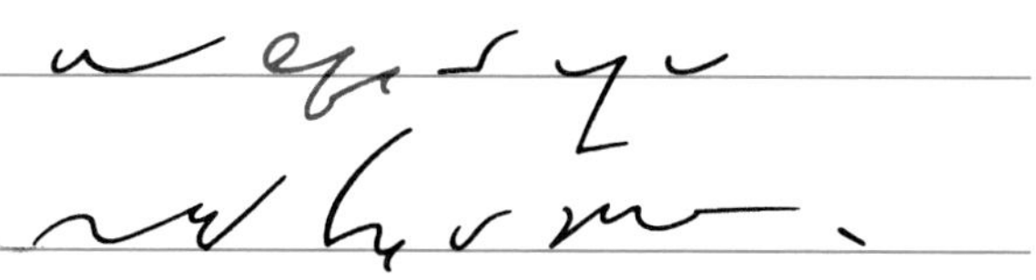

3 *[shorthand outline]*

4 *[shorthand outline]*

5 *[shorthand outline]*

¶ **Business Meeting**

[shorthand outlines]

23.

[shorthand outlines]

27.

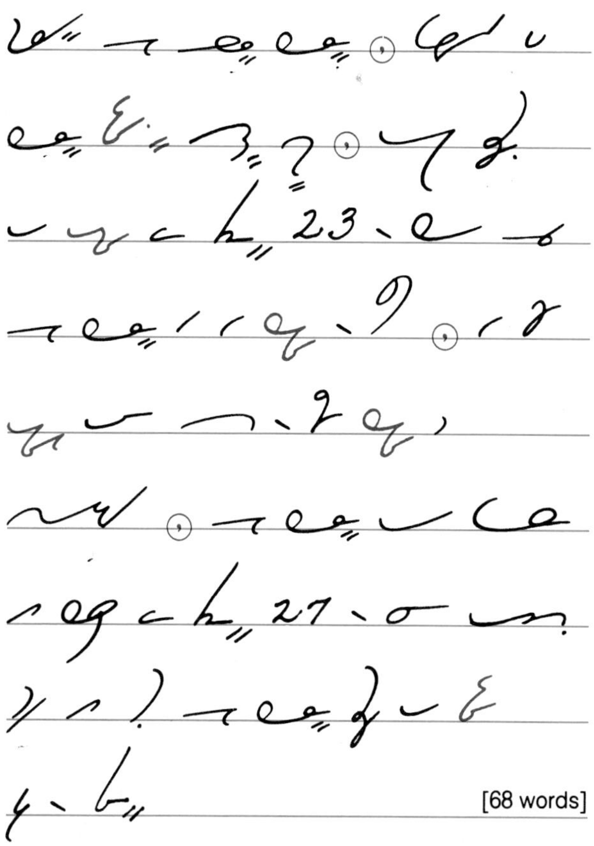

[68 words]

SOUND OF EA

The sound of *e* followed by an *a* as in *area* is represented by an *a* circle with a dot in it. The dot is added after the body of the outline has been written. We call this symbol *e ah*.  *○*

Example: area *[shorthand outline]*

Ea Words

area *(shorthand)*

areas *(shorthand)*

create *(shorthand)*

created *(shorthand)*

creation *(shorthand)*

creative *(shorthand)*

piano *(shorthand)*

appreciate *(shorthand)*

appreciates *(shorthand)*

appreciated *(shorthand)*

associate *(shorthand)*

associated *(shorthand)*

associating *(shorthand)*

Gloria *(shorthand)*

Garcia *(shorthand)*

Ea Practice
25.2

1 *(shorthand outline)*

2 *(shorthand outline)*

3 *(shorthand outline)*

4 *(shorthand outline)*

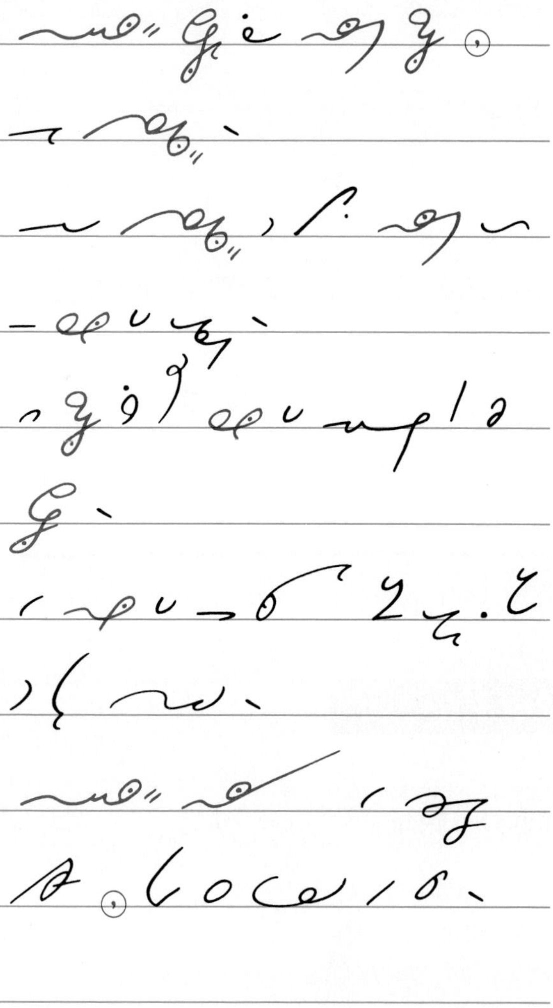

5 *(shorthand outline)*

¶ **Advertising Material**

(shorthand outline)

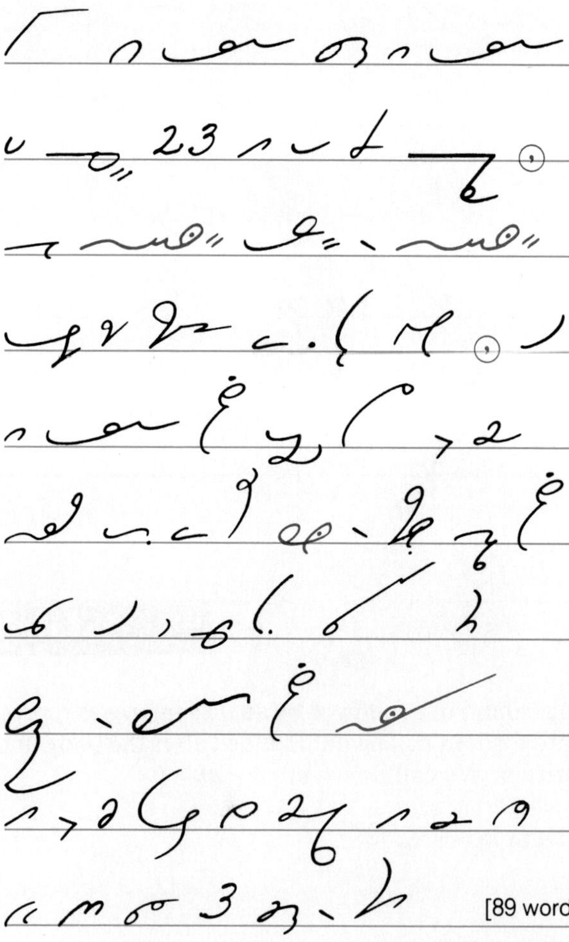

[89 words]

DAYS AND MONTHS

The sound of the first syllable is written for each day of the week; *fri* for *Friday*, for example. The sound of the first syllable is written for each month of the year except for the five months *March* through *July*, which are easy to write in full.

Days

Sunday _____   Wednesday _____   Saturday _____

Monday _____   Thursday _____

Tuesday _____   Friday _____

Months

January _____   May _____   September _____

February _____   June _____   October _____

March _____   July _____   November _____

April _____   August _____   December _____

Days and Months Practice
25.3

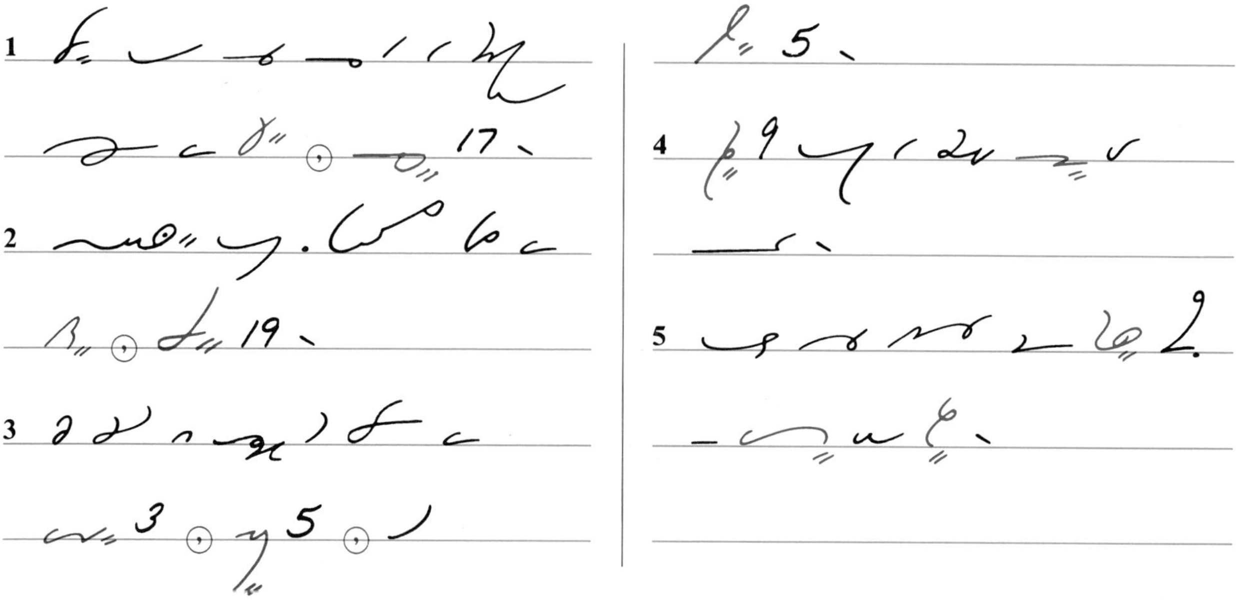

[shorthand notes]

[94 words]

Executives who take shorthand notes during a meeting capture the main points being discussed and note any actions that must be taken afterward.

25.4 Dictation Speed Letter

[shorthand outlines]

[60 words]

25.5 Department Merger

[shorthand outlines]

1 Richards

[shorthand outlines]

[82 words]

2 Boyd   3 devised   4 merge   5 division
6 developed   7 overhead   8 listen   9 possible

LESSON

26

- Seven brief forms
- Word beginnings *en-* and *un-*
- Symbols for the sounds of *ya* and *ye*
- Shorthand for personal use

BRIEF FORMS

any	manufacture	very
gentlemen	morning	
insure, insurance	time	

Brief-Form Derivatives

anybody	anytime	manufacturer
anyone	insuring	timed
anything	insured	timely
anyway	gentleman	sometime
anywhere ■	manufactured	mornings

■ In the compound word *anywhere*, the *e* is dropped from *any* for ease of writing.

Brief-Form Phrases

at this time	by this time	very much

Brief-Form Practice

26.1

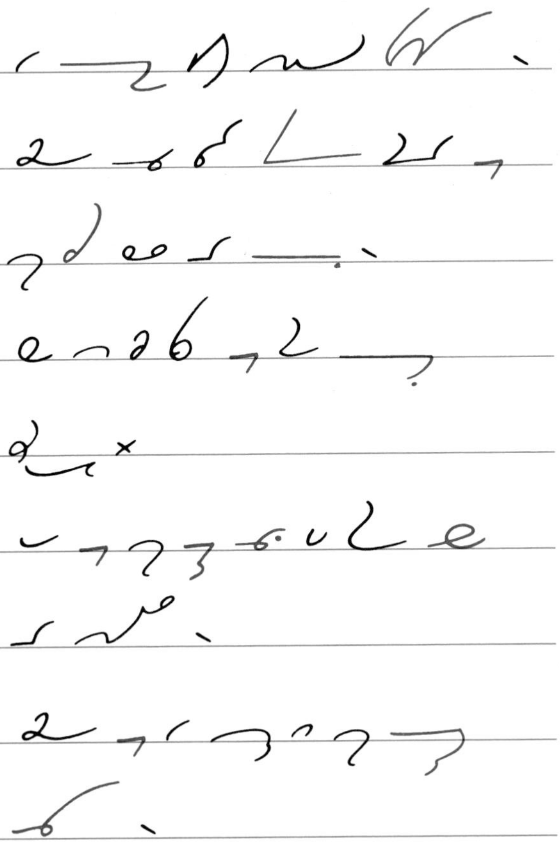

¶ **Insurance Policy**

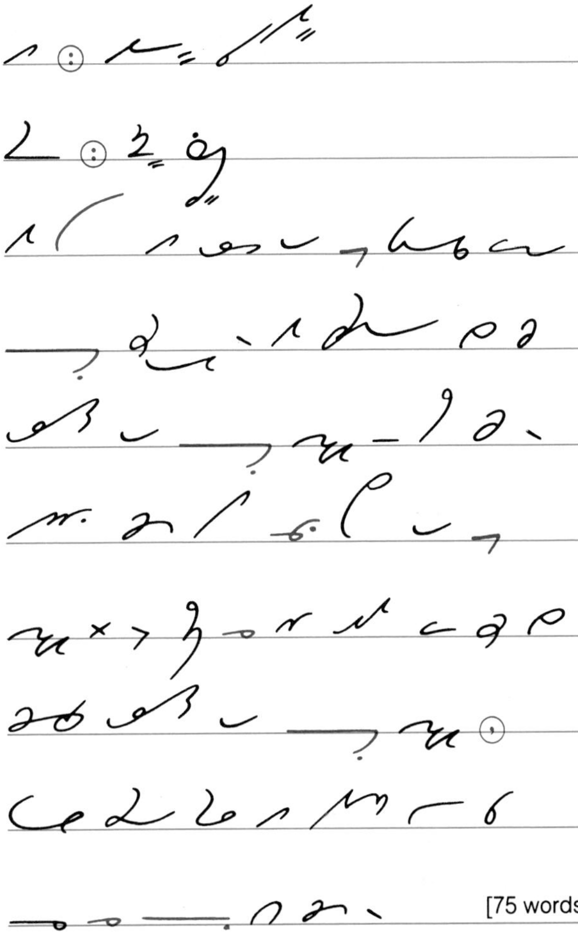

[75 words]

WORD BEGINNINGS EN-, UN-

The word beginning *en-* as in *enjoy* and the word beginning *un-* as in *until* are represented by the *n* symbol. You have been using the letter *n* for the similar word beginning *in-* ever since you learned the brief form *in* in Lesson 4.

Examples: enjoy  until 

En- Words

enjoy

enroll

enrolled

enrollment

engine

engineers

encourages

encouragement

endeavor

engagement

enforce

environment

Un- Words

until

unless

unlikely

unload

unloaded

unrelated

unfair

unwilling

unpaid

But: When a vowel follows *en-*, *un-*, or *in-*, the initial vowel is also written.

enable

unable

innovative

En-, Un- Practice
26.2

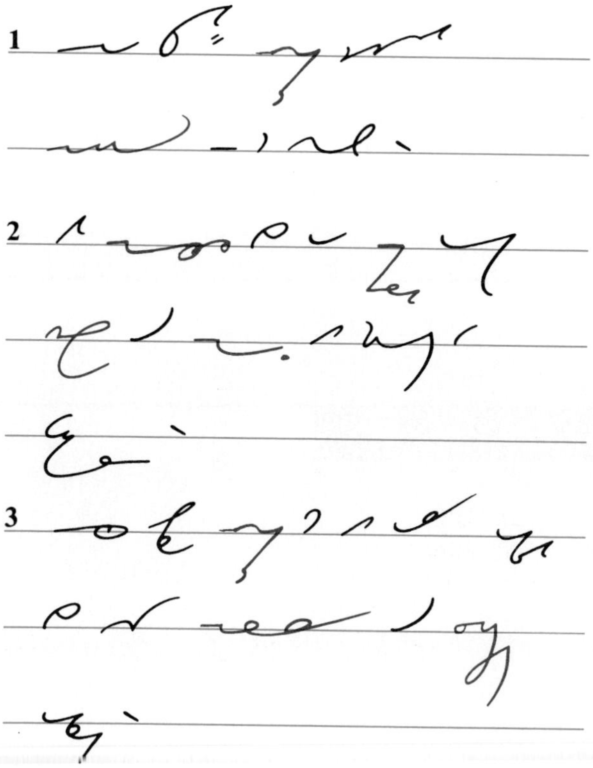

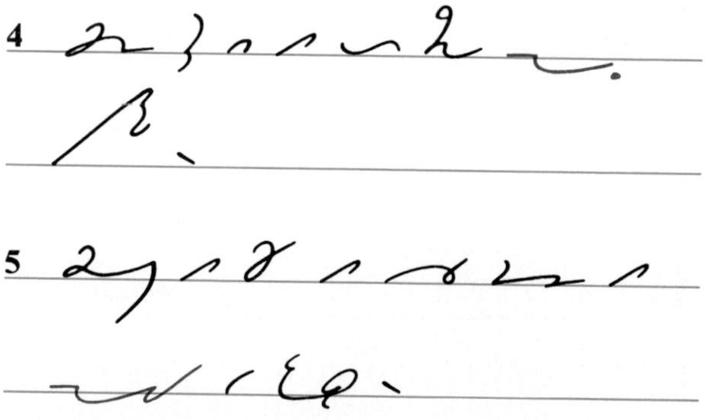

1

2

3

4

5

¶ **Payment Collections**

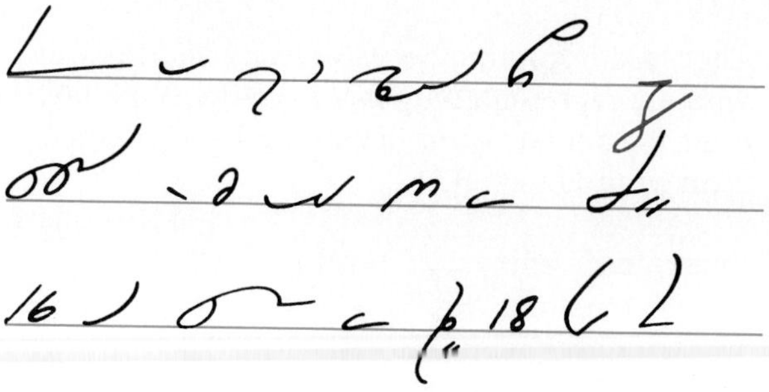

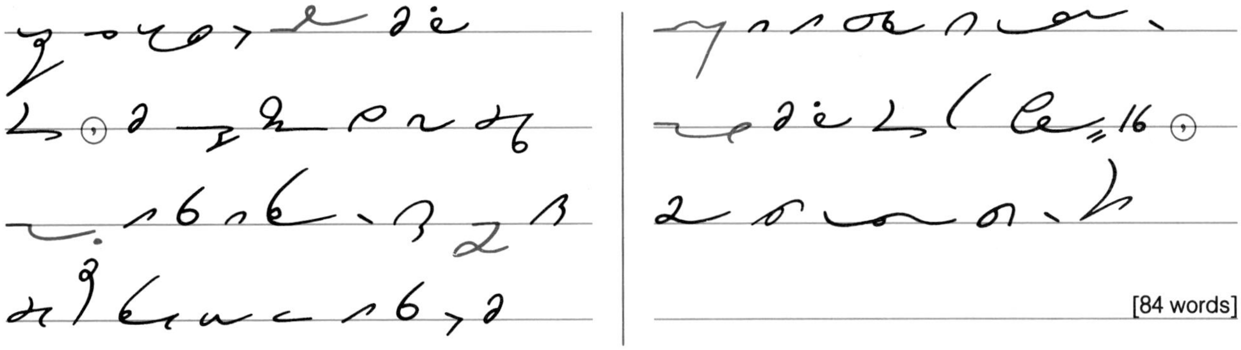

[shorthand outlines]

[84 words]

SOUNDS OF YA, YE

The sounds of *ya* as in *yard* and *ye* as in *year* are expressed by dropping the *y* and simply writing the *a* or the *e* that follows.

ya *⟋*   ye *∘*

Examples: yard *⟋*   year *⟍*

Ya Words

yard *⟋*   yarn *⟍*   Yale *⟍*

Ye Words

year *⟍*   yield *⟍*   yielded *⟍*

years *⟍*   yielding *⟍*   yes *9*

yellow *⟍*   yields *⟍*   yet *6*

Ya, Ye Practice
26.3

1 *[shorthand outline]*

2 *[shorthand outline]*

3 *[shorthand outline]*

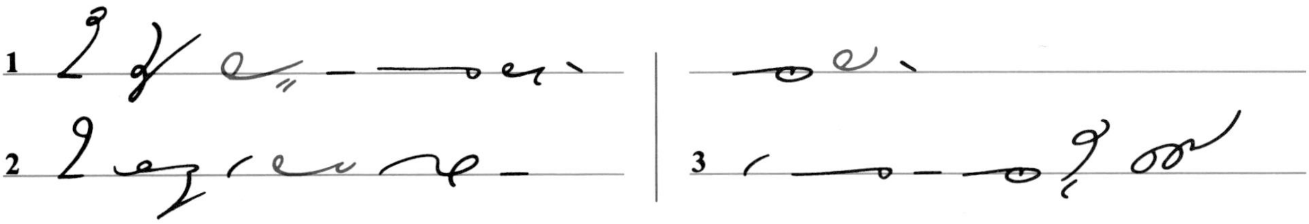

(shorthand symbols)

4 *(shorthand symbols)*

5 *(shorthand symbols)*

¶ **Furniture Manufacturer**

(shorthand symbols)

[67 words]

Using Shorthand for "To Do" Lists

Shorthand has many valuable uses both on the job and in one's personal life. Instructions about projects that need to be done, shopping lists, lists of appointments, and other personal reminders can all be easily written in shorthand.

In order to really learn and to retain shorthand, you must write it all the time. Once you have acquired the habit of using shorthand for all your personal notes, you will become so proficient in its use that you will wish you never had to write longhand again!

Here is an example of a personal "to do" list:

Done	Priority	To Do December 16
	A	*(shorthand symbols)*
	B	*(shorthand symbols)*
	B	*(shorthand symbols)*

Reading and Writing Practice

26.4 Dictation Speed Letter

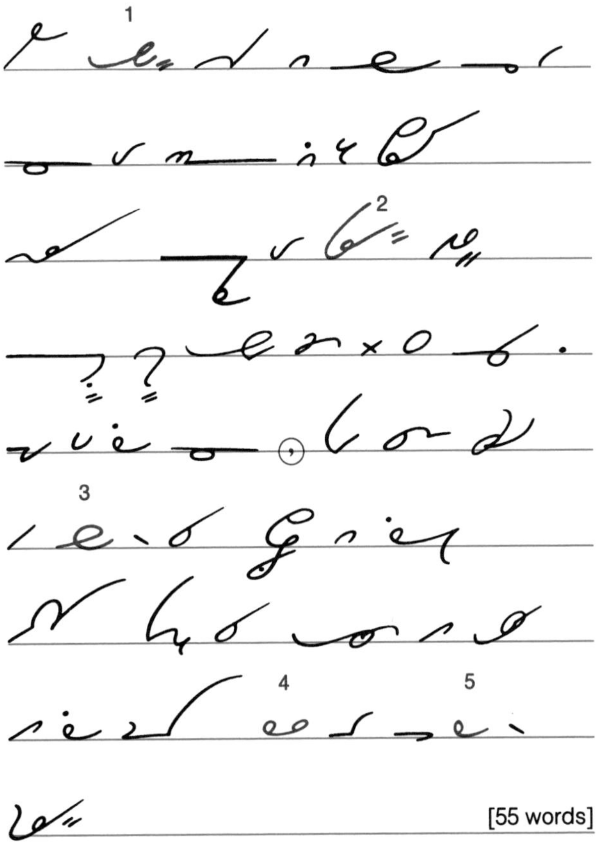

[Shorthand outlines]

[55 words]

1 Leo 2 Boyd 3 anywhere 4 early
5 year

26.5 Personal Note

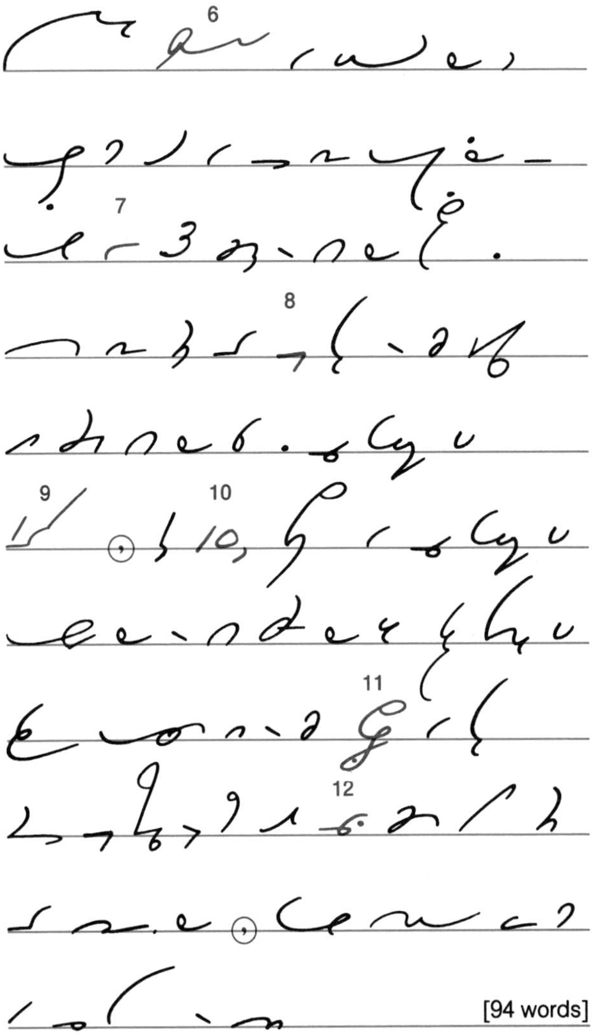

[Shorthand outlines]

[94 words]

6 Tyler   7 than   8 insurance   9 $100,000
10 10 percent   11 appreciate   12 anything

LESSON 27

NEW IN LESSON 27

- Word ending *-ification*
- Word beginning *mis-*
- New symbol for *w*
- Handling interruptions during dictation

WORD ENDING -IFICATION

The word ending *-ification* as in *notification* is represented by a disjoined *f* and is written close to the last symbol.

Example: notification

-ification Words

notification   modifications   specifications

classification   justification   identification

classifications   ratification   certification

modification   specification   clarification

However, note that the word ending *-ify* is written according to the "minor-vowel-omitted" rule.

Example: ratify

Minor-Vowel-Omitted Words

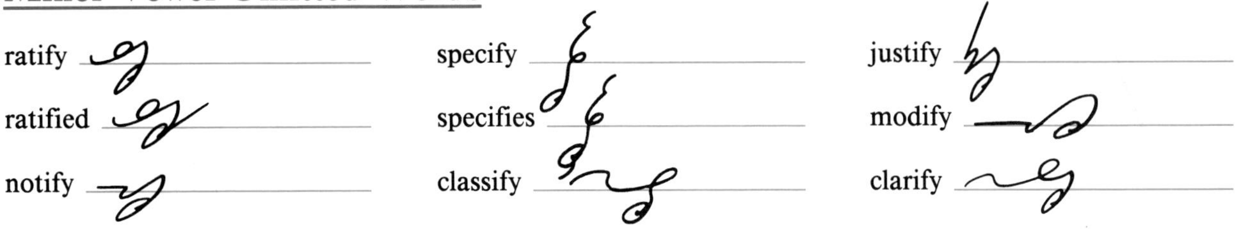

ratify _[shorthand]_

specify _[shorthand]_

justify _[shorthand]_

ratified _[shorthand]_

specifies _[shorthand]_

modify _[shorthand]_

notify _[shorthand]_

classify _[shorthand]_

clarify _[shorthand]_

-ification Practice
27.1

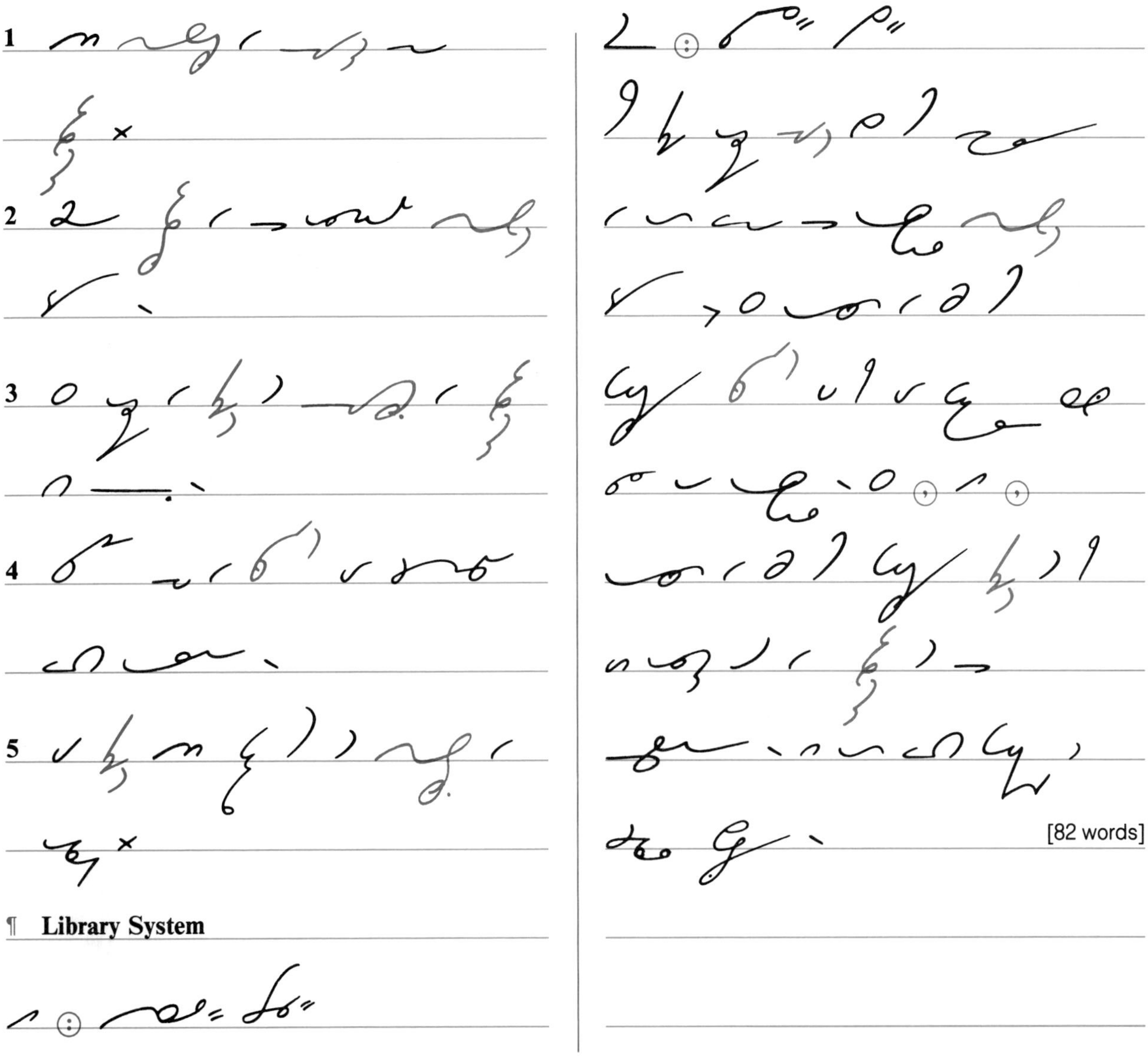

1 _[shorthand outlines]_

2 _[shorthand outlines]_

3 _[shorthand outlines]_

4 _[shorthand outlines]_

5 _[shorthand outlines]_

¶ **Library System**

[shorthand outlines]

[shorthand outlines]

[82 words]

The word beginning *mis-* as in *mistake* is abbreviated with the *m* and *s* symbols.

Example: mistake _(shorthand)_

Mis- Words

mistake _(shorthand)_	misplace _(shorthand)_	misprint _(shorthand)_
mistakes _(shorthand)_	mislead _(shorthand)_	mystery _(shorthand)_
mistaken _(shorthand)_	misleading _(shorthand)_	misrepresent _(shorthand)_

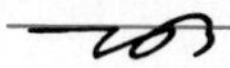

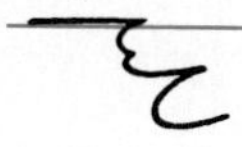

Mis- Practice
27.2

(shorthand practice sentences numbered 1–5)

¶ **Thank-You Letter**

(shorthand)

[64 words]

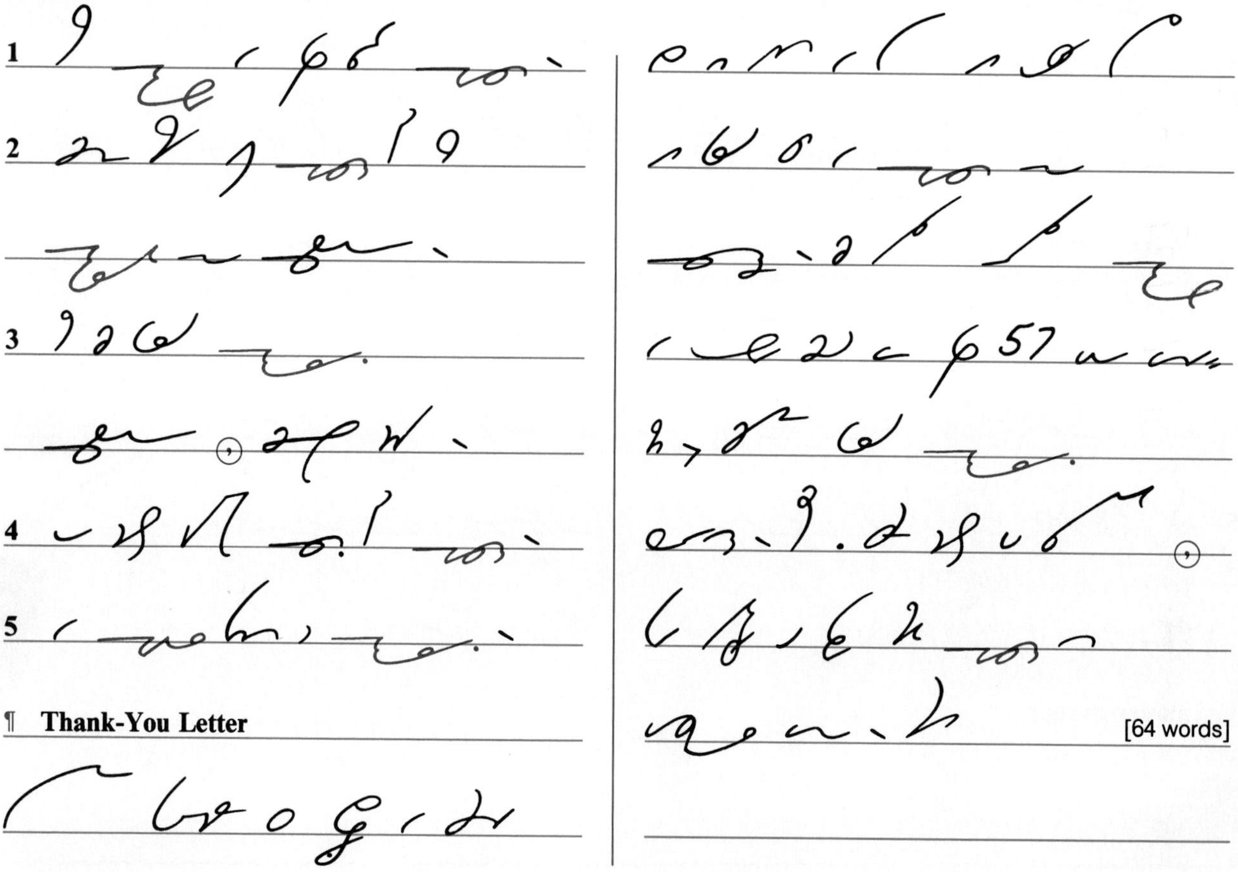

In Lesson 6 you learned that the *oo* symbol represents the sound of *w* or *wh* at the beginning of words. A *w* within the body of a word is represented by a short dash *underneath the following vowel*. The dash is written after the body of the outline. ⎯

Example: quick ⟋

W Dash Words

quick ⟋

quickly ⟋⟋

quit ⟋

quote, quart ⟋

quoted ⟋

quarterly ⟋

qualify ⟋

quite ⟋

always ⟋

Broadway ⟋

square ⟋

hardware ⟋

W Dash Practice
27.3

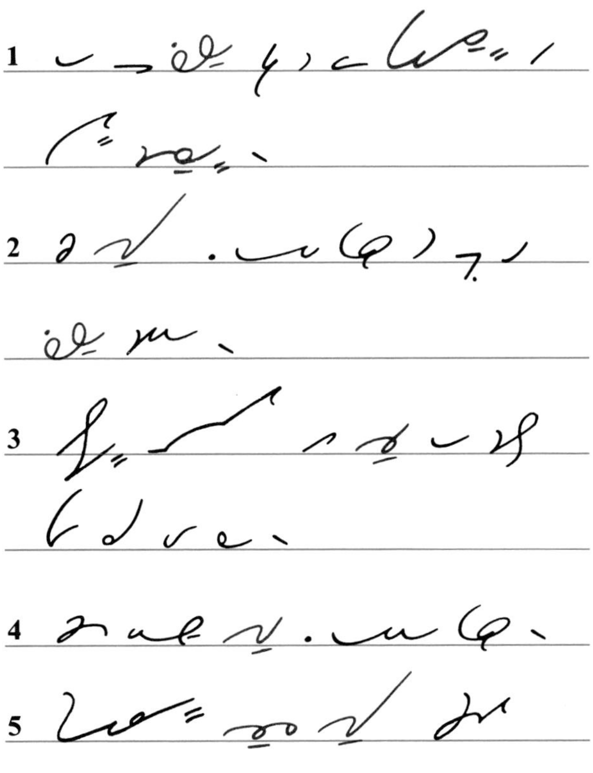

¶ **Insurance Quotes**

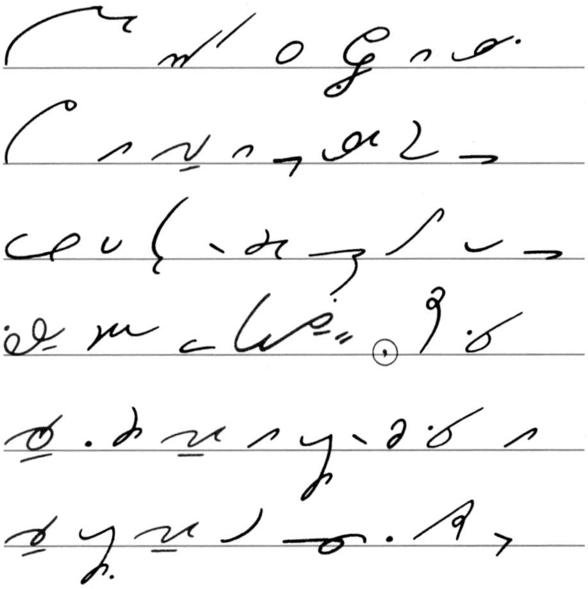

An executive may leave a meeting in order to dictate information that must be transcribed and brought back into the meeting.

Handling Interruptions During Dictation

One of the realities of taking dictation in an office is that executives are frequently interrupted. They may be interrupted by the telephone, they may search for a file, or they may simply take a long pause in order to collect their thoughts. These interruptions can be of benefit to the secretary who is writing shorthand.

During a pause, the secretary should quickly scan the notes that have just been written to see if they are readable. Missing outlines can usually be supplied from memory while the dictation is "fresh." Poorly written outlines may be rewritten so that they will be readable during transcription later on. If it is found that outlines are missing or unreadable, the interruption is a good time for the secretary to ask for clarification before the dictation resumes.

Reading and Writing Practice

27.4 Dictation Speed Letter

(shorthand outlines)

[45 words]

27.5 Factory Plan

(shorthand outlines)

1 recent   2 Let us   3 Moreno

(shorthand outlines)

[73 words]

4 specifications   5 construction   6 Peoria
7 study   8 whatever   9 appreciate

NEW IN LESSON 28

- Eight brief forms
- Word beginning *ex-*
- Salutations and complimentary closings
- Differentiating between *correspondence*, *correspondents* and *accept*, *except*

BRIEF FORMS

correspond, correspondence

equip

never

opinion

order

product

regular

thank

Brief-Form Derivatives

corresponds

corresponded

correspondent

correspondents

equipment

equipped

opinions

orders

ordered ■

ordering

products

production

regularly

thanks ■ ■

thanking

■ The jog is used to distinguish the *d* in *order* from the *d* representing past tense.

■ ■ The *dot* is dropped and replaced by the *s*.

Brief-Form Phrases

In order to increase writing speed, the dot is omitted from the brief
form *thank* in the following *thank* phrases.

in order	*(outline)*	thank you for the	*(outline)*
your order ■	*(outline)*	thank you for your	*(outline)*
thank you	*(outline)*	thank you for your order ■	*(outline)*
thank you for	*(outline)*	thank you for your letter	*(outline)*

■ For ease of writing, the *o* in *order* is eliminated when phrased with *you* and
your.

Brief-Form Practice
28.1

1

2

3

4

5

¶ **Lost Shipment**

[96 words]

The word beginning *ex-* as in *extra* is written with the *e* and *s* symbols, depending on the symbol that follows *ex*.

ex- ⟋ or ℓ

Examples: extra ⟋◡ expire ℰ

Ex- Words

extra	⟋◡	exactly	⟋◡	export	ℰ
exam	⟋	exciting	⟋	expect	ℰ
examine	⟋	expire	ℰ	expected	ℰ
extreme	⟋◡	expired	ℰ	expense	ℰ
extremely	⟋◡◦	expand	ℰ	expenses	ℰ
exact	⟋◡	expert	ℰ	expensive	ℰ

Ex- Practice
28.2

1 *(shorthand outlines)*

2 *(shorthand outlines)*

3 *(shorthand outlines)*

4 *(shorthand outlines)*

5 *(shorthand outlines)*

¶ **Study Notes**

(shorthand outlines)

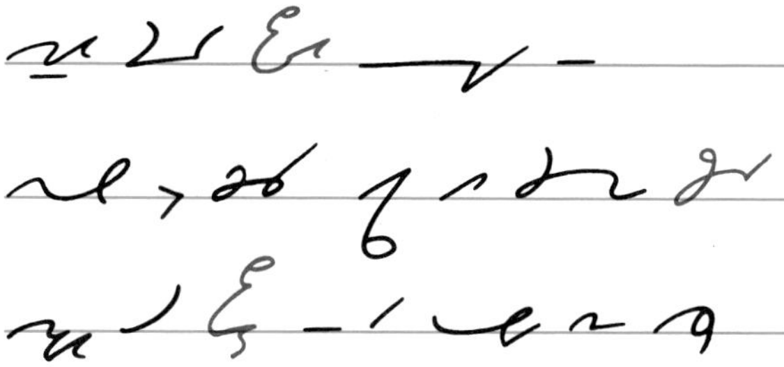

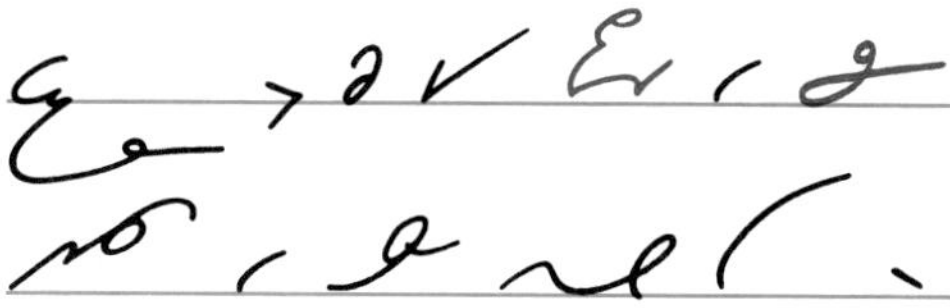

[shorthand outlines] [65 words]

SALUTATIONS AND COMPLIMENTARY CLOSINGS

Eight salutations and complimentary closings were presented in Lesson 12. Here are the remaining six for which we have special outlines.

Dear Ms.  _[shorthand]_   Sincerely yours _[shorthand]_   Yours sincerely _[shorthand]_

Very cordially yours _[shorthand]_   Very sincerely yours _[shorthand]_   Yours very sincerely _[shorthand]_

Salutation and Complimentary Closing Practice
28.3

1 _[shorthand]_

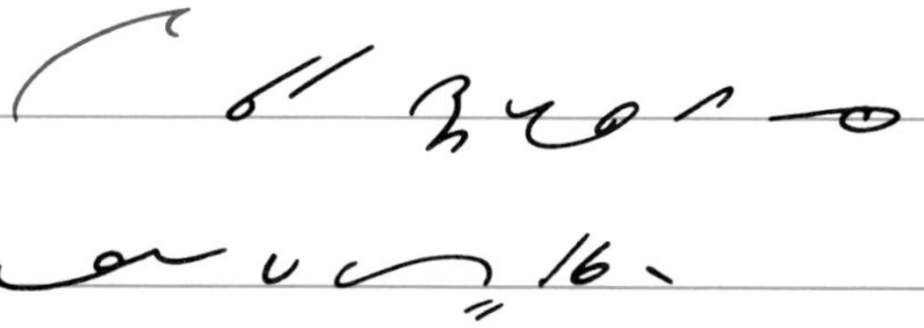

2 _[shorthand]_

3 _[shorthand]_

4 _[shorthand]_

5 _[shorthand]_

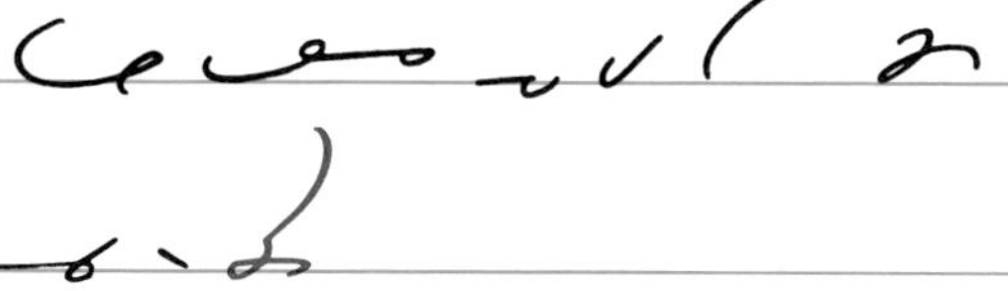

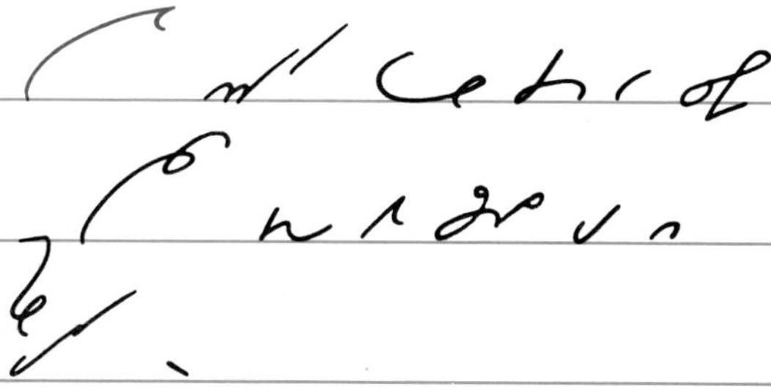

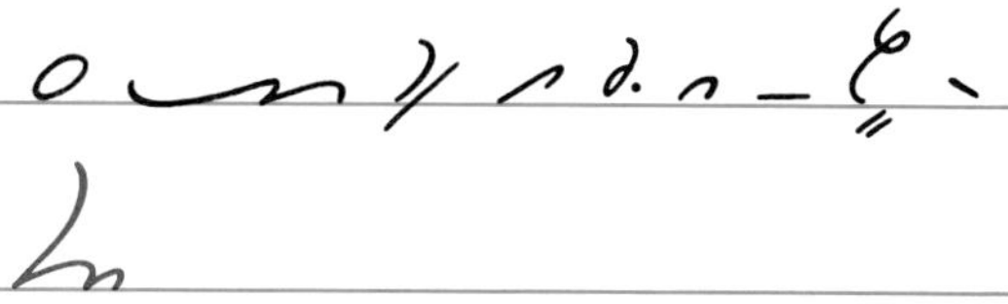

Communication Skill Builder

Similar Words: correspondence, correspondents

correspondence: letters and other communications

correspondents: people who communicate by letter or who contribute news and articles to the news media; plural of *correspondent*

[shorthand notation]

I have much *correspondence* to read by Friday.

[shorthand notation]

The news agency has news *correspondents* all over the country.

Similar Words: accept, except

accept: to agree to; to receive

except: (prep.) other than; excluding

[shorthand notation]

We *accept* your offer to pay $480 for our boat.

[shorthand notation]

Everyone *except* Bill enjoyed the book.

Reading and Writing Practice

28.4 Dictation Speed Letter

[shorthand notation]

[52 words]

1 appreciation   2 quality   3 opinions

4 Maybe   5 campaign

28.5 Relocation

(shorthand outlines)

6 Paul   7 export   8 necessary

[84 words]

9 council   10 official   11 exciting

Secretaries are often required to attend important meetings in order to record the minutes.

U N I T

VIII

LESSON 29

- Symbol for the sound of *ia*
- Word beginnings *inter-* and *enter-*
- Outlines for cities and states
- Differentiating between similar words *quit*, *quite*, and *quiet*

SOUND OF IA

The sound of *long i* followed by soft *a* as in *client* is represented by the *long i* symbol in which the tail of the *i* is closed as a second circle.

ia $\mathcal{O}$

Example: client ～○

Ia Words

client ～○   riot ○   dryer ～○

quiet ○   trial ～○   dryers ～○

science ○   appliances ○   O'Bryan ○

prior ○   reliance ○   Ryan ○

Ia Practice
29.1

1 [shorthand outline]

[shorthand outline]

[shorthand outline]

2 [shorthand outline]

[shorthand outline]

3 [shorthand outline]

[shorthand outline]

4 [shorthand outline]

[shorthand outline]

5 [shorthand outline]

[shorthand outline]

¶ **Business Letter**

[shorthand outlines]

[58 words]

WORD BEGINNINGS INTER-, ENTER-

The word beginnings *inter-* as in *interest* and *intr-* as in *introduce* are written with a disjoined *n*. The word beginnings *enter-* as in *entertain* and *entr-* as in *entrance* are also written with a disjoined *n*. Line placement of the *inter-* word beginning is generally halfway between the lines of writing.

Examples: interest [outline] introduce [outline] entertain [outline] entrance [outline]

Inter- Words

interest _／_ interviewing _⌐ん._ international _￢℮_

interested _ノ_ interfere _￣ユ_ interrupted _￣-✓_

interests _ュ_ interfered _￣ユ_ introduce _￣ノ_

interview _￣ユ_ interval _￣ユ_ introduction _￣ᴧ_

Enter- Words

enter _￣_ entertain _／_ enterprises _￣Ϭ_

entering _￣·_ entertainment _／_ entrance _￣ᴢ_

entered _／_ enterprise _￣Ϭ_ entrances _￣ᴦ_

Inter-, Enter- Practice
29.2

1 _℮ Ϭϑノ ￢℮ ᴧ·_

2 _ᴜᴧ ᴄᴊ ￣ ᴧ ノᴢ_

_℮ᴧ ￢℮ ᴜᴦ·_

3 _ᴦᴧϭᴅϭ Ϭᴢ_

4 _ϑノ ᴦᴧ ノ￣✓ ᴦ_

_ノᴅ ᴜᴊ Ϭ=·_

5 _￣ᴧ ᴥ✓ノ·_

¶ **Job Interview**

ᴦ ℮ϑᴦ·ᴧᴥᴜ ᴦ

_ユ ℮ᴋ·ᴢ ✓ ℮ᴧ ᴜ/_

_ノ ᴦ ᴧ℮ᴊᴦ ᴜ Ϭ·⊙'_

ᴜ ᴧᴅϭϑ ᴦᴢᴄ

ᴜᴦ· ᴄ℮ᴊᴦᴥ ￣ᴦ

_ᴑ ᴧ ᴧᴜ ᴜᴩ_

ᴧᴦノ ᴑ ￢℮ ᴊ·

_ᴑᴧ ᴧ ℮ᴥ ￣ ᴜᴥ·_

_ᴜᴩ ᴦ⊙ ￢℮= Ϭ·_

_ᴧ_

[87 words]

The state abbreviations are simply shorthand versions of the standard two-letter state abbreviations used with ZIP Codes. The complete lists of state abbreviations and abbreviations for many cities are appendices to the *Gregg Shorthand Dictionary*. Here are several examples.

Cities

Chicago

Boston

Philadelphia

San Francisco

Los Angeles

St. Louis

Denver

New Orleans

Seattle

States

The shorthand outline for each state abbreviation is based upon the two-letter ZIP Code abbreviation. The following guidelines were used to determine the shorthand symbol:

1 The *c* is represented by *k* in CA, CO, CT, NC, and SC.
2 The *y* is represented by *i* in KY, NY, and WY.
3 The *short i* is represented by *e* in IL, IN, and WI.
4 The *w* is represented by *oo* in WA, WV, WI, and WY.

Massachusetts

Illinois

Pennsylvania

California

Missouri

Wyoming

Georgia

Florida

New York

Similar abbreviations are used for the following:

America

American

United States

Cities and States Practice
29.3

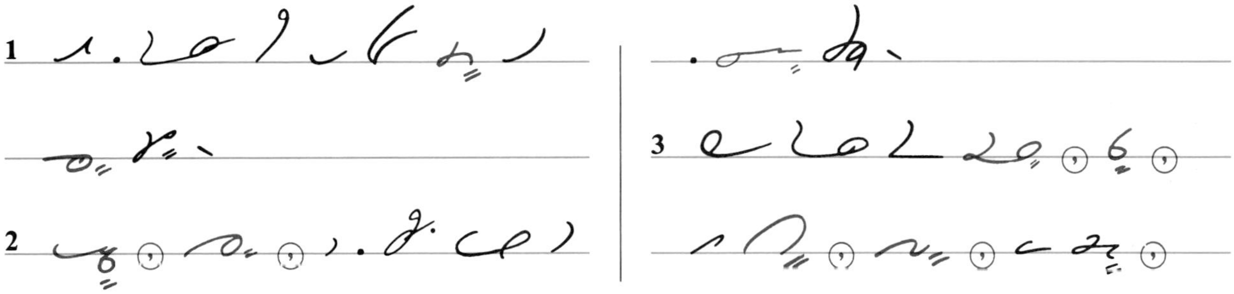

1

2

3

~ 23 ~

4 *[shorthand]*

5 *[shorthand]*

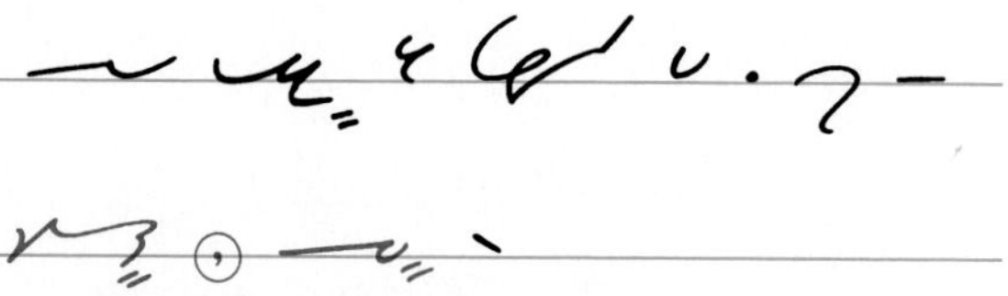

¶ **Geography Class Notes**

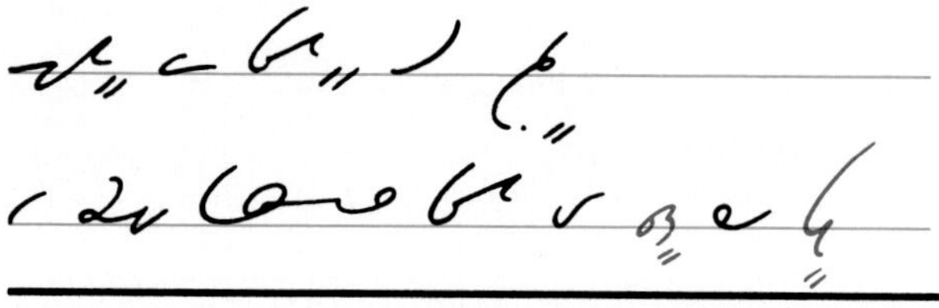

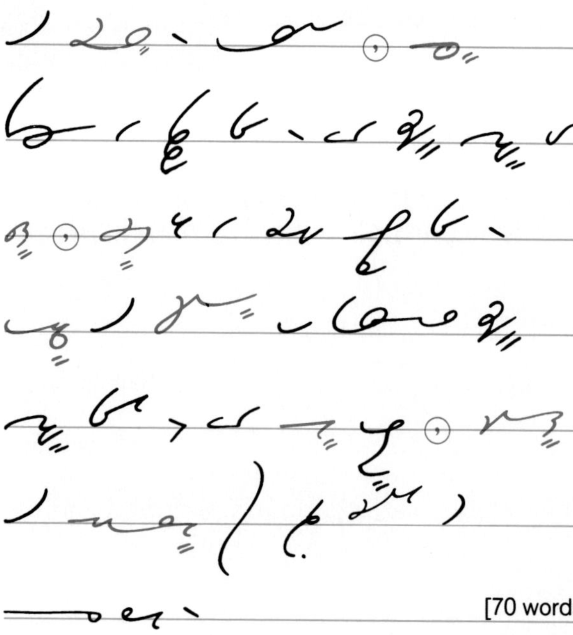

[shorthand]

[shorthand] [70 words]

Communication Skill Builder

Similar Words: quit, quite, quiet

quit: to stop

quite: entirely; somewhat or rather

quiet: without noise

[shorthand]

Mark says he will *quit* smoking.

[shorthand]

I am *quite* pleased with my grades.

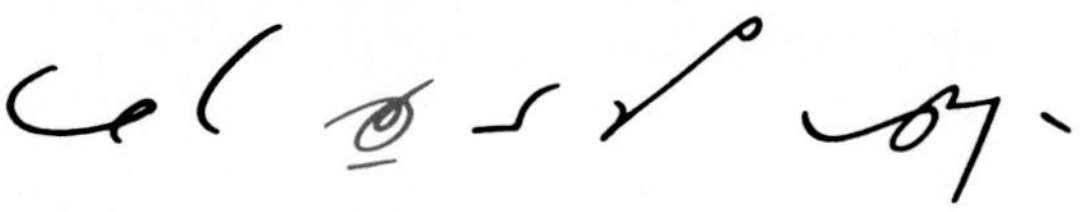

[shorthand]

Please be *quiet* in the study lounge.

29.4 Contribution Appreciation

[60 words]

29.5 Letter of Condolence

1 generous   2 Science   3 supported   4 Glenn

[80 words]

5 death   6 Jennings   7 regrets   8 Enterprises
9 entertainment   10 broadcast   11 media

LESSON 30

NEW IN LESSON 30

- Eight brief forms
- Word ending *-tribute*
- Word ending *-ful*
- Using shorthand for confidentiality

BRIEF FORMS

enclose _____

envelope _____

newspaper _____

probable _____

property _____

recognize _____

throughout _____

usual _____

Brief-Form Derivatives

enclosed _____

enclosure _____

envelopes _____

probably _____

recognized _____

recognition _____

recognizes _____

usually _____

unusual _____

Brief-Form Practice
30.1

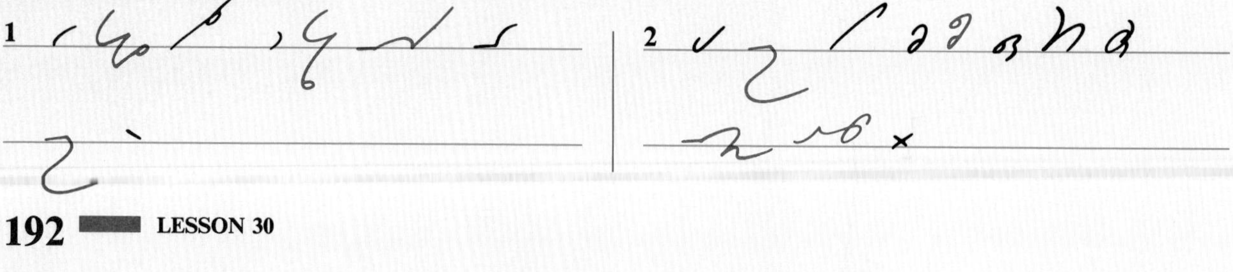

1 _____

2 _____

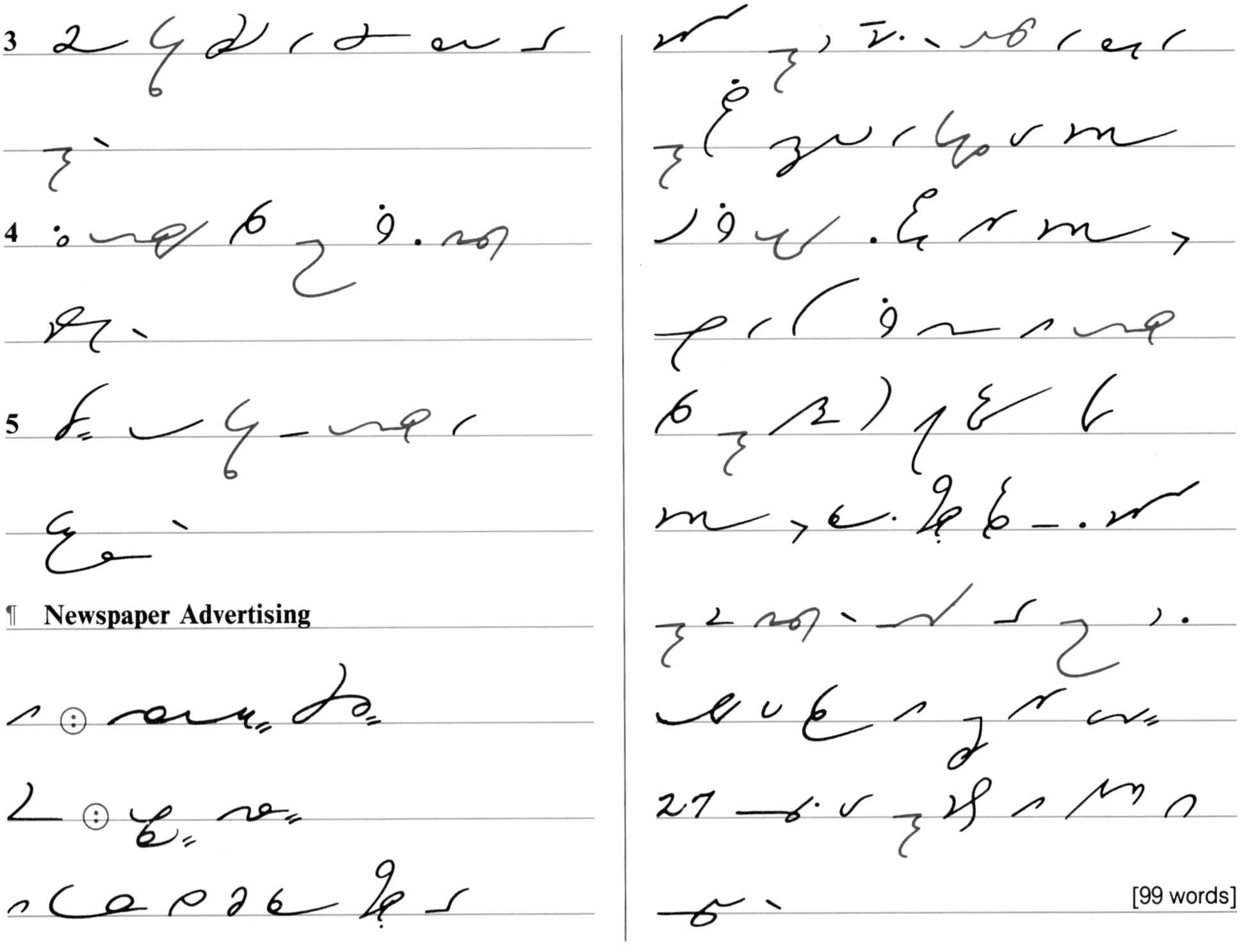

3 [shorthand outline]

4 [shorthand outline]

5 [shorthand outline]

¶ **Newspaper Advertising**

[shorthand outlines]

[shorthand outlines]

[99 words]

WORD ENDING -TRIBUTE

The word ending -*tribute* as in *contribute* is written with the *t r e b* symbols.

-tribute [shorthand outline]

Example: contribute [shorthand outline]

-tribute Words

contribute [shorthand]	distribute [shorthand]	distributes [shorthand]
contribution [shorthand]	distributed [shorthand]	attributes [shorthand]
contributor [shorthand]	distribution [shorthand]	attributed [shorthand]

-tribute Practice
30.2

1 *[shorthand]*

2 *[shorthand]*

3 *[shorthand]*

4 *[shorthand]*

5 *[shorthand]*

¶ **Distribution Routes**

[shorthand]

[64 words]

An attorney can quickly record information and draft questions in shorthand.

The word ending *-ful* as in *grateful* is expressed with the *f* symbol.

Example: grateful   〰️

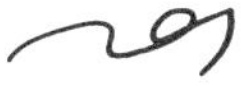

-ful Words

grateful _____

successful ■ _____

successfully ■ _____

helpful _____

useful _____

careful _____

carefully _____

meaningful _____

beautiful _____

wonderful _____

hopefully _____

delightful _____

thoughtful _____

doubtful _____

thankful ■ _____

■ Brief-form derivative.

-ful Practice
30.3

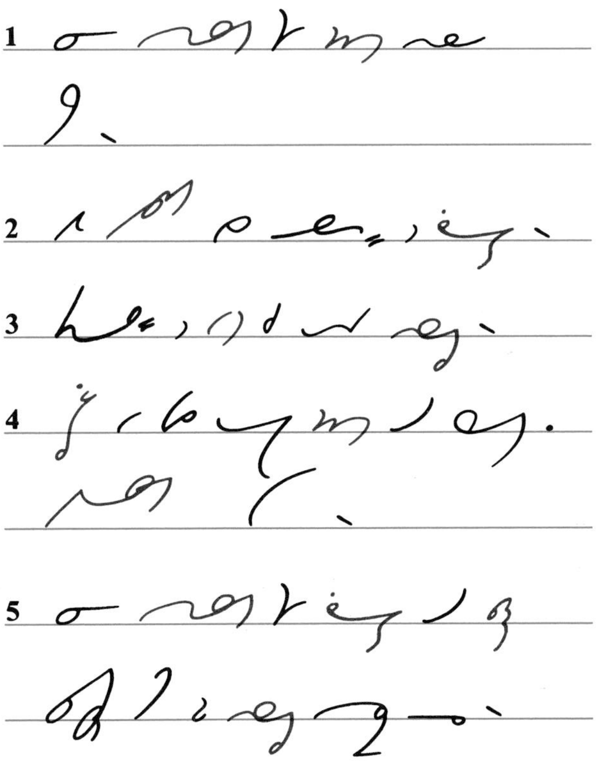

1 _____

2 _____

3 _____

4 _____

5 _____

¶ **Research Report**

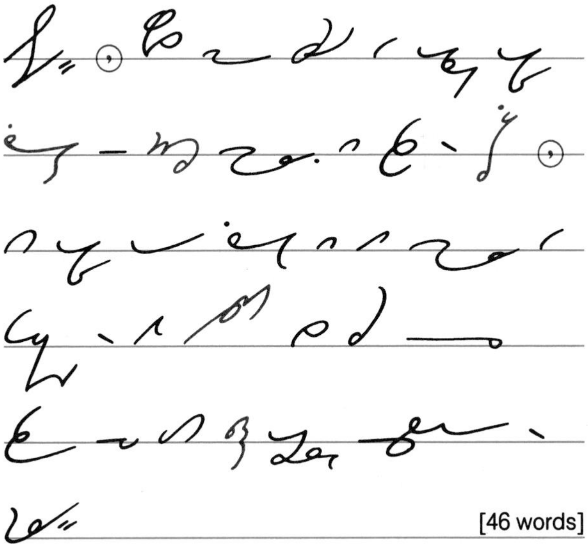

[46 words]

Using Shorthand for Confidentiality

A practical definition of a secretary or an administrative assistant is "the executive's closest and most trusted employee." By working so closely with an executive, a secretary naturally learns information that must be kept confidential. This is one more aspect of office work in which shorthand proves to be valuable.

When an executive wants to dictate a document, the strictest confidentiality may be important. The executive can then dictate to the private secretary who takes shorthand rather than have an anonymous person in a steno pool or word processing center transcribe a voice recording.

Reading and Writing Practice

30.4 Dictation Speed Letter

[75 words]

1 property   2 clipping

30.5 Survey Report

3 Klein   4 response   5 unusually   6 effort
7 comments

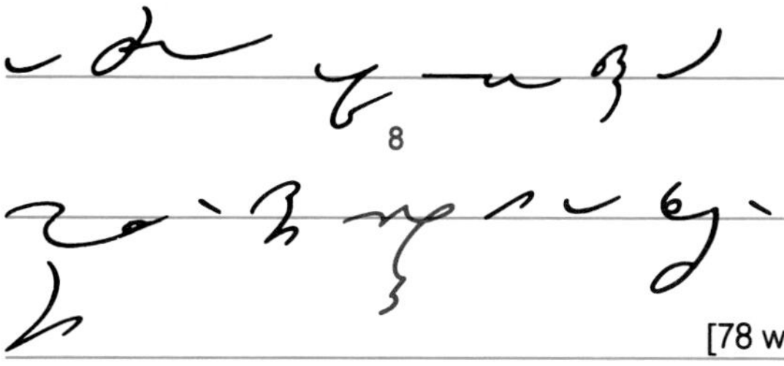

(shorthand outline)

[78 words]

8 contributions

30.6 Message

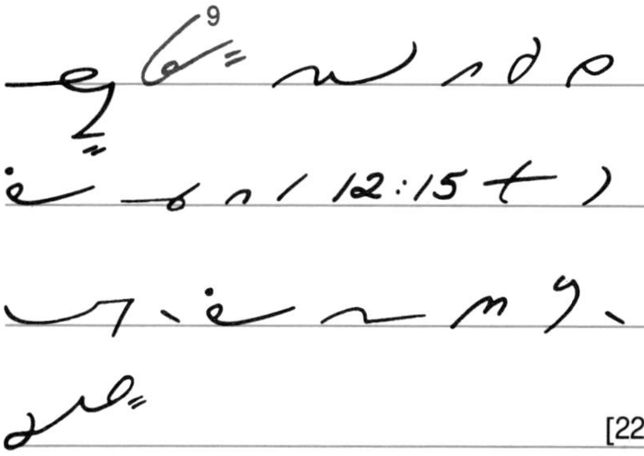

(shorthand outline) 12:15

[22 words]

9 Boyd

LESSON 31

NEW IN LESSON 31

- Symbol for the sounds of *md* and *mt*
- Symbol for the sound of *x*
- Word beginning *al-*
- Coding notes

SOUNDS OF MD, MT

The sounds of *md* as in *seemed* and *mt* as in *prompt* are written with a blend that represents a combination of the *m* and *d* symbols. The same symbol represents both sounds and is a long under curve written on the slope of the *d* symbol.

m ——— + d ╱ = md, mt ╱

Examples: seemed ⌒ prompt ⌒

Md, Mt Words

seemed ⌒

named ⌒

blamed ⌒

framed ⌒

claimed ⌒

informed ⌒

confirmed ⌒

unconfirmed ⌒

welcomed ⌒

prompt ⌒

promptly ⌒

empty ⌒

Md, Mt Practice
31.1

1

2

3

4

5

¶ **Letter of Recommendation**

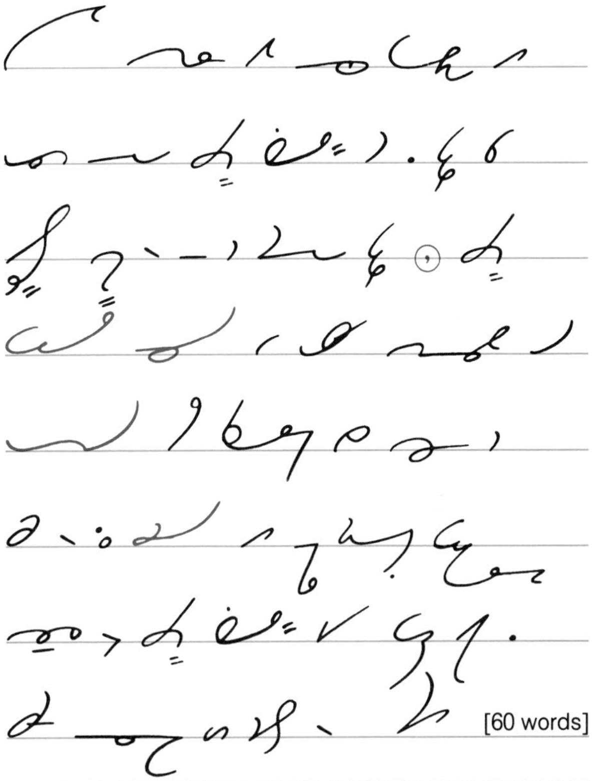

[60 words]

SOUND OF X

The letter *x* in shorthand is represented by a slanted right or left *s* symbol. Compare the examples below.

Examples: mess — mix —

fees  — fix —

X Words

mix _____ index _____ boxes _____

tax _____ indexing _____ fix _____

taxes _____ box _____ fixed _____

X Practice
31.2

1 *(shorthand outline)*

(shorthand outline)

2 *(shorthand outline)*

(shorthand outline)

3 *(shorthand outline)*

4 *(shorthand outline)*

(shorthand outline)

5 *(shorthand outline)* 10, *(shorthand outline)*

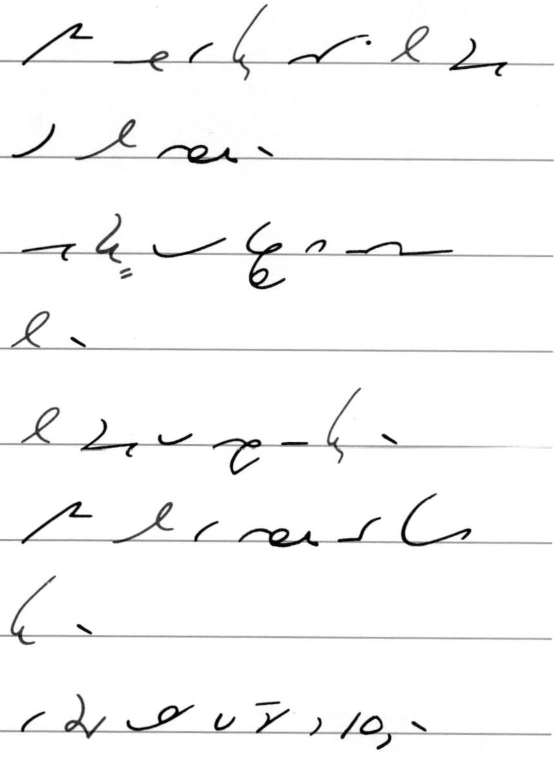

¶ **Storage of Records**

(shorthand outlines)

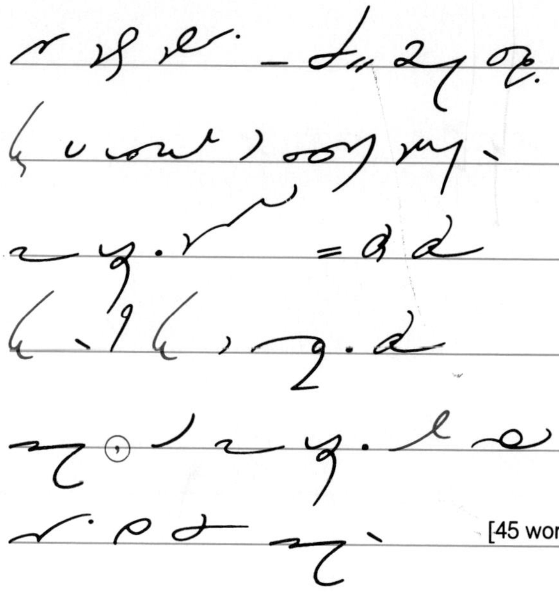

[45 words]

The word beginning *al-* as in *also* is represented by the *o* symbol for ease of writing. *ᴗ*

Example: also *Ɛ*

Al- Words

<u>al</u>so *Ɛ*   <u>al</u>together *ᴗᵒ*   <u>al</u>though *ᴗ*

<u>al</u>ready *ᴗᵒ*   <u>al</u>most *ᴗ*   <u>al</u>tered *ᴗ*

But: *Always* retains the *l* to make a more readable outline.

always *ᴗℓ*

Al- Practice
31.3

1 *(shorthand outline)*

2 *(shorthand outline)*

¶ **Accounting Club**

3 *(shorthand outline)*

4 *(shorthand outline)*

5 *(shorthand outline)*

[45 words]

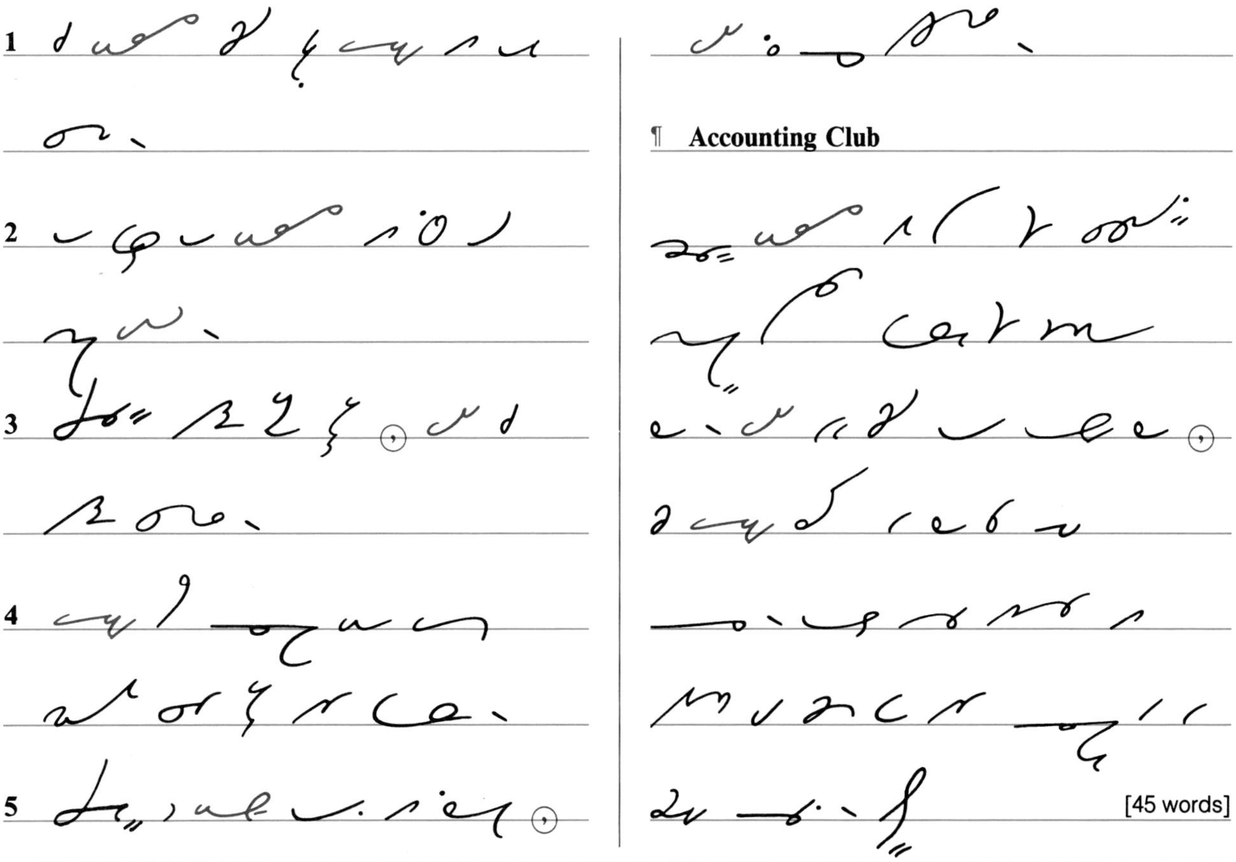

Coding Notes

A person who knows shorthand and has good listening habits has a tremendous advantage over other people in terms of personal efficiency. To the student, knowing shorthand means that all the key points of a lecture can be recorded in class notes for later study. In order to make notes even more useful, they should be coded.

Whenever an assignment is made by the teacher, the student should print an *A* and draw a circle around it. Such an assignment code stands out clearly when the student quickly scans the notebook pages later.

While the student may assume that anything presented in a class is likely to be tested, sometimes a teacher will specifically state that information will be on a test. Information that will be tested should be preceded in the notes by a printed letter *T* with a circle drawn around it. During later study, the items preceded by the test code can be given the most careful review.

Often during meetings people receive instructions from their supervisors or make commitments to complete projects on behalf of the group. Notes explaining such commitments should be preceded by a printed letter *C* with a circle drawn around it.

Students, secretaries, and executives all benefit from coding notes. Coded notes ensure that once a class or meeting has been concluded, details of agreements will be remembered and commitments met.

Reading and Writing Practice

31.4   Dictation Speed Letter

1 200   2 10,000   3 farther   4 Yale

[80 words]

31.5 Company Shareholder

[shorthand outlines]

5 Booth   6 shareholder   7 Office   8 Products
9 manufacturer   10 index   11 informed

[97 words]

12 quarterly   13 receiving

Shorthand can be used to record testimony during legal proceedings.

LESSON

32

- **Eight brief forms**
- **Word ending -quire**
- **Symbols for the sounds of ng and nk**
- **Differentiating between some and sum**

BRIEF FORMS

experience   _ℰ_

satisfy, satisfactory   _ℓ_

under   _⌒_

include   _o/_

short   _v_

worth   _ᴎ_

progress   _ᒧ_

suggest   _ᴋ_

Brief-Form Derivatives

experienced   _ℰ_

progressive   _ᒧ_

suggested   _ᴋ_

includes   _o/_

satisfying   _ℓ_

suggestion   _ᴋ_

included   _o/_

shortage   _ᴎ_

underneath   _⌒_

including   _o/_

shortly   _vᵖ_

understand   _⌒_

inclusion   _o/_

shorthand   _v_

worthless   _ᴎℓ_

progressed   _ᒧ_

suggests   _ᴋ_

worthwhile ■   _ᴎᵒ_

■ In the compound word *worthwhile*, *while* has been simplified for ease of writing.

Brief-Form Practice

32.1

1 [shorthand outline]

2 [shorthand outline]

3 [shorthand outline]

4 [shorthand outline]

5 [shorthand outline]

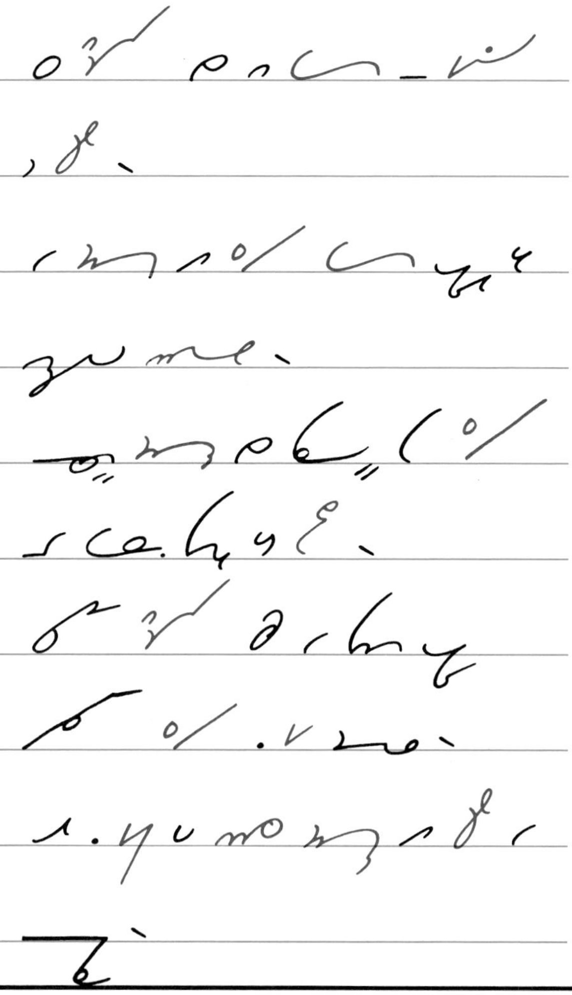

¶ **Sales Suggestion**

[shorthand outlines]

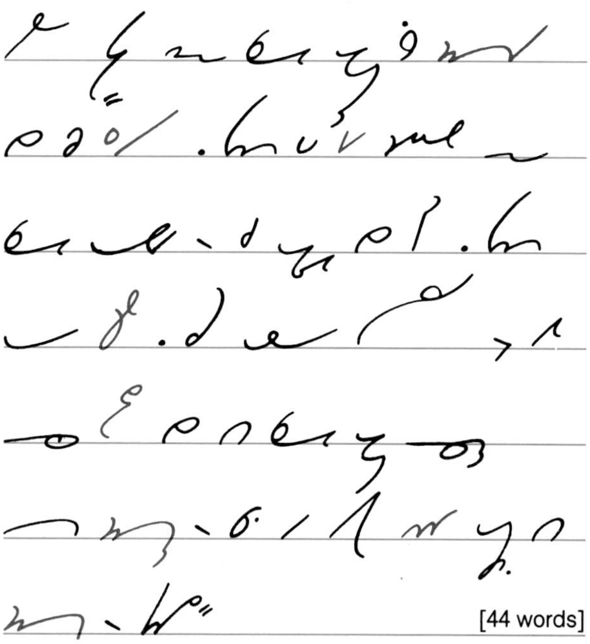

[44 words]

WORD ENDING -QUIRE

The word ending *-quire* as in *require* is represented by the *k* and *i* symbols. [shorthand outline]

Example: require [shorthand outline]

-quire Words

require _(outline)_   requirements _(outline)_   inquires _(outline)_

requires _(outline)_   acquire _(outline)_   inquiry _(outline)_

required _(outline)_   inquire _(outline)_   inquired _(outline)_

-quire Practice
32.2

1. _(shorthand outlines)_

2. _(shorthand outlines)_

3. _(shorthand outlines)_

4. _(shorthand outlines)_

5. _(shorthand outlines)_

¶ **Business Letter**

(shorthand outlines)

[50 words]

SOUNDS OF NG, NK

The sounds of *ng* as in *single* and *nk* as in *sink* are represented by *downward* slanting straight strokes the size of *n* and *m*.

ng _(stroke)_   nk _(stroke)_

Examples: single _(outline)_   sink _(outline)_

Ng Words

single _(shorthand)_ belong _(shorthand)_ strong _(shorthand)_

long _(shorthand)_ bring _(shorthand)_ stronger _(shorthand)_

longer _(shorthand)_ spring _(shorthand)_ younger _(shorthand)_

Nk Words

sink _(shorthand)_ blank _(shorthand)_ Franklin _(shorthand)_

ink _(shorthand)_ rank _(shorthand)_ uncle _(shorthand)_

bank _(shorthand)_ frank _(shorthand)_ Lincoln _(shorthand)_

banker _(shorthand)_ frankly _(shorthand)_ anxious _(shorthand)_

Ng, Nk Practice
32.3

1 _(shorthand outlines)_

2 _(shorthand outlines)_

¶ **Letter**

3 _(shorthand outlines)_

4 _(shorthand outlines)_

5 _(shorthand outlines)_

(shorthand outlines)

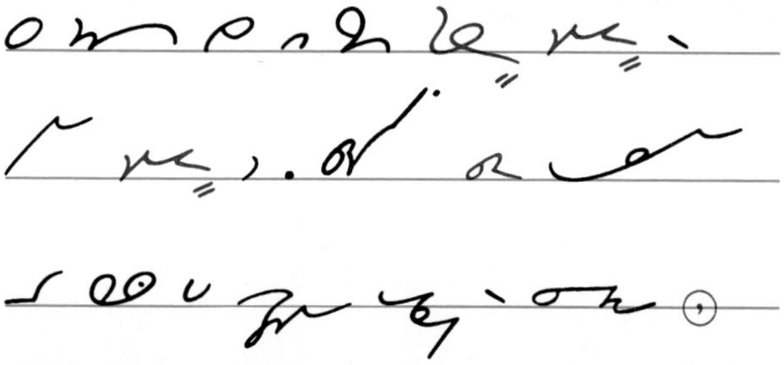

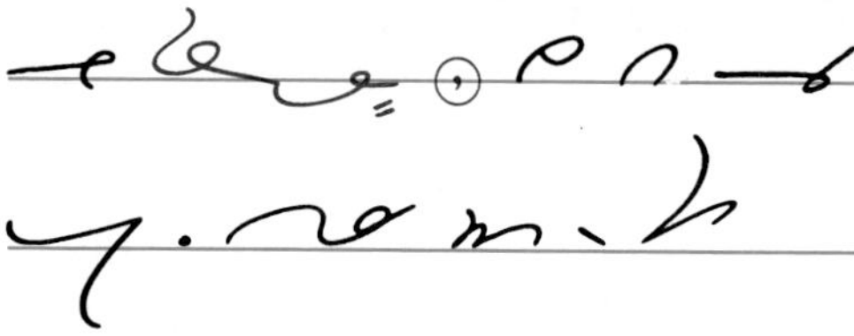

(shorthand outlines)

[85 words]

Communication Skill Builder

Similar Words: some, sum

some: a few; a part of

sum: a total; an amount of money

(shorthand outline)

The students raised *some* concerns about the test.

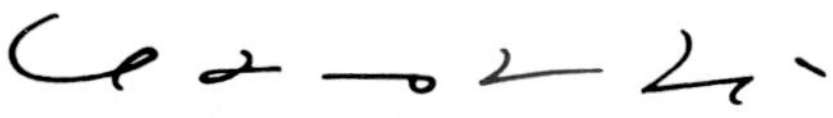

(shorthand outline)

Please send me *some* forms.

(shorthand outline)

Mark received a large *sum* of money.

Reading and Writing Practice

32.4 Dictation Speed Letter

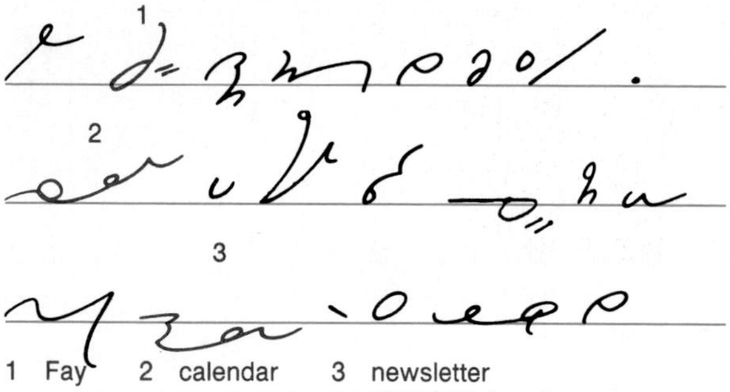

4

(shorthand outlines)

1 Fay   2 calendar   3 newsletter

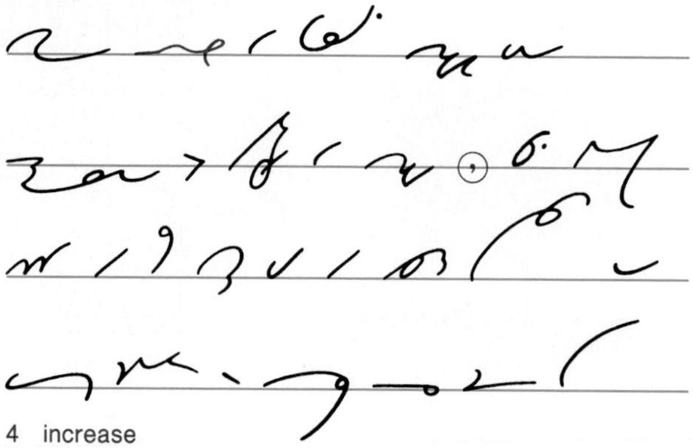

4 increase

[shorthand outline] [70 words]

32.5 Advertising Solicitation

[shorthand outline]

[shorthand outline] [92 words]

Shorthand-writing secretaries are valuable to attorneys who wish to capture legal details quickly and accurately.

U N I T

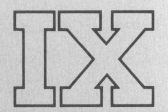

LESSON
33

NEW IN LESSON 33

- Word endings *-ition* and *-ation*
- Word ending *-hood*
- Symbol for the sound of *ul*
- Shorthand as an aid to research

WORD ENDINGS -ITION, -ATION

The circle vowel sounds *a* and *e* are omitted between *t, d, n, m* and the word ending *-tion*. The following eight word endings are thus abbreviated: *-tition, -tation, -dition, -dation, -nition, -nation, -mition,* and *-mation*.

Example: addition

-ition, -ation Words

addi<u>tion</u>

addi<u>tional</u>

condi<u>tion</u>

condi<u>tions</u>

condi<u>tional</u>

edi<u>tion</u>

sta<u>tion</u>

sta<u>tioned</u>

ad<u>mission</u> ■

per<u>mission</u> ■

invi<u>tation</u>

auto<u>mation</u>

accommo<u>dation</u>

repe<u>tition</u>

presen<u>tation</u> ■ ■

repu<u>tation</u>

do<u>nation</u>

informa<u>tion</u>

■ Although *admission* and *permission* end in *-mission*, *-mission* has the same sound as *-mition* words and the same rule applies.

■ ■ Brief-form derivative.

-ition, -ation Practice

33.1

1 [shorthand outline]

2 [shorthand outline]

3 [shorthand outline]

4 [shorthand outline]

5 [shorthand outline]

[shorthand outline]

[71 words]

Secretaries who deal with numerous tasks daily find shorthand a valuable skill for recording information quickly and accurately.

WORD ENDING -HOOD

The word ending *-hood* as in *boyhood* is represented by a disjoined *d*.

Example: boyhood

-hood Words

boyhood	girlhood	neighborhood
childhood	likelihood ■	neighborhoods
fatherhood	motherhood	parenthood

■ Transcription Alert.

-hood Practice

33.2

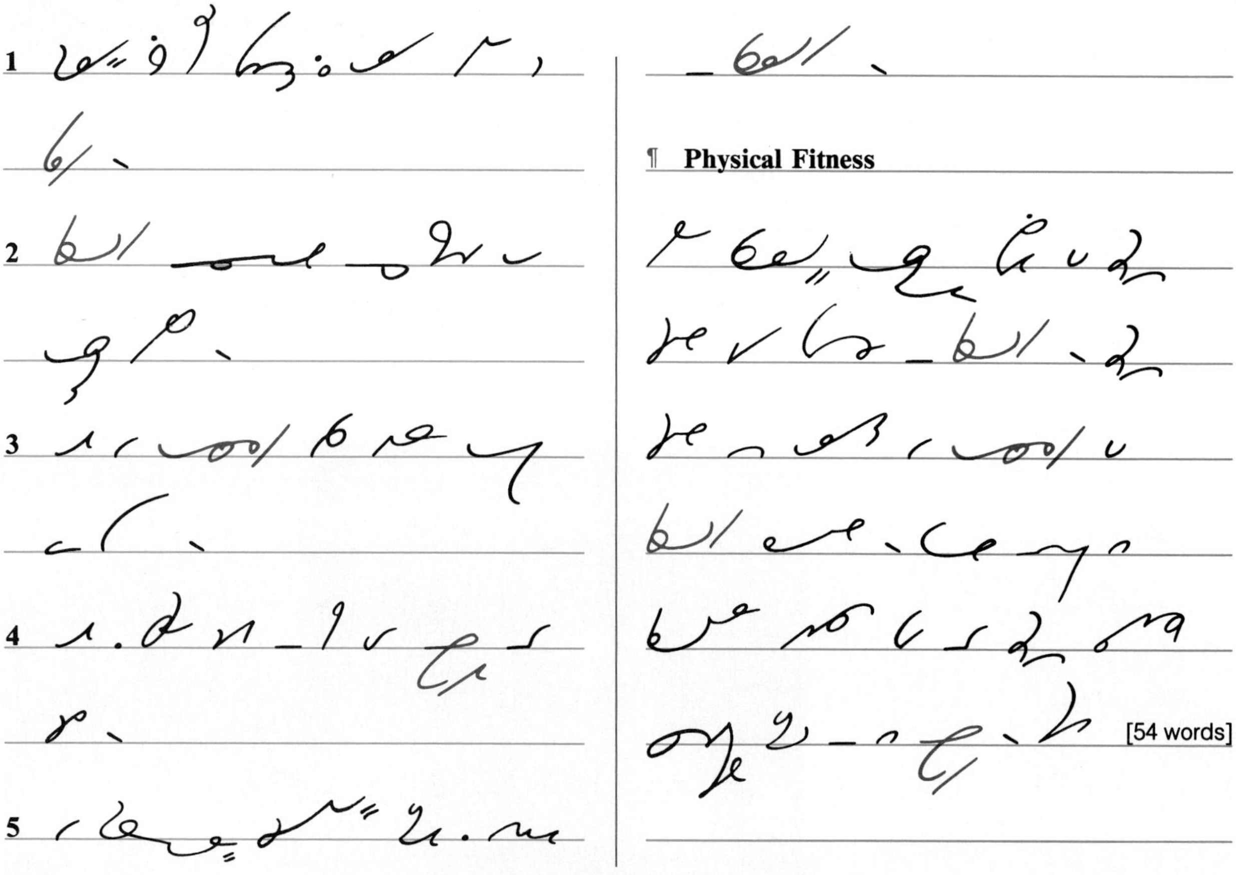
1
2
3
4
5
¶ Physical Fitness
[54 words]

The sound of *ul* as in *adult* is represented by the *oo* symbol. ⌒

Example: adult *[shorthand symbol]*

Ul Words

adult *[shorthand]*

adulthood *[shorthand]*

consult *[shorthand]*

consultant *[shorthand]*

insult *[shorthand]*

result *[shorthand]*

resulted *[shorthand]*

ultimate *[shorthand]*

ultimately *[shorthand]*

Ul Practice
33.3

[shorthand outlines numbered 1–5 and continuing in the right column]

¶ **Sales Lead**

[shorthand outlines]

[109 words]

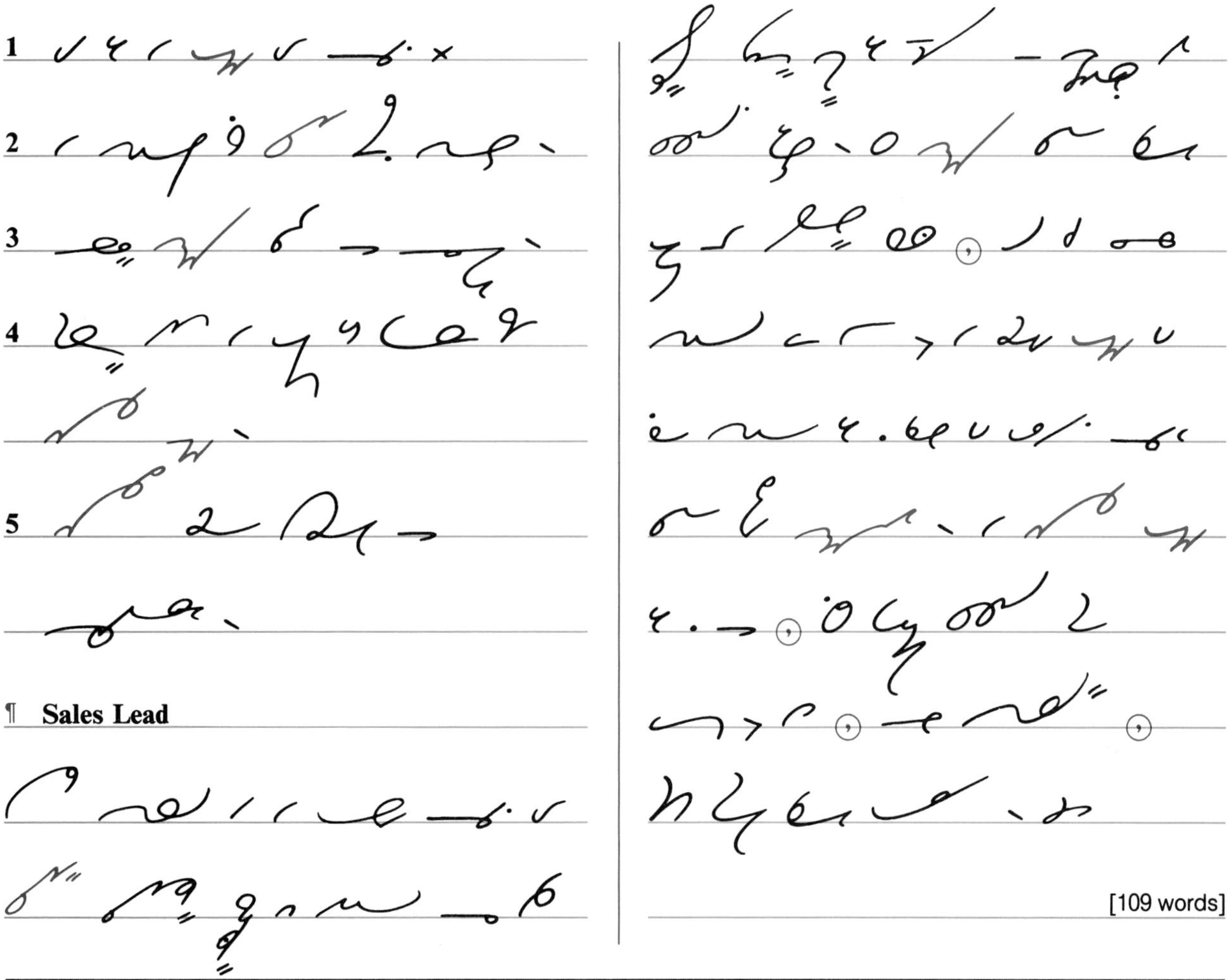

Using Shorthand for Research Notes

An assignment that most students face is to write a research paper based upon resources available in the library. Business people—executives and secretaries—are also called upon to prepare reports that involve extensive research. Anyone who has written such a paper knows the long hours of painstaking work that can be involved in taking longhand notes from research data. While photocopies can be made, this becomes a costly process if a great number of pages must be copied, for photocopy machines cannot edit. They copy an entire page, even though the researcher may desire to quote only a sentence or two.

The person who knows shorthand has an advantage when it comes to taking research notes. Data can be quickly scanned, with major points noted in shorthand. Crucial data and quotations that support those major points are also easily noted in shorthand. Since shorthand can be written at a speed several times that of longhand, it can easily cut research time in half. Virtually everyone can appreciate that kind of contribution to more effective time management.

Reading and Writing Practice

33.4 Dictation Speed Letter

[73 words]

33.5 Additional Copies Required

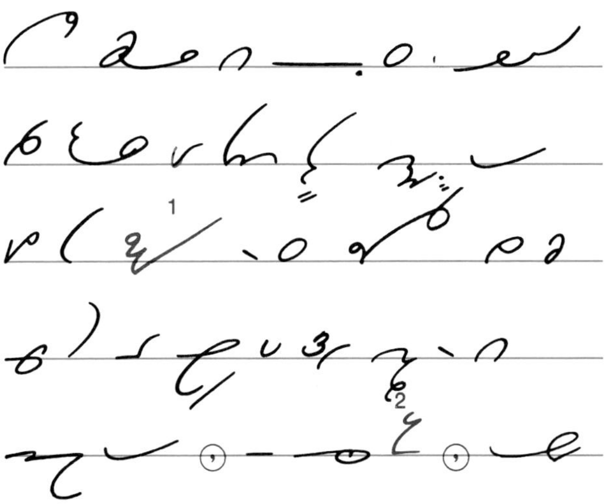

1 exhausted   2 opinion

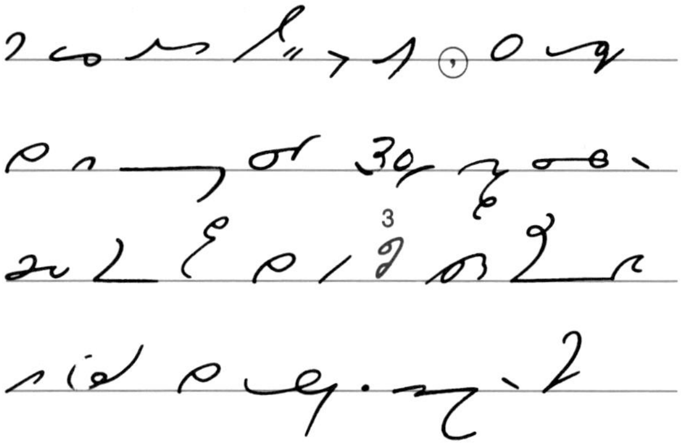

3 usually

[87 words]

LESSON 34

NEW IN LESSON 34

- **Eight brief forms**
- **Symbols for the sounds of *ern, erm***
- **Word endings *-titute* and *-titude***
- **Differentiating between *know* and *no***

BRIEF FORMS

appropriate ■ *(shorthand)*

executive *(shorthand)*

object *(shorthand)*

particular ■ *(shorthand)*

program *(shorthand)*

quantity *(shorthand)*

subject *(shorthand)*

wish *(shorthand)*

■ Transcription Alert.

Brief-Form Derivatives

appropriately *(shorthand)*

appropriation *(shorthand)*

executives *(shorthand)*

objects *(shorthand)*

objected *(shorthand)*

objection *(shorthand)*

objective *(shorthand)*

particularly *(shorthand)*

programs *(shorthand)*

programmed *(shorthand)*

programmer *(shorthand)*

programming *(shorthand)*

quantities *(shorthand)*

subjected *(shorthand)*

subjects *(shorthand)*

wishes *(shorthand)*

wished *(shorthand)*

wishful *(shorthand)*

Brief-Form Practice

34.1

1 [shorthand outlines]

2 [shorthand outlines]

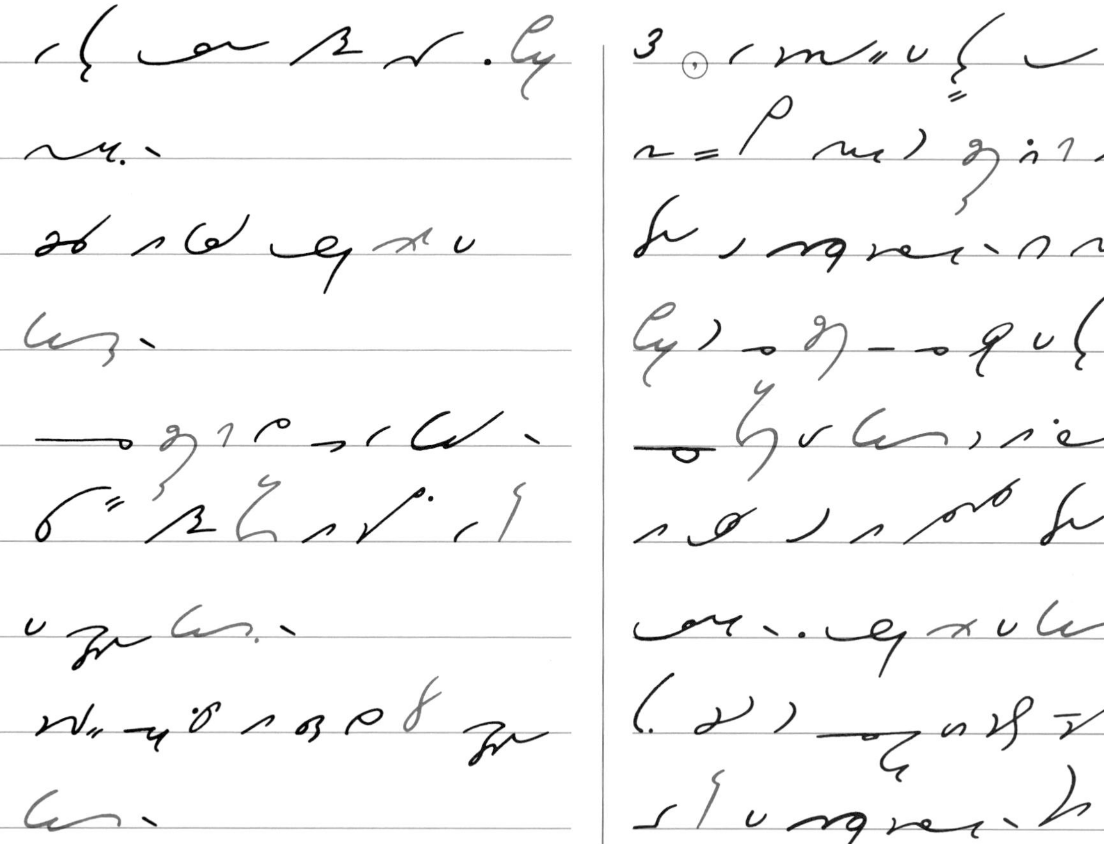

3 [shorthand outlines]

4 [shorthand outlines]

5 [shorthand outlines]

¶ **Communications Course**

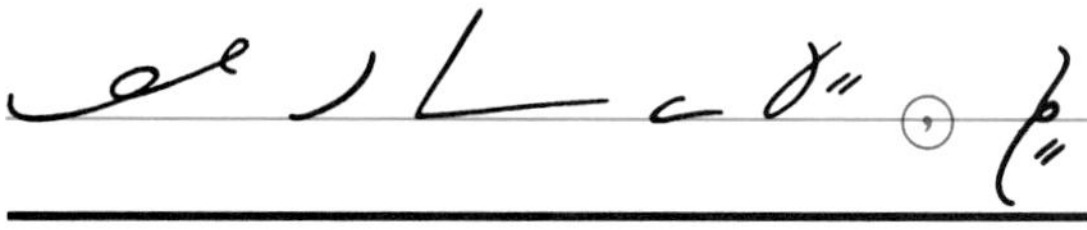

[shorthand outlines]

[91 words]

SOUNDS OF ERN, ERM

The sounds of *ern* and *erm* as in *turn* and *term* are abbreviated by the deletion of the *r* symbol.

Examples: turn [shorthand outline]   term [shorthand outline]

Ern, Erm Words

turn _(shorthand)_

turns _(shorthand)_

return _(shorthand)_

returned _(shorthand)_

eastern _(shorthand)_

western _(shorthand)_

modern _(shorthand)_

southern _(shorthand)_

alternate _(shorthand)_

alternated _(shorthand)_

alternative _(shorthand)_

term _(shorthand)_

terminal _(shorthand)_

termination _(shorthand)_

determine _(shorthand)_

determined _(shorthand)_

determination _(shorthand)_

thermometer _(shorthand)_

Ern, Erm Practice
34.2

1 _(shorthand)_

2 _(shorthand)_

3 _(shorthand)_

4 _(shorthand)_

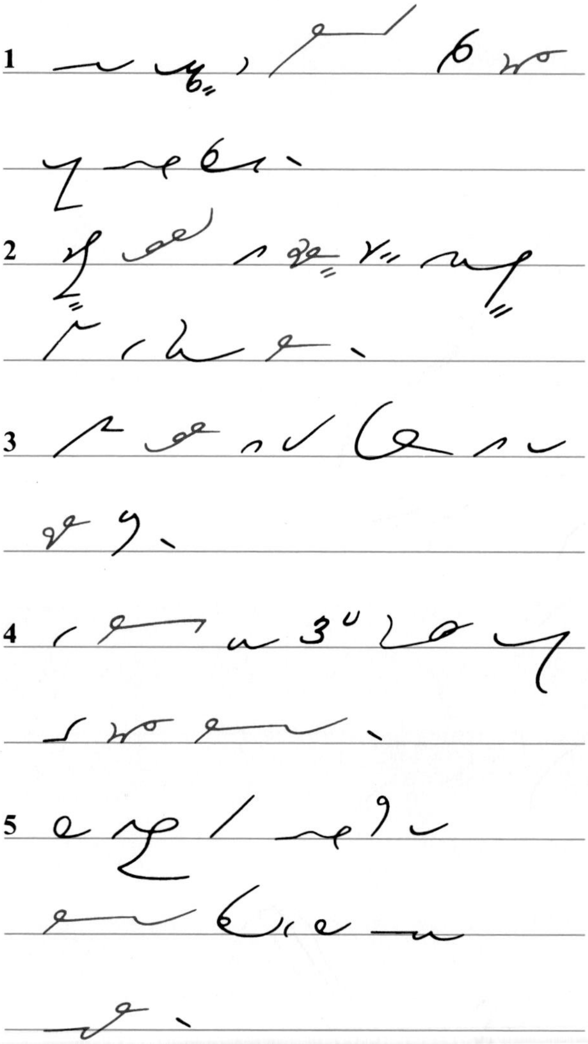

5 _(shorthand)_

¶ **Printing Needs**

(shorthand)

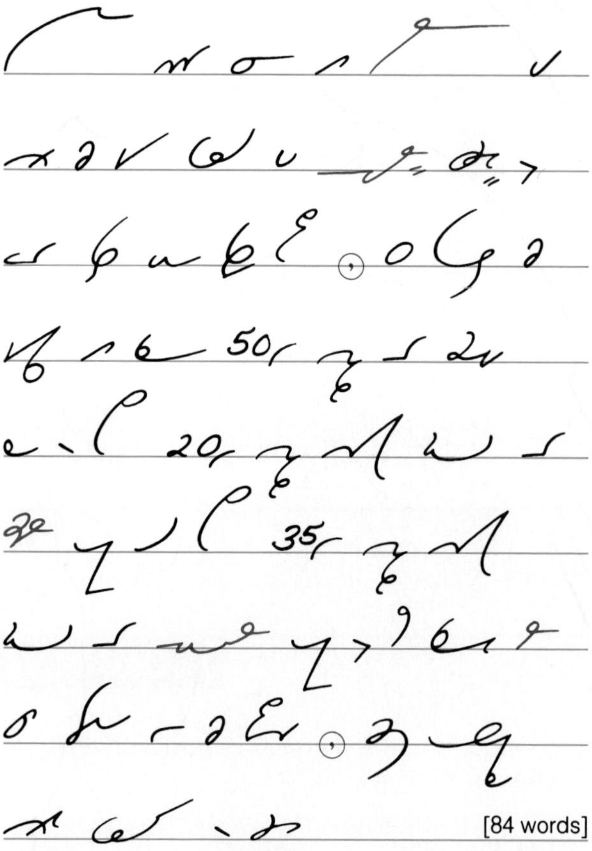

[84 words]

WORD ENDINGS -TITUTE, -TITUDE

The word endings -*titute* and -*titude* as in *constitute* and *attitude* are abbreviated *t e t*.

-titute, -titude ⟋

Examples: constitute ⟋ attitude ⟋

-titute, -titude Words

constitute ⟋ _____ | instituted ⟋ _____ | attitudes ⟋ _____

constitution ⟋ _____ | institution ⟋ _____ | aptitude ⟋ _____

institute ⟋ _____ | attitude ⟋ _____ | gratitude ⟋ _____

-titute, -titude Practice
34.3

1 ⟋ _____

2 _____

3 _____

4 _____

5 _____

¶ **Future Plans**

[62 words]

Communication Skill Builder

Similar Words: know, no

know: to have knowledge

no: not any

[shorthand]

Floyd does not *know* that typing class has been canceled.

[shorthand]

There will be *no* typing class on Wednesday.

Reading and Writing Practice

34.4 Dictation Speed Message

[shorthand]

[44 words]

34.5 Approval of Constitution

[shorthand]

1 terminate   2 William

[shorthand]

[70 words]

3 constitution   4 owe   5 gratitude   6 agenda
7 objective

LESSON 35

NEW IN LESSON 35

- **Minor vowels omitted**
- **Word beginnings *ah-* and *aw-***
- **Word ending *-ingly***
- **Differentiating between *principle* and *principal***

MINOR VOWELS OMITTED

When two vowels occur together, such as the *e us* sounds in *previous*,
the minor vowel may be omitted.

Example: previous ⟍

Minor-Vowel-Omitted Words

previous	situated	various
previously	situation	theory
period	serious	continue
genuine	seriously	obvious

Minor-Vowel-Omitted Practice
35.1

1 _____

2 _____

3 _____

[shorthand outlines]

4 *[shorthand outlines]*

5 *[shorthand outlines]*

¶ **Student's "To Do" List**

① *[shorthand outlines]*

[shorthand outlines]

② *[shorthand outlines]*

③ *[shorthand outlines]* 16

④ *[shorthand outlines]*

[64 words]

WORD BEGINNINGS AH-, AW-

In the word beginnings *ah-* and *aw-*, the sound of *a* is represented by a dot.

Examples: ahead *[shorthand]*   away *[shorthand]*

Ah-, Aw- Words

ahead *[shorthand]*   awaits *[shorthand]*   aware *[shorthand]*

away *[shorthand]*   awake *[shorthand]*   ward *[shorthand]*

await *[shorthand]*   awaken *[shorthand]*   awards *[shorthand]*

Ah-, Aw- Practice
35.2

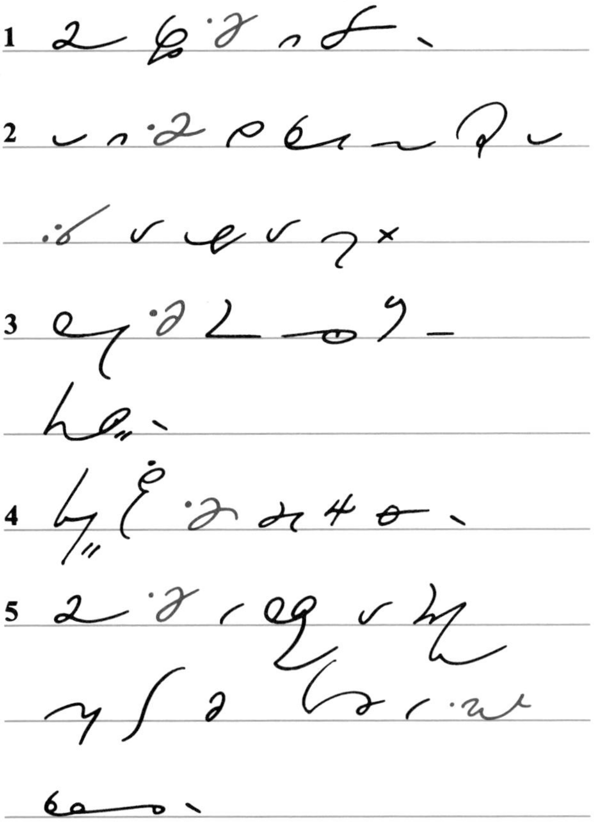

1 *[shorthand outline]*

2 *[shorthand outline]*

3 *[shorthand outline]*

4 *[shorthand outline]*

5 *[shorthand outline]*

[shorthand outline]

¶ **Vacation Schedule**

[shorthand outlines]

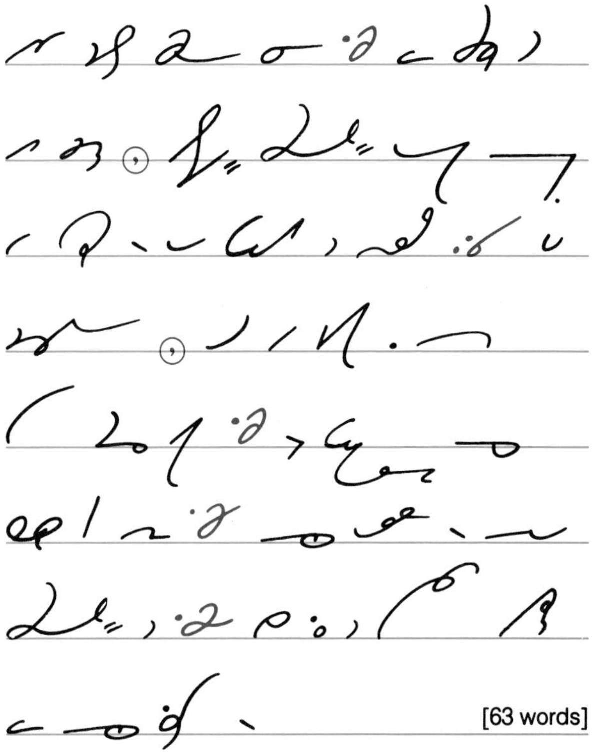

[63 words]

WORD ENDING -INGLY

The word ending *-ingly* as in *knowingly* is represented by a disjoined *-ly* circle. *[shorthand symbol]*

Example: knowingly *[shorthand outline]*

-ingly Words

knowingly *[shorthand outline]*

willingly ■ *[shorthand outline]*

■ Brief-form derivative.

increasingly *[shorthand outline]*

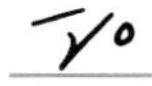

exceedingly *[shorthand outline]*

interestingly *[shorthand outline]*

convincingly *[shorthand outline]*

-ingly Practice
35.3

1 [shorthand outline]

2 [shorthand outline]

3 [shorthand outline]

4 [shorthand outline]

5 [shorthand outline]

¶ **Executive Training**

[shorthand outlines]

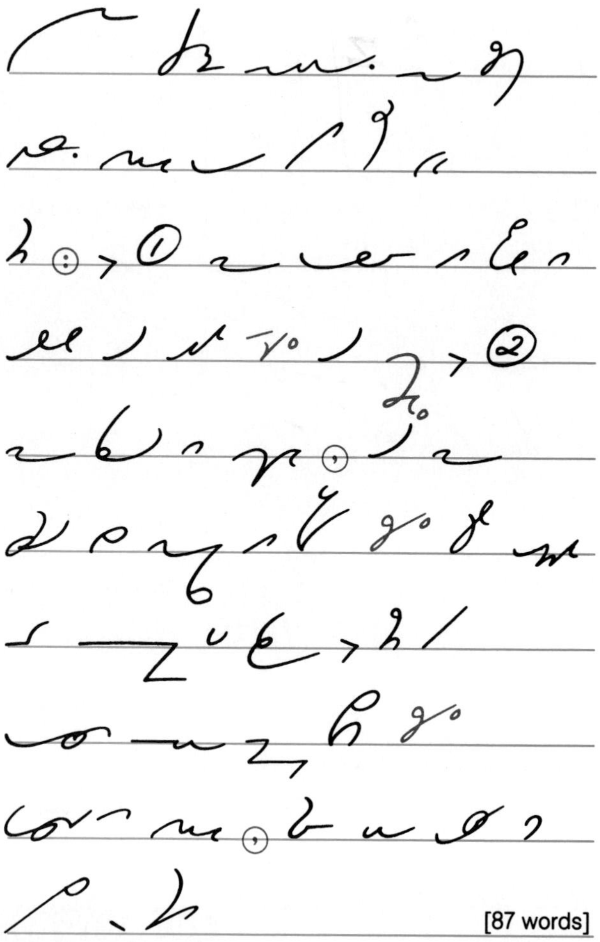

[87 words]

Communication Skill Builder

Similar Words: principle, principal

principle: a rule or fundamental belief

principal: (n.) sum of money that earns interest; chief official of a school; **(adj.)** chief

She believes in the *principle* of free speech.

Your loan payment equals *principal* plus interest.

Her father was the *principal* of the high school.

Leo will be the *principal* actor in the play.

Reading and Writing Practice

35.4 Dictation Speed Letter

[67 words]

1 Frank 2 sincere 3 appreciation 4 Albany
5 theories

6 exceedingly 7 convincingly

35.5 Years of Service

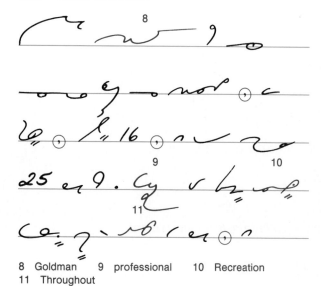

8 Goldman 9 professional 10 Recreation
11 Throughout

12 contribution

[78 words]

In the sports field, shorthand is a useful planning tool in determining a detailed schedule of events.

LESSON 36

NEW IN LESSON 36

NEW IN LESSON 36

- Six brief forms
- Word beginning *super-*
- Word ending *-ulate*
- Word ending *-quent*
- Differentiating between *advise* and *advice*

BRIEF FORMS

anniversary _____

next _____

convenient, convenience ■ _____

public _____

incorporate _____

reluctant, reluctance _____

■ Transcription Alert.

Brief-Form Derivatives

conveniently _____

publicly _____

inconvenient, inconvenience _____

reluctantly _____

incorporated _____

Brief-Form Phrases

next time _____   next year _____   next month _____

Brief-Form Practice

36.1

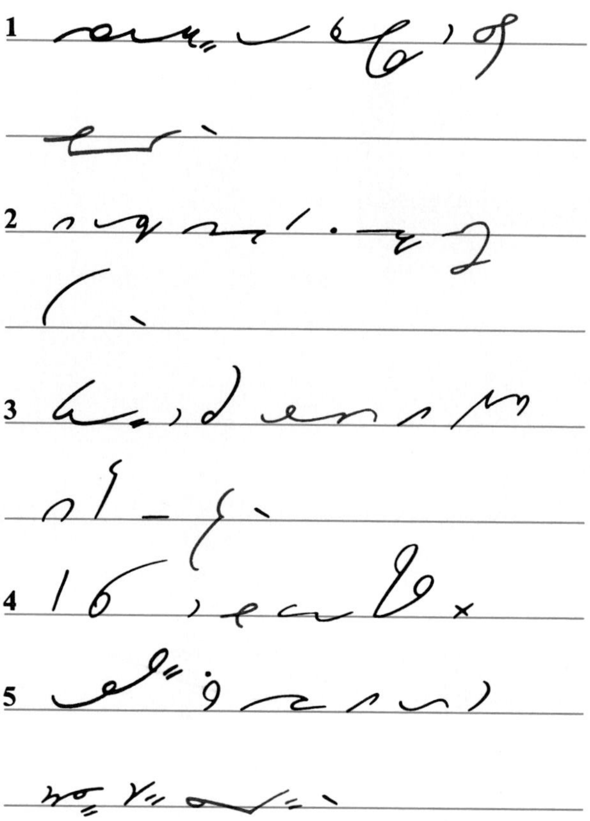

¶ **Plans to Incorporate**

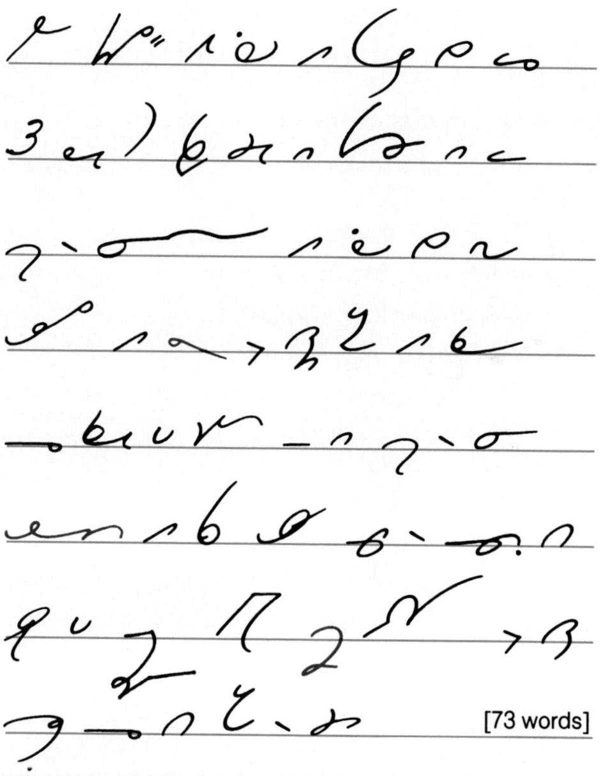

1 [shorthand outlines]

2 [shorthand outlines]

3 [shorthand outlines]

4 [shorthand outlines]

5 [shorthand outlines]

[73 words]

WORD BEGINNING SUPER-

The word beginning *super-* as in *supervise* is written with a disjoined comma *s*.

Example: supervise *[shorthand outline]*

Super- Words

supervise *[shorthand]*	supervises *[shorthand]*	supervision *[shorthand]*
supervised *[shorthand]*	supervisor *[shorthand]*	supersede ■ *[shorthand]*

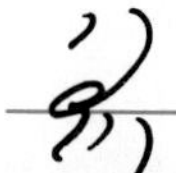

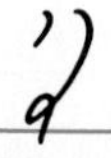

■ Transcription Alert.

superintendent ⟋⁓　　　superior ⟍　　　superb ⟍

Super- Practice
36.2

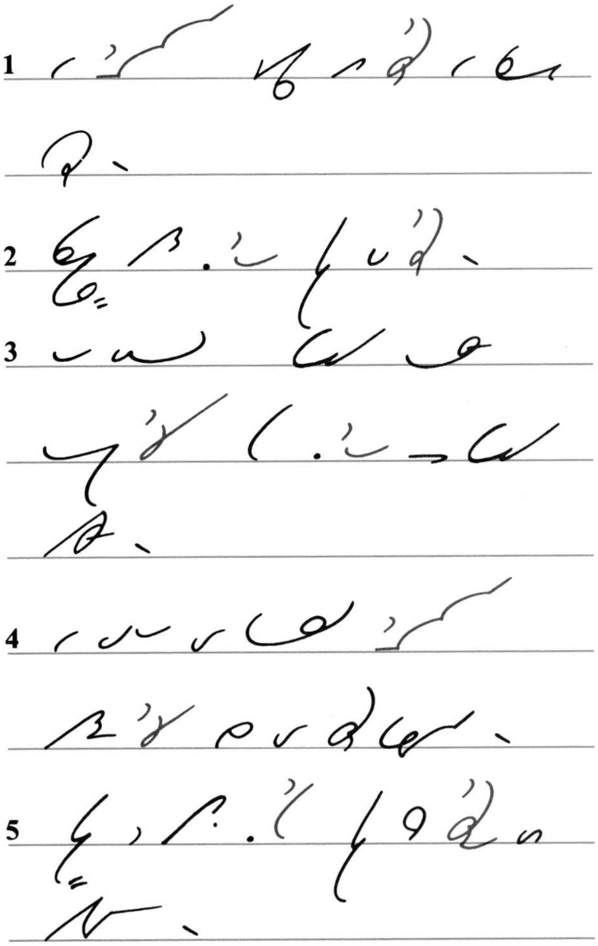

1 [shorthand outlines]

2 [shorthand outlines]

3 [shorthand outlines]

4 [shorthand outlines]

5 [shorthand outlines]

¶ **Job Opening**

[shorthand outlines]

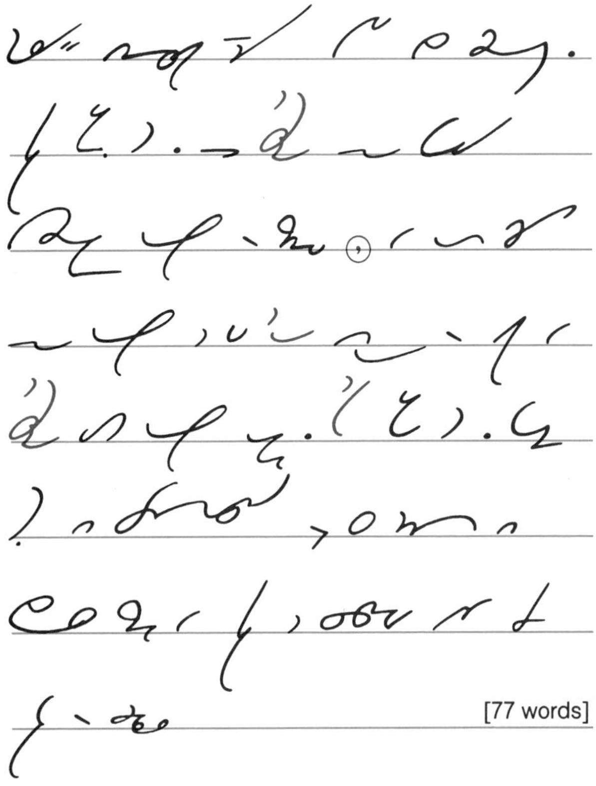

[77 words]

The word ending -*ulate* as in *regulate* is represented by a disjoined *oo* and is written close to the last symbol. The word ending -*ulation* is represented by the disjoined *oo* and *ish*.

Examples: regulate ⟳ regulation ⟳

-ulate Words

regulate ⟳

regulation ⟳

regulates ⟳

formulate ⟳

formulated ⟳

congratulate ■ ⟳
■ Transcription Alert.

congratulations ⟳

circulate ⟳

circulation ⟳

calculate ⟳

calculated ⟳

calculator ⟳

-ulate Practice
36.3

1 ⟳

2 ⟳

3 ⟳

4 ⟳

5 ⟳

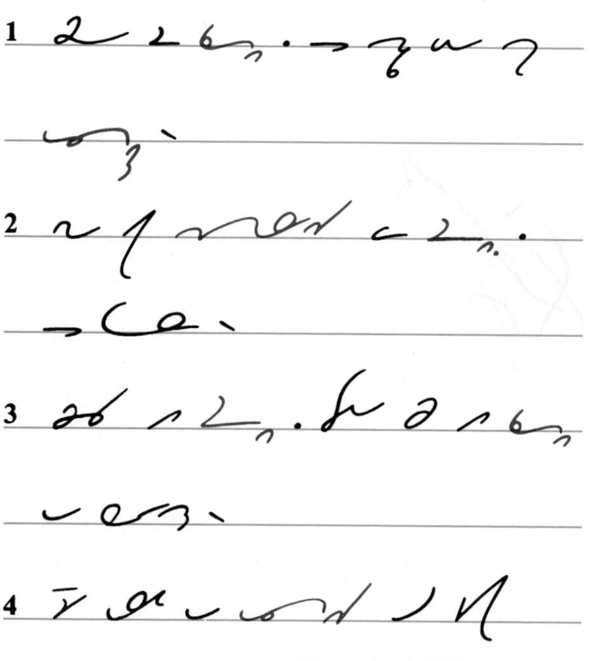

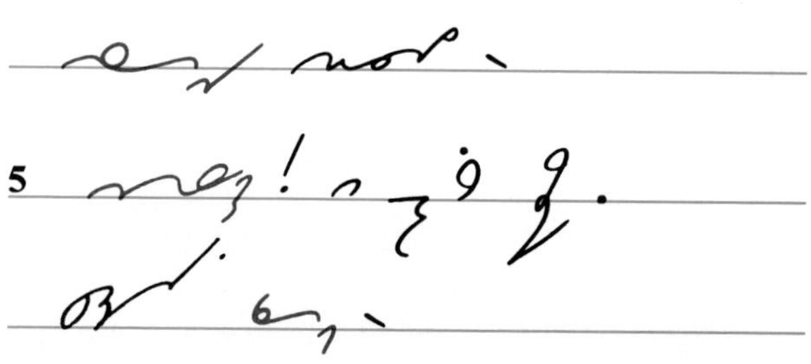

¶ **Company Policy**

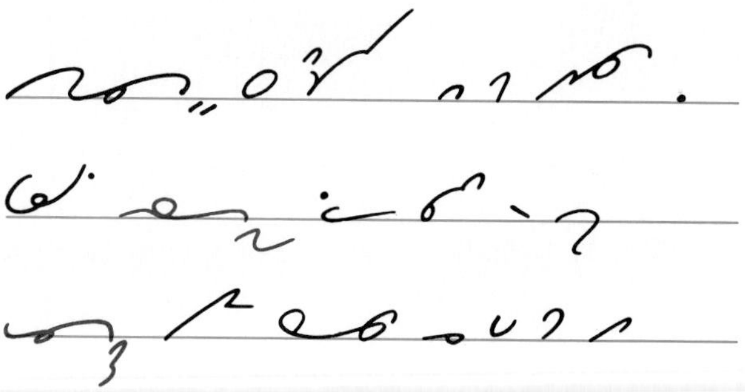

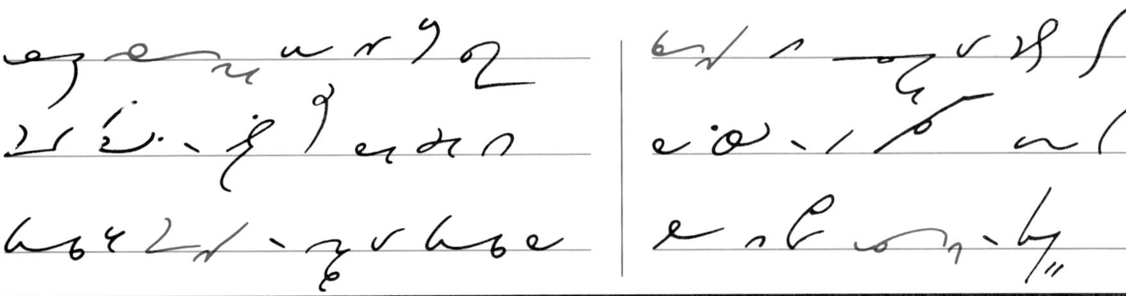

(shorthand outlines) [80 words]

WORD ENDING -QUENT

The word ending *-quent* as in *frequent* is represented by a joined *k*.

-quent ⌐

Example: frequent ⌐

-quent Words

frequent ⌐

frequently ⌐

frequency ⌐

consequent, consequence ⌐

consequently ⌐

eloquent ⌐

-quent Practice
36.4

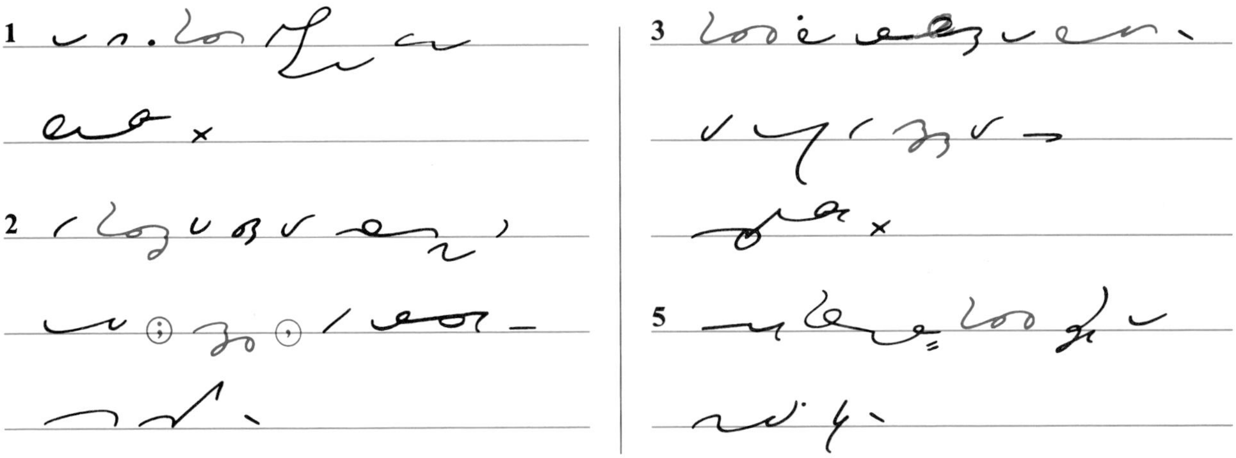

(shorthand practice exercises 1-5)

(shorthand outlines)

[88 words]

Shorthand is a portable skill that can be used to record information at any time.

Communication Skill Builder

Similar Words: advise, advice

advise: (v.) to inform; to give counsel

advice: (n.) information; recommendation

[shorthand]

Please *advise* me about your discount policy.

[shorthand]

Thank you for giving me *advice* about my career.

Reading and Writing Practice

36.5 Dictation Speed Letter

[shorthand]

[73 words]

1 leasing   2 cost effective

36.6 Contribution Request

[shorthand]

[77 words]

3 contribute   4 requests   5 equipment
6 formulate   7 donations

LESSON 37

NEW IN LESSON 37

- **Word ending *-ship***
- **Word beginnings *im-* and *em-***
- **Word beginning *trans-***
- **Shorthand and the immediate deadline**

WORD ENDING -SHIP

The word ending *-ship* as in *ownership* is represented by a disjoined
ish and is written close to the last symbol in the root word. ╱

Example: ownership   ⌐↻

-ship Words

owner**ship** ⌐↻	member**ship** ⌐⤳	relationship**s** ✒
leader**ship** ⤳	relation**ship** ✒	friend**ship** ✒

-ship Practice
37.1

1 ⌐ ⟋ʒⳑ ⌐ⳑ ᵒ ⟋⌐⟍

2 ʒ ⟋ⳑʹ ⟋ ⌐ ℯ

ℯ⟍

3 ⟊ ⟍ʹ ʒⳑ. ⌐⟍ ʹℯ

⌐ ⟍

4 [shorthand outlines]

5 [shorthand outlines]

¶ **Club Membership**

[shorthand outlines]

[shorthand outlines]

[57 words]

WORD BEGINNINGS IM-, EM-

The word beginnings *im-* and *em-* as in *improve* and *employ* are represented by the *m* symbol. ———

Examples: improve [shorthand] employ [shorthand]

Im- Words

improve [shorthand]

improvement [shorthand]

impress [shorthand]

impressed [shorthand]

impressive [shorthand]

import [shorthand]

imports [shorthand]

impact [shorthand]

impartial [shorthand]

Em- Words

employ [shorthand]

employed [shorthand]

employment [shorthand]

employee [shorthand]

employees [shorthand]

empire [shorthand]

embarrass [shorthand]

embarrassed [shorthand]

emphatically [shorthand]

But: *Im-* and *em-* are written in full when followed by a vowel.

immodest *[shorthand outline]*   emotional *[shorthand outline]*

Im-, Em- Practice
37.2

1 *[shorthand outline]*

2 *[shorthand outline]*

3 *[shorthand outline]*

4 *[shorthand outline]*

5 *[shorthand outline]*

¶ **Profitability Statements**

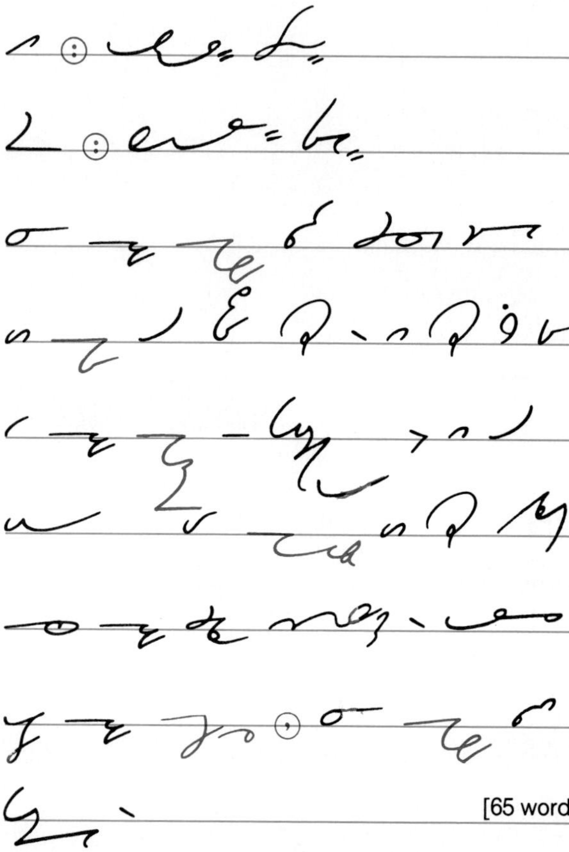

[shorthand outlines]

[65 words]

WORD BEGINNING TRANS-

The word beginning *trans-* as in *transfer* is represented by a disjoined *t*. The disjoined *t* is written in the middle of the writing line and close to the first symbol in the second outline.

Example: transfer

Trans- Words

transfer
transferred
transact
transaction
transacted
translation
transmit
transmission
transport
transportation
transcribe
transistor

Trans- Practice

37.3

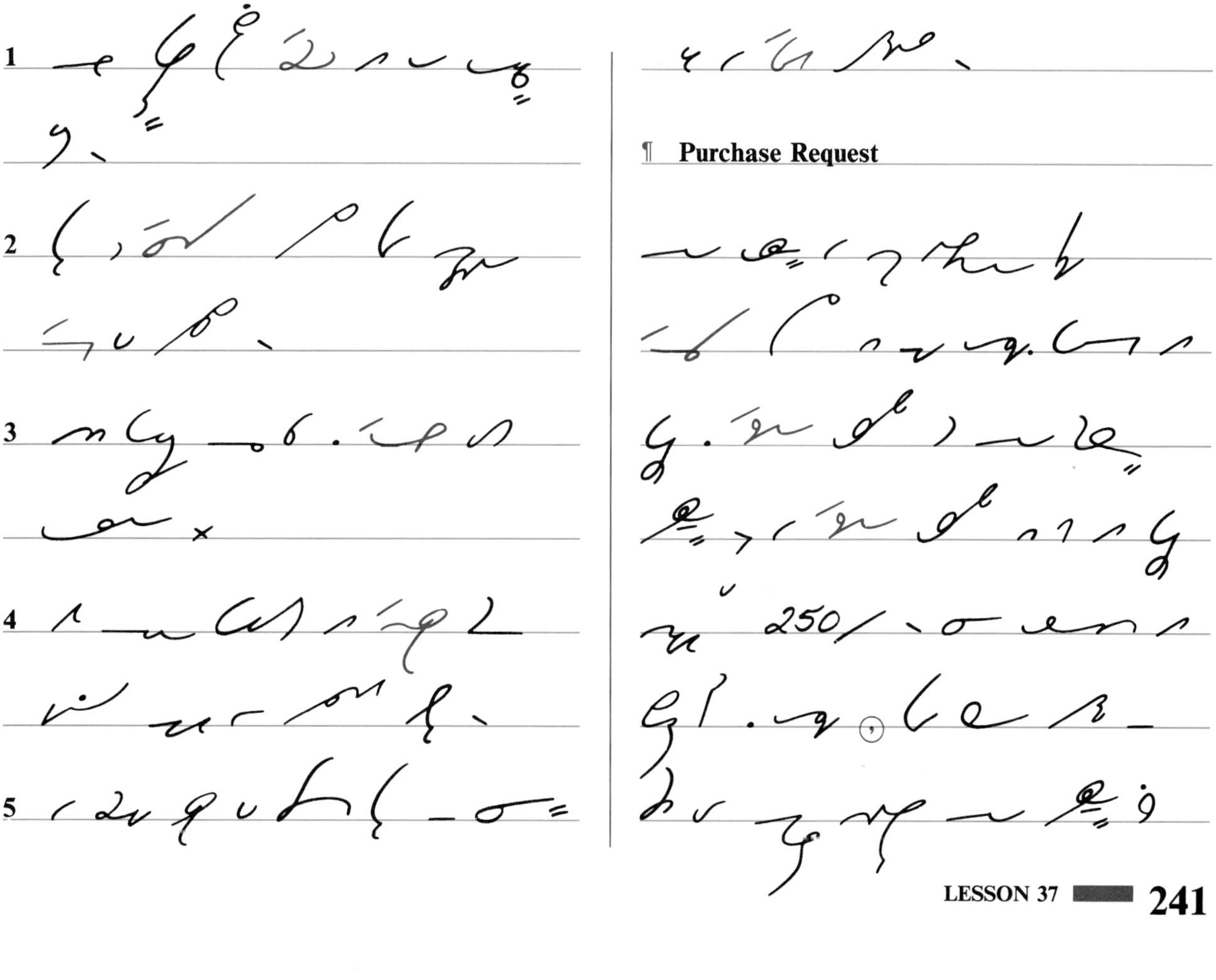
1
2
3
4
5
¶ Purchase Request
250

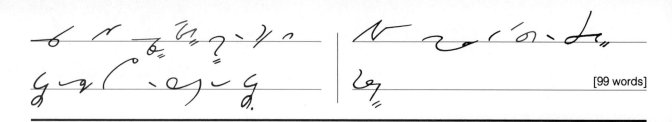

[99 words]

Shorthand and the Immediate Deadline

The concept of "turnaround time" is becoming more and more important as people are increasingly concerned with office productivity. Simply put, turnaround time is the number of minutes or hours that elapse from the time an executive finishes dictating a letter until that letter is ready for the executive's signature.

The executive who knows how to dictate and the secretary who is a good transcriber form an unbeatable team in the quest for rapid turnaround time. An executive with a private secretary knows exactly what the secretary's work priorities are. The executive with a private secretary also knows from experience what level of productivity to expect when the secretary is under pressure. No steno pool or word processing center is likely to beat the turnaround time of a private secretary who has just been told, "Take this letter in shorthand and give me a typewritten transcript now!"

Reading and Writing Practice

37.4 Dictation Speed Letter

[72 words]

1 noticed   2 omitted   3 auditors   4 agreed

5 included

37.5 Rising Costs

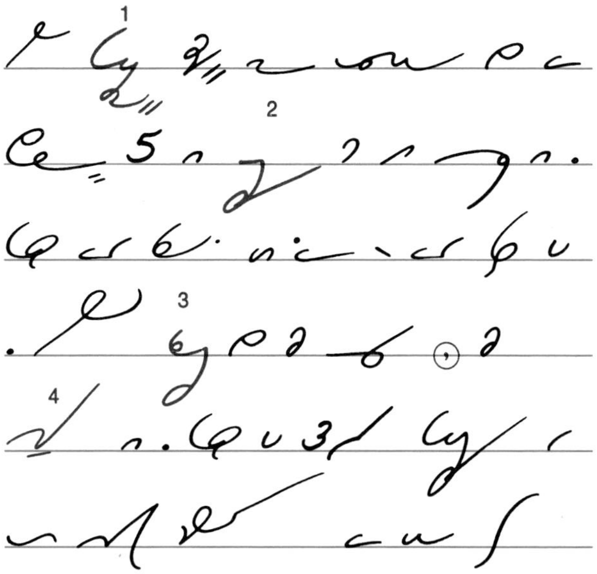

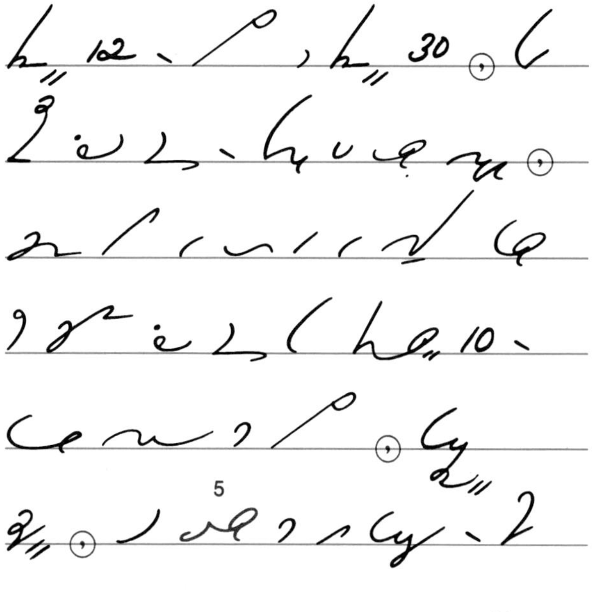

(shorthand outline)

1 Professor   2 invited   3 survey   4 quoted

5 authorize

[96 words]

LESSON 38

NEW IN LESSON 38

- **Eight brief forms**
- **Word ending** *-ily*
- **Word beginning** *sub-*
- **Differentiating between** *piece* **and** *peace*

BRIEF FORMS

electric

memorandum

equivalent

significant, significance

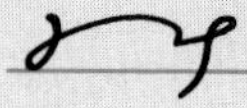

idea

speak

important, importance

world

Brief-Form Derivatives

electrical

electricity

speakers

electronic

ideas ■

significantly

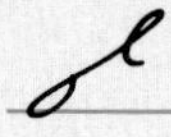

electronically

speaks

worldwide

■ The *e* in *ideas* is written counterclockwise for ease of writing the *s*.

Brief-Form Practice

38.1

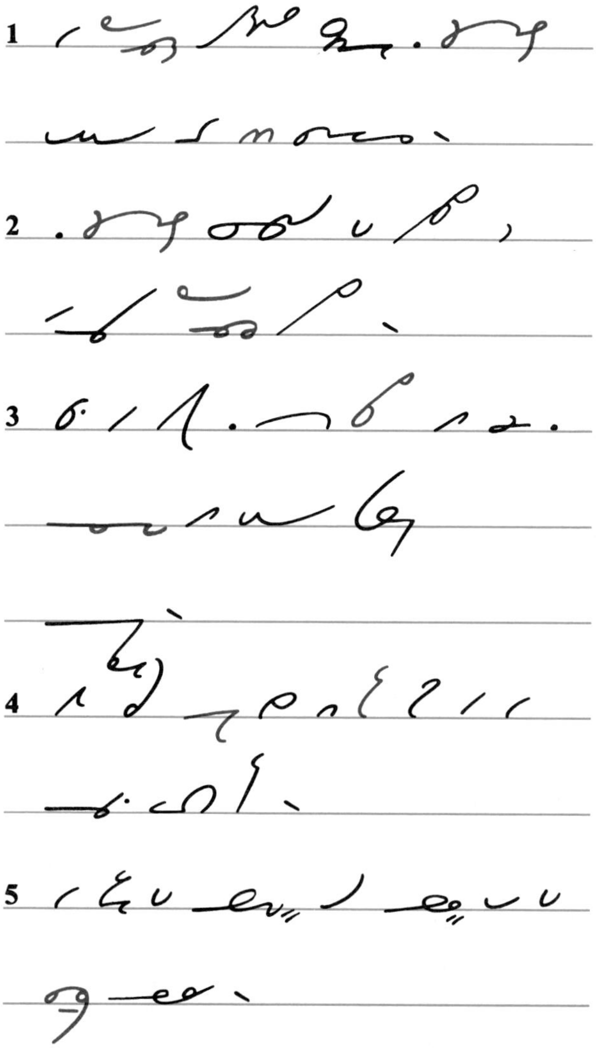

1 *[shorthand outlines]*

2 *[shorthand outlines]*

3 *[shorthand outlines]*

4 *[shorthand outlines]*

5 *[shorthand outlines]*

¶ **Business Communication**

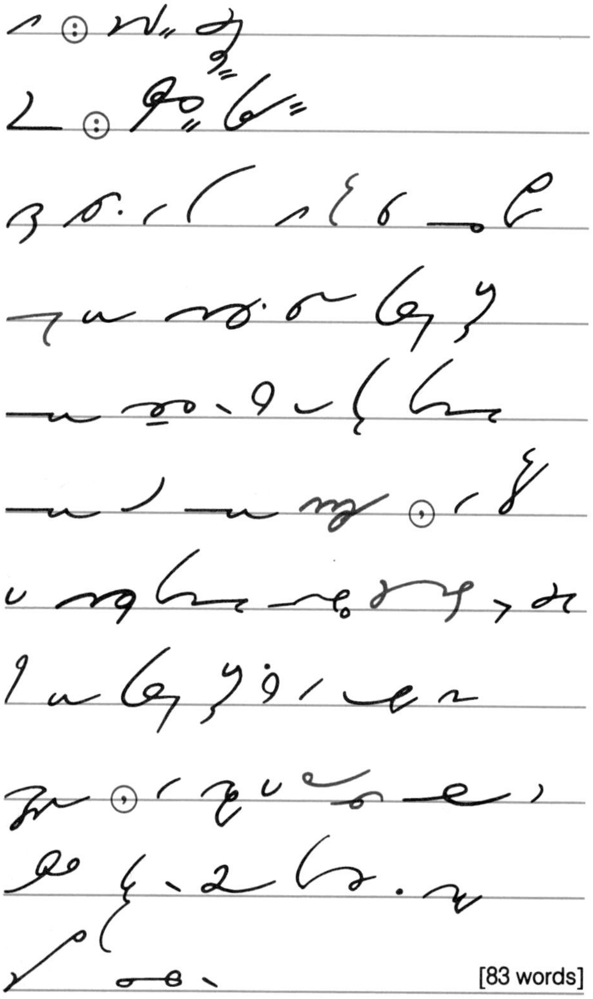

[shorthand outlines]

[83 words]

WORD ENDING -ILY

The word ending *-ily* as in *readily* is represented by a *-ly* circle which is flattened into a loop. *o*

Example: readily *[shorthand outline]*

Compare with *ready* *[shorthand outline]*

-ily Words

readily *[shorthand]* families *[shorthand]* steadily *[shorthand]*

family *[shorthand]* easily *[shorthand]* temporarily *[shorthand]*

-ily Practice
38.2

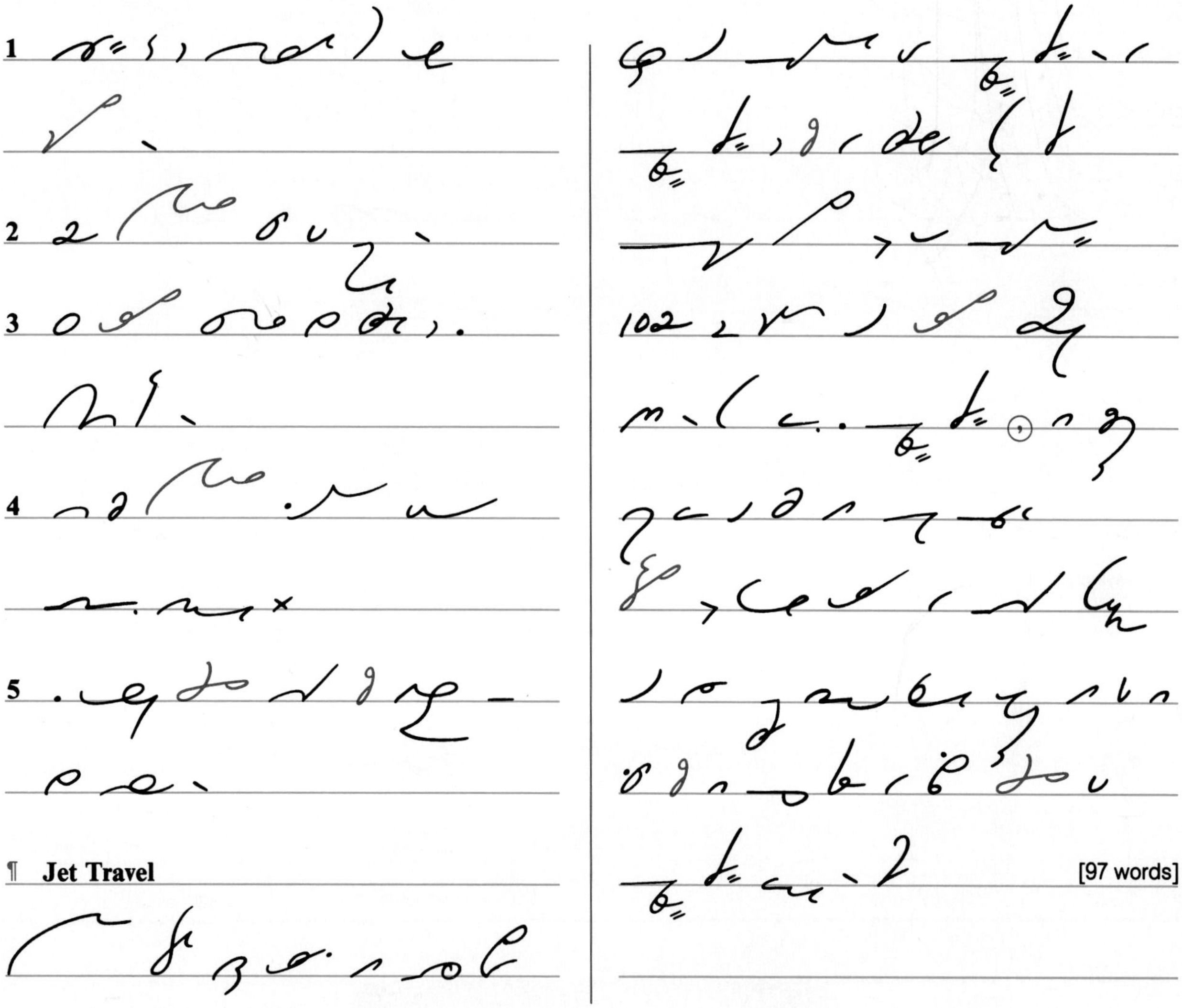

1 *[shorthand outlines]*

2 *[shorthand outlines]*

3 *[shorthand outlines]*

4 *[shorthand outlines]*

5 *[shorthand outlines]*

¶ **Jet Travel**

[shorthand outlines]

[shorthand outlines]

102 *[shorthand outlines]*

[97 words]

The word beginning *sub-* as in *submit* is written with a joined *left* or *right* *s* symbol, depending on the symbol that follows.

Examples: submit _⟋_   suburb _⟍_

Sub- Words

submit _⟋_	subscription _⟍_	substance _⟍_
subsequent _⟋_	subway _⟍_	substantial _⟍_
subscribe _⟋_	subdivide _⟍_	suburb _⟍_
subscribes _⟋_	subdivision _⟍_	suburban _⟍_

Sub- Practice
38.3

1 _（shorthand outline）_

2 _（shorthand outline）_

3 _（shorthand outline）_

4 _（shorthand outline）_

5 _（shorthand outline）_

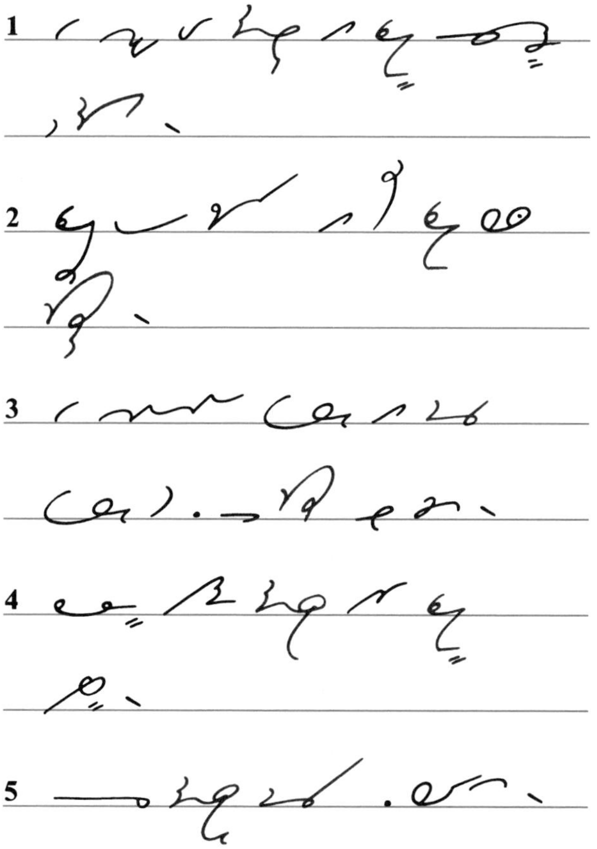

¶ **Newspaper Delivery**

（shorthand outlines）

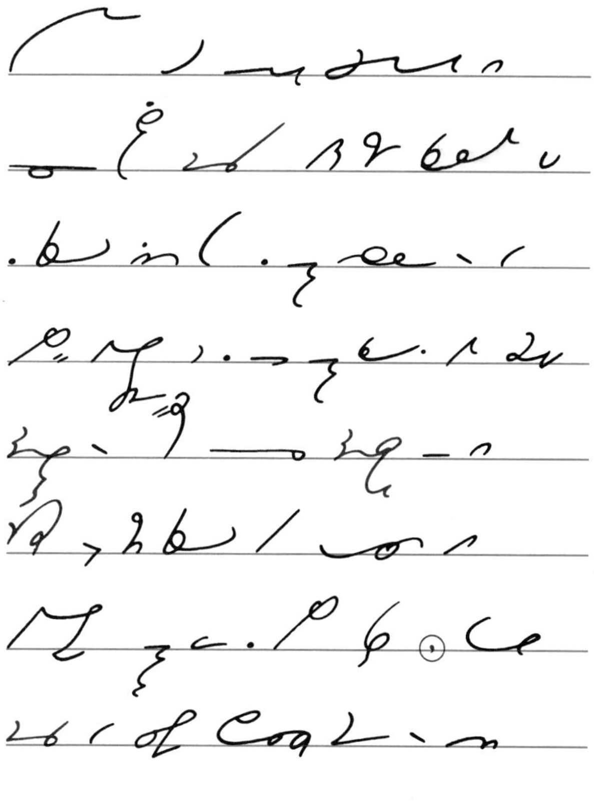

[70 words]

The need for shorthand-writing secretaries is prominent in the fashion industry.

Communication Skill Builder

Similar Words: piece, peace

piece: a single part; a portion
peace: the absence of conflict

Please attach your photograph to this form with a *piece* of tape.

Since he resigned, we have had *peace* in the office.

Reading and Writing Practice

38.4   Dictation Speed Letter

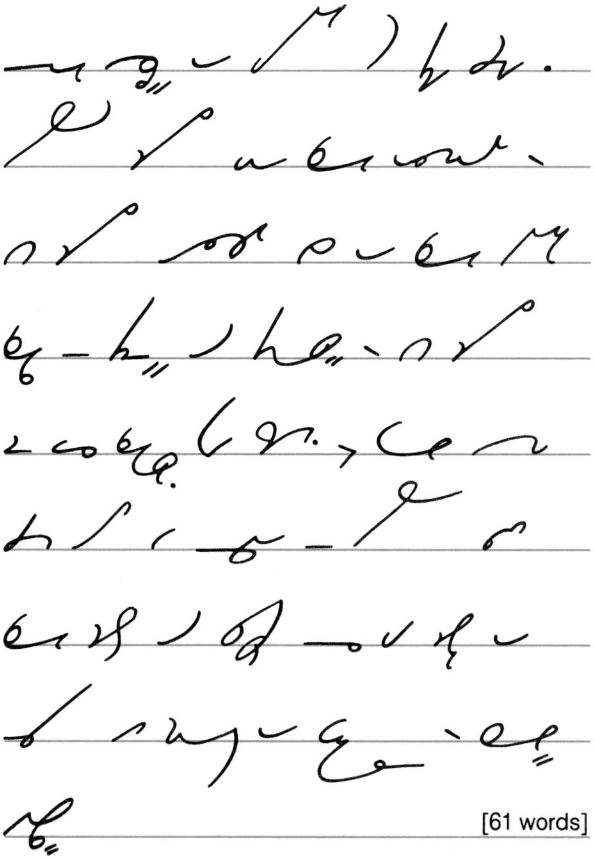

[shorthand content]

[61 words]

38.5   Magazine Article

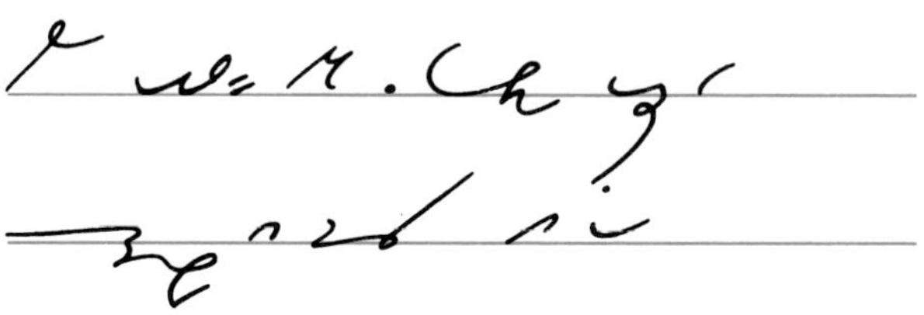

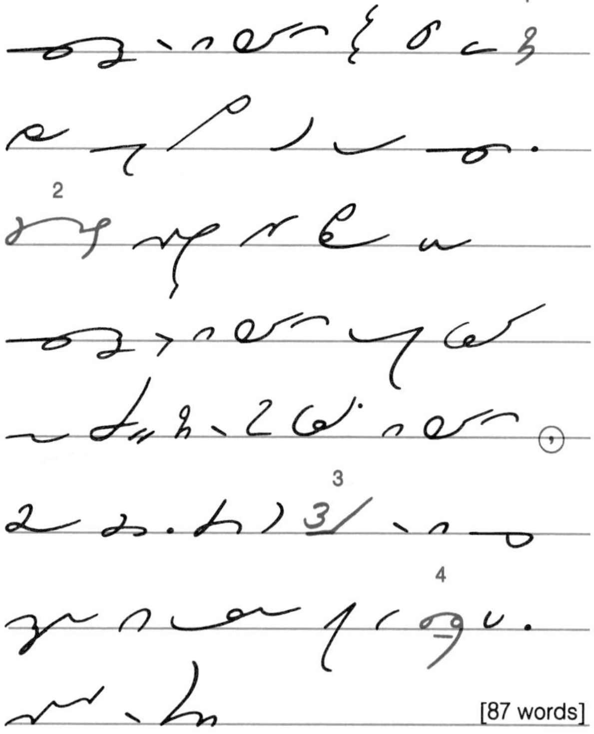

[shorthand content]

[shorthand content]

[87 words]

38.6   Reminder

[shorthand content]

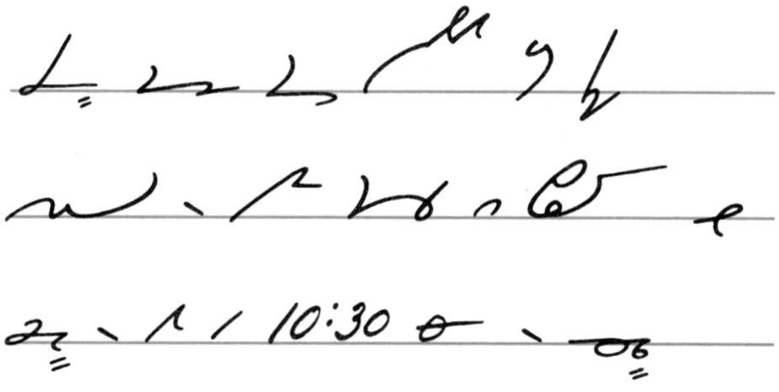

[21 words]

1 issues   2 significant   3 $300   4 equivalent

LESSON 39

NEW IN LESSON 39

- Word ending *-ology*
- Word beginning and ending *self*
- Word ending *-iety*
- Linking shorthand and English competence

WORD ENDING -OLOGY

The word ending *-ology* as in *apology* is abbreviated with the *o* and *l* symbols.

Example: apology

-ology Words

apology

apologies

apologize

psychology

psychological ■

psychologically ■

sociology

biology

technology

technological ■

■ Notice that the disjoined *k* is added for the *-ical* ending.

1 *[shorthand outline]*

2 *[shorthand outline]*

3 *[shorthand outline]*

4 *[shorthand outline]*

5 *[shorthand outline]*

¶ **Note of Apology**

[shorthand outlines]

[46 words]

WORD BEGINNING AND ENDING SELF

The word beginning *self-* as in *selfish* is represented by a disjoined left *s* and is written in the middle of the line. *[shorthand symbol]*

Example: selfish *[shorthand symbol]*

Self- Words

selfish *[shorthand]*

selfishness *[shorthand]*
■ **Transcription Alert.**

self-addressed ■ *[shorthand]*

self-confident ■ *[shorthand]*

self-confidence ■ *[shorthand]*

self-improvement ■ *[shorthand]*

The word ending *-self* as in *myself* and *yourself* is represented by a joined *s*.

Examples: myself *[shorthand]*   yourself *[shorthand]*

-Self Words

myself _[shorthand]_   itself _[shorthand]_   ourselves _[shorthand]_

herself _[shorthand]_   yourself _[shorthand]_   themselves _[shorthand]_

himself _[shorthand]_   yourselves _[shorthand]_

Self-, -self Practice
39.2

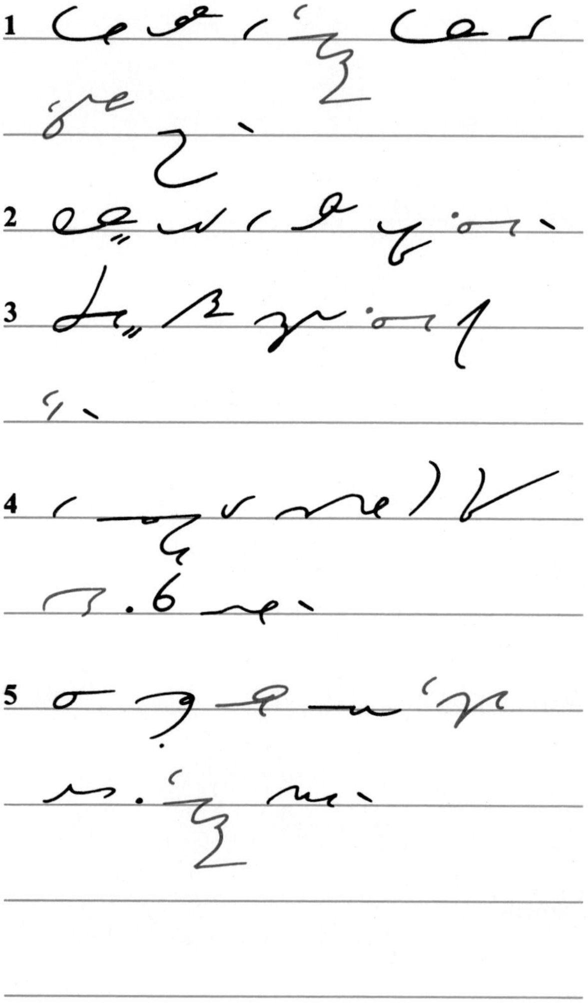

1 _[shorthand outline]_

2 _[shorthand outline]_

3 _[shorthand outline]_

4 _[shorthand outline]_

5 _[shorthand outline]_

¶ **Letter**

[shorthand outline]

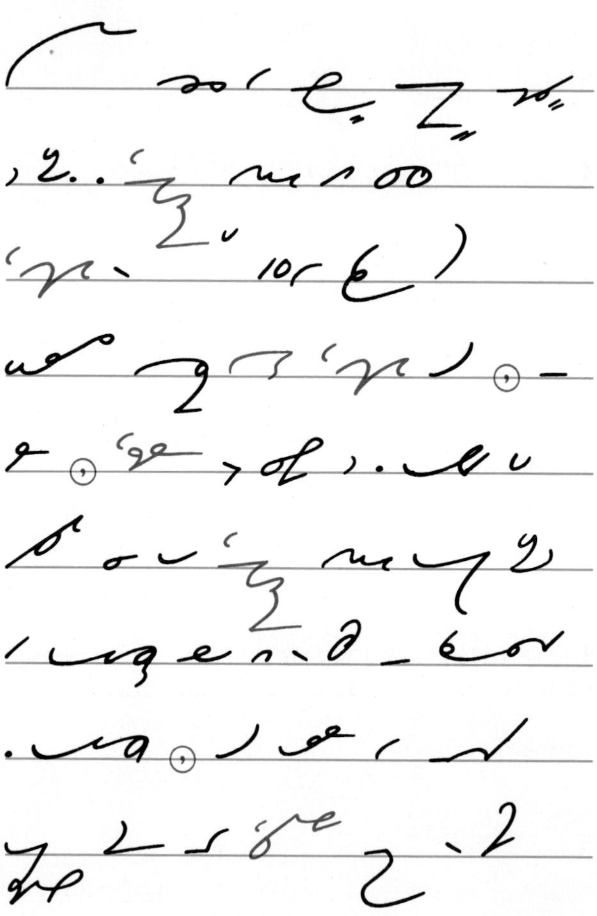

[83 words]

WORD ENDING -IETY

The word ending *-iety* as in *variety* is abbreviated with the *i* symbol. ⟋

Example: variety ⟋⟍

-iety Words

variety ⟋⟍ _____   society ⟍ _____   notoriety ⟋⟍ _____

anxiety ⟍ _____

-iety Practice
39.3

1 [shorthand outline]

2 [shorthand outline]

3 [shorthand outline]

4 [shorthand outline]

5 [shorthand outline]

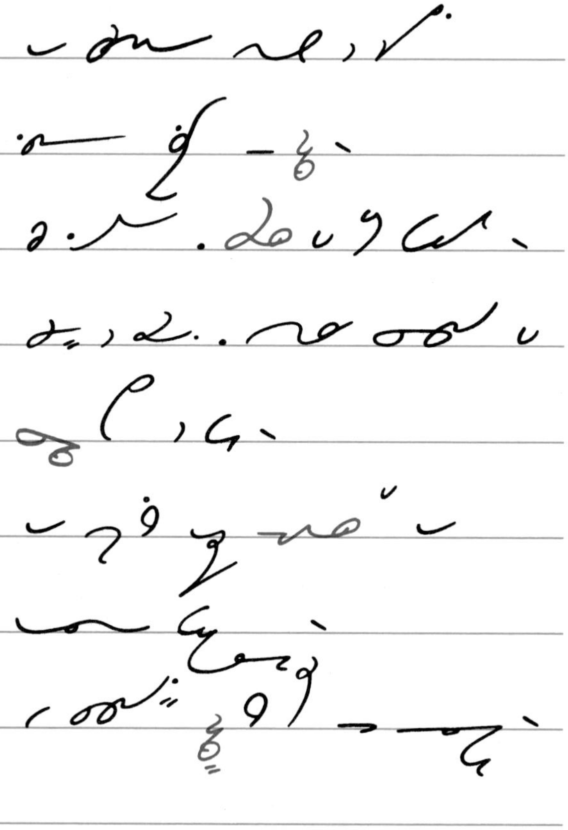

¶ **Accounting Presentation**

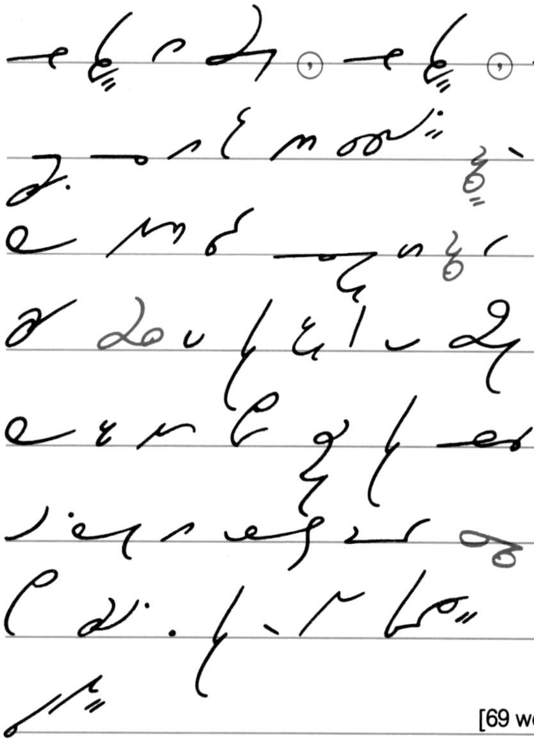

[shorthand outlines]

[69 words]

Shorthand and English Competence

For many people, the study of shorthand is the event that makes them feel that they are really beginning to master the English language. Students cannot help but improve their knowledge of the English language by studying Gregg Shorthand, and they apply that knowledge when transcribing their shorthand notes.

Employers recognize the value of the study of shorthand in a secretary's background. In a recent survey, an overwhelming majority of business executives stated that they believe the study of shorthand makes a better secretary.

Because of the English competence gained through the study of Gregg Shorthand, people who have studied Gregg Shorthand make better typists, better word processing operators, better editors of their bosses' correspondence, and better writers of communications that are delegated to them for composition. Best of all, employers appreciate these advantages.

A secretary who has studied Gregg Shorthand has the best chance of being hired, being promoted, and being self-assured on the job.

Reading and Writing Practice

39.4 Dictation Speed Letter

[72 words]

39.5 Retirement Plan

1 Mendez   2 Self-Employment   3 Law
4 deduction   5 15 percent

6 classification 7 yourself 8 anxiety 9 years

[80 words]

LESSON 40

NEW IN LESSON 40

- Eight brief forms
- Common name endings *-ington*, *-ingham*, *-ville*, and *-burgh*
- Differentiating between *sense* and *cents*

BRIEF FORMS

character _____ ordinary _____ question _____

circular _____ privilege ■ _____ statistic _____

circumstance _____ publish, publication _____

■ Transcription Alert.

Brief-Form Derivatives

characters _____ ordinarily _____ questions _____

circulars _____ privileges _____ questionable _____

circumstances _____ published _____ questionnaire ■ _____

extraordinary ■ _____ publications, publishes _____ statistical _____

■ Transcription Alert.

Brief-Form Practice
40.1

1 *[shorthand outlines]*

2 *[shorthand outlines]*

3 *[shorthand outlines]*

4 *[shorthand outlines]*

5 *[shorthand outlines]*

¶ **Publication Announcement**

[shorthand outlines]

[73 words]

Recording the requirements of the client quickly in shorthand is an aid to the sales representative.

-ington

The name ending -ington is represented by a disjoined *ten* blend.

Washington  _____   Lexington _____   Wilmington _____

-ingham

The name ending -ingham is represented by a disjoined *m*. ——

Buckingham _____   Cunningham _____   Framingham _____

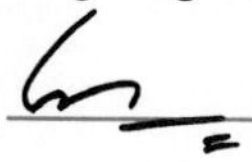

-ville

The name ending -ville is represented by the *v* symbol.

Nashville  _____   Jacksonville _____   Evansville _____

-burgh

The name ending -burg(h) is represented by the *b* symbol.

Pittsburgh, Pittsburg  _____   Harrisburg _____   Greensburg _____

Names Practice
40.2

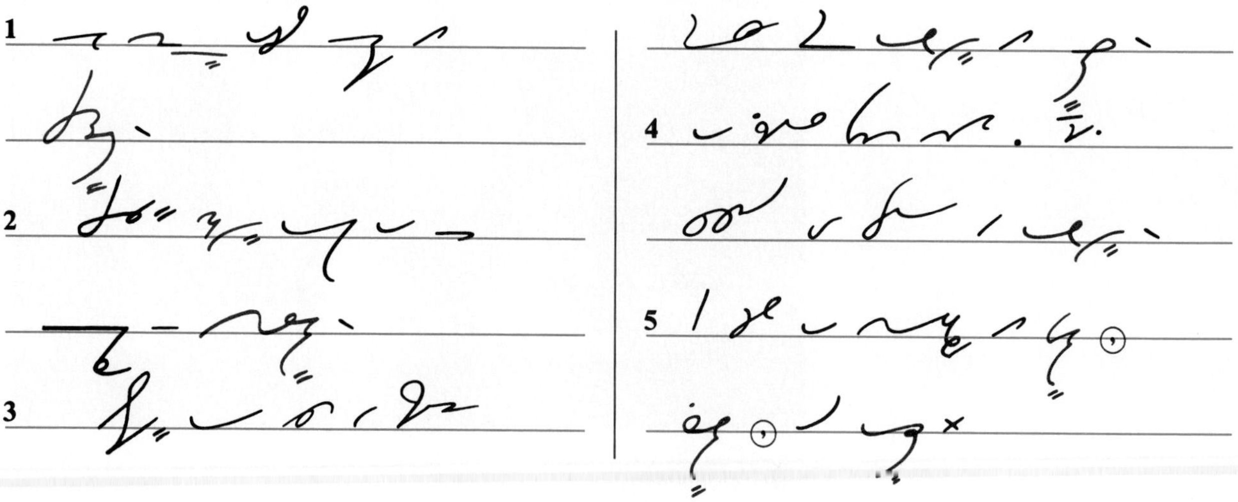

1 _____

2 _____

3 _____

4 _____

5 _____

[shorthand writing]

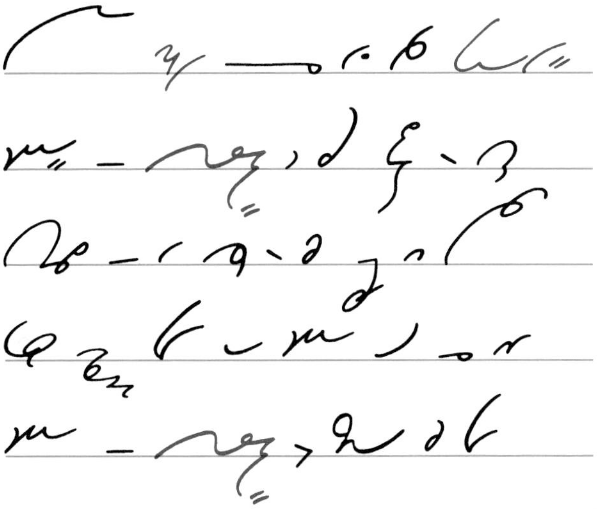

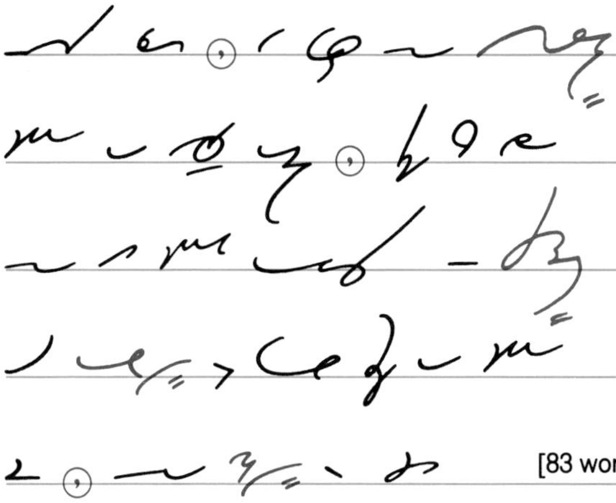

[83 words]

Communication Skill Builder

Similar Words: sense, cents

sense: good judgment

cents: pennies

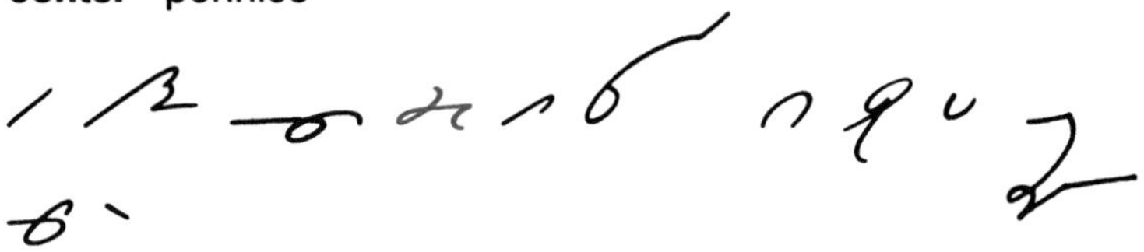

[shorthand writing]

It does not make *sense* to attempt this type of investment now.

[shorthand writing]

The new advertising campaign is bad business in terms of dollars and *cents*.

Congratulatory Message

Congratulations! Your study of Gregg Shorthand theory is complete. Though millions of people have learned Gregg Shorthand before you, you still have the satisfaction of acquiring knowledge that places you in an elite class of professionals who handle communications most efficiently.

At this point you probably feel that you know the basic Gregg alphabet, as well as most of the early brief forms, quite well. You may not yet have complete confidence in your knowledge of many of the abbreviated word beginnings and endings and some of the recent brief forms. As you continue your shorthand study, your knowledge of the system will become more and more certain and your writing speed will increase.

The ability to take notes quickly in shorthand during a fashion show can be important for a buyer.

Reading and Writing Practice

40.3 Speed Dictation Memo

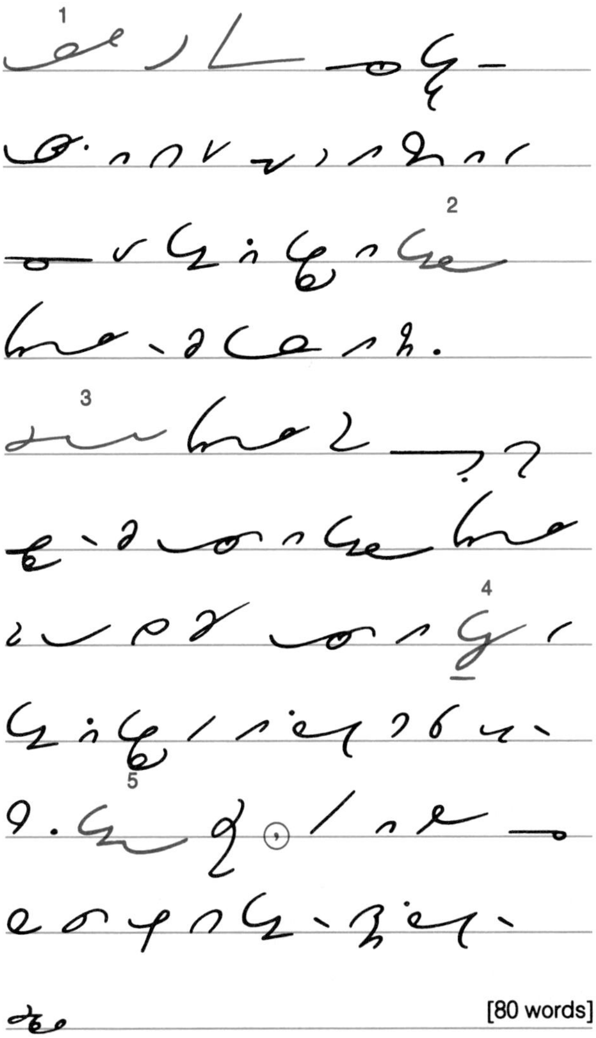

[Shorthand outlines]

[80 words]

1 Ladies and Gentlemen   2 personnel   3 similar
4 persuade   5 personal

40.4 Payment Request

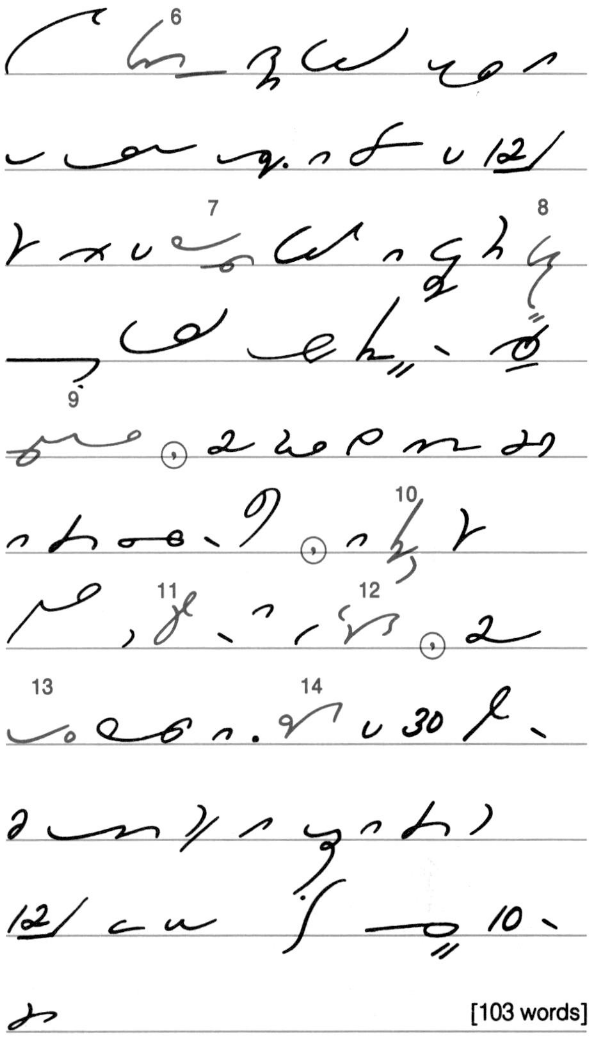

[Shorthand outlines]

[103 words]

6 Buckingham   7 electronic   8 Pittsburgh
9 naturally   10 justification   11 satisfactory
12 circumstances   13 willingly   14 extension

U N I T

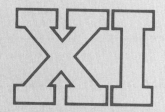

ADMITTING SUPERVISOR

LESSON 41

NEW IN LESSON 41

- **Dictation speed building**
- **Transcription skill development**
- **Related numbers in a sentence**

DICTATION SPEED BUILDING

The shorthand outlines below appear in the speed dictation practice which follows. Practice writing these words using the shorthand outlines. Then, using the key below, dictate the words to yourself.

Theory Words

Brief Forms

Phrases

Key *Theory*: forgotten, expired, slipped, lapse, minutes, return, together

  Brief Forms: insurance, never, this, enclosed, form, envelope, that

  Phrases: I am sure, will you please, with your, in the

Speed Dictation Practice

41.1 Expiration of Insurance

[shorthand notation]

[60 words]

TRANSCRIPTION SKILL DEVELOPMENT

Transcribe the following words and phrases, noting spelling and capitalization. Then transcribe the transcription letter which follows.

Transcription Warmup

41.2

[shorthand notation]

■ Transcription Hint: *Mrs.* will be capitalized and followed by a period.

Transcription Practice

41.3   Credit Reference

(shorthand outlines)

[80 words]

Related Numbers in a Sentence

In previous lessons the following number rules were presented:

Spell out the numbers *one through ten* within a sentence.
Use figures for the numbers *11 and above* within a sentence.
If a number is used at the *beginning of a sentence*, spell it out.

An additional number rule is listed below with examples:

If there is a series of related numbers *one through ten* in a sentence, express all of them in words. If one or more of the related numbers is *above ten*, write all of them in *figures*.

(shorthand outline)

There are *five* secretaries and *eight* assistants.

(shorthand outline)

We ordered *6* notebooks and *30* envelopes.

(shorthand outline)

We purchased *15* tapes and *20* records.

Reading and Writing Practice

41.4 Communications Bulletin

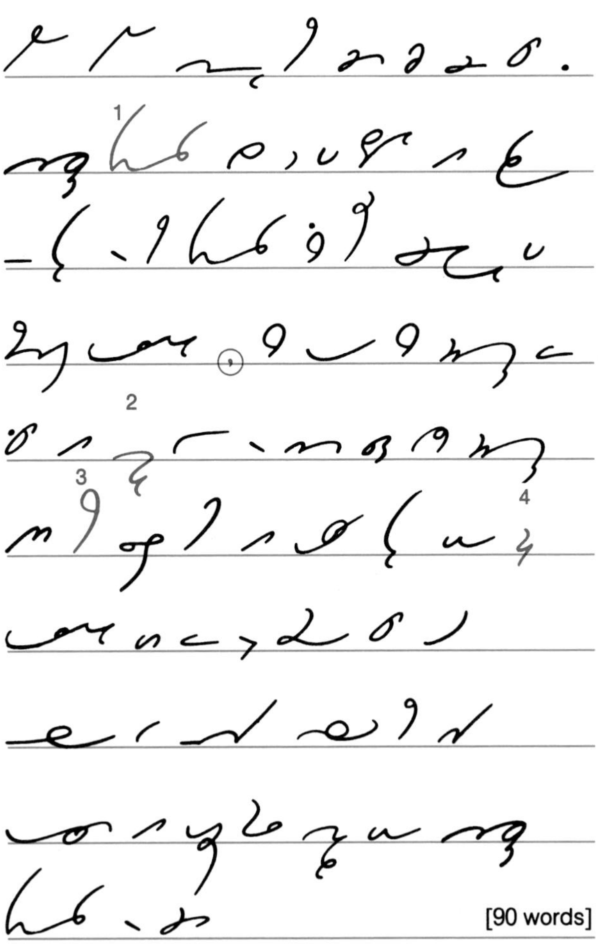

[shorthand outlines]

1 bulletin   2 compose   3 advantage   4 social

[90 words]

41.5 Finance Update

[shorthand outlines]

5 Harris   6 financial   7 review   8 difficult
9 organization   10 representatives   11 success
12 adequate   13 replacements   14 progress
15 15 percent   16 considerable

[91 words]

LESSON 42

NEW IN LESSON 42

- Dictation speed building
- Transcription skill development
- Punctuation: commas in a series (series comma)

DICTATION SPEED BUILDING

The shorthand outlines below appear in the speed dictation practice which follows. Practice writing these words using the shorthand outlines. Then, using the key below, dictate the words to yourself.

Theory Words

Brief Forms

Phrases

Key *Theory*: pleasure, receive, various, items, return, handle, account, forward
      Brief Forms: office, products, enclosed, represents, order, satisfied, business
      Phrases: it was, in our, to us, this will, we hope that, you will be, with our, with you

Speed Dictation Practice

42.1 Purchase Request

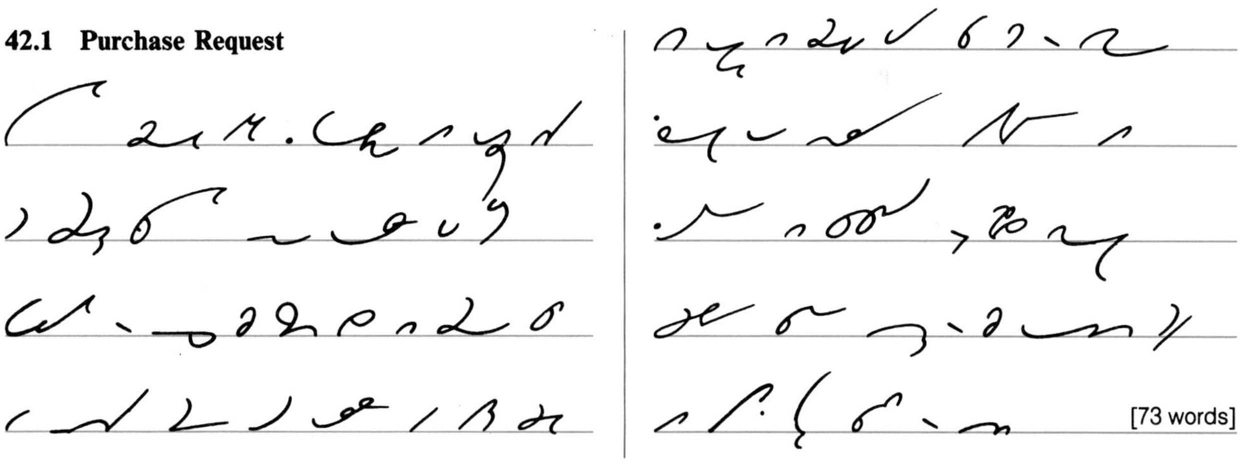

[shorthand outlines]

[73 words]

Transcribe the following words and phrases, noting spelling and capitalization. Then transcribe the transcription letter which follows.

Transcription Warmup

42.2

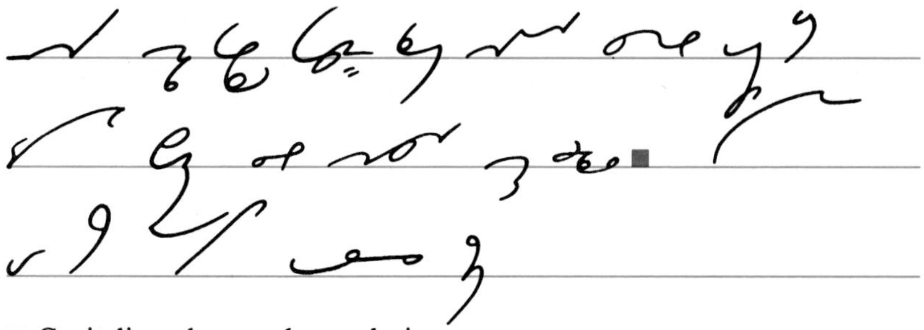

[shorthand outlines]

■ Capitalize when used as a closing.

Transcription Practice

42.3   Contract Review

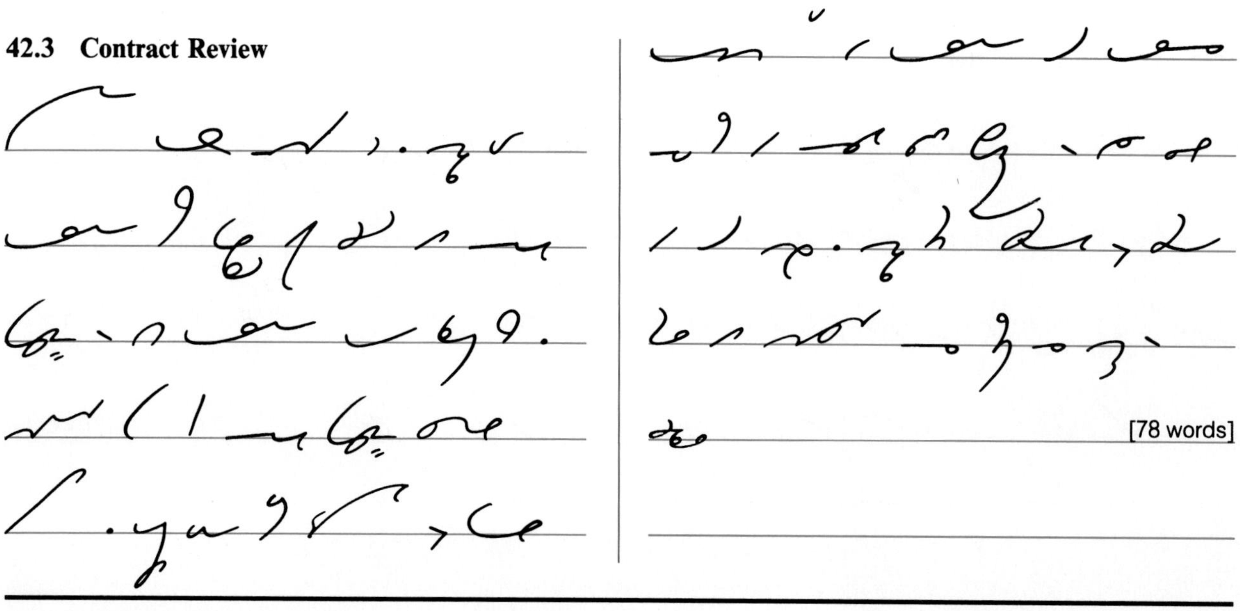

[shorthand outlines]

[78 words]

Punctuation: Commas in a Series

When three or more items are listed in a series and the last item is preceded by the word *and*, *or*, or *nor*, place a comma before the conjunction and between the other items.

The *series comma* is indicated by ⊙̦

[shorthand outlines]

The folder contained *letters*, *memos*, and *forms*.

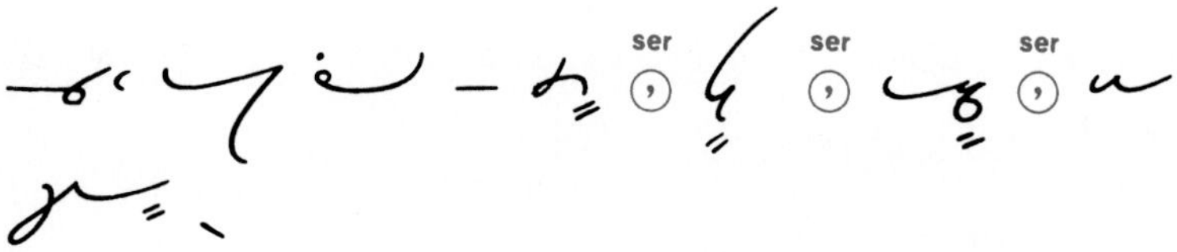

[shorthand outlines]

Meetings will be held in *Chicago*, *Boston*, *Los Angeles*, or *Seattle*.

42.4 Appreciation Letter

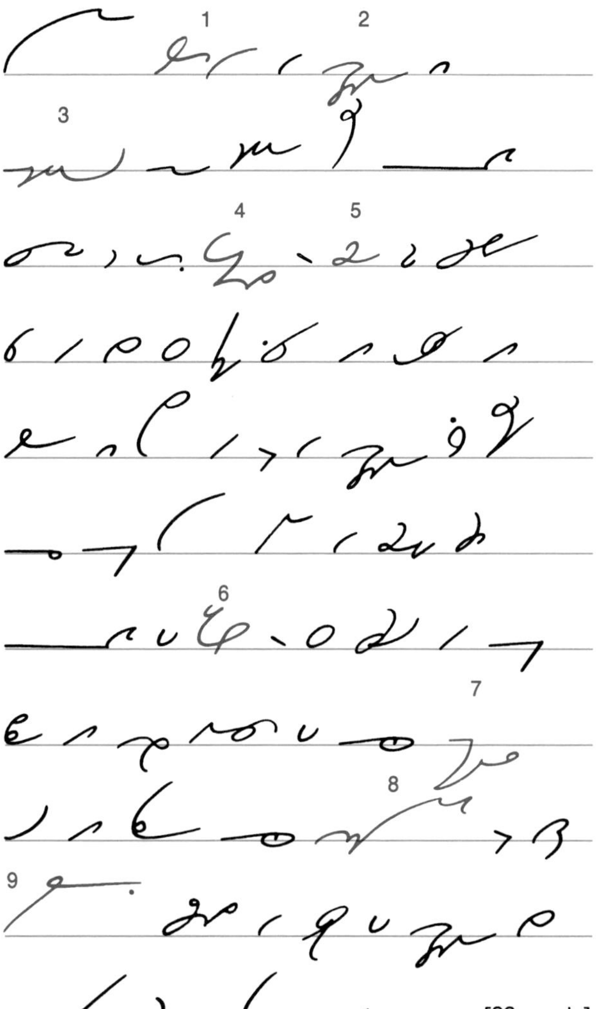

(shorthand outlines)

[83 words]

1 Tarkington   2 computer   3 installed
4 perfectly   5 We are   6 operation   7 inventory
8 customers   9 determining

42.5 Income Tax

(shorthand outlines)

[84 words]

10 Hastings   11 enclosed   12 federal
13 government   14 engaged   15 insurance
16 furnish   17 difficulty

NEW IN LESSON 43

- Dictation speed building
- Transcription skill development
- Differentiating between *stationary* and *stationery*

DICTATION SPEED BUILDING

The shorthand outlines below appear in the speed dictation practice which follows. Practice writing these words using the shorthand outlines. Then, using the key below, dictate the words to yourself.

Theory Words

Phrases

Key *Theory*: Drake, magazine, article, effective, collection, just, kind, item, creative, patience, months, accommodate

  Phrases: thank you, very much, it is, from our, at this time, to be, in which, that will

Speed Dictation Practice

43.1 Magonine Article

[shorthand symbols]

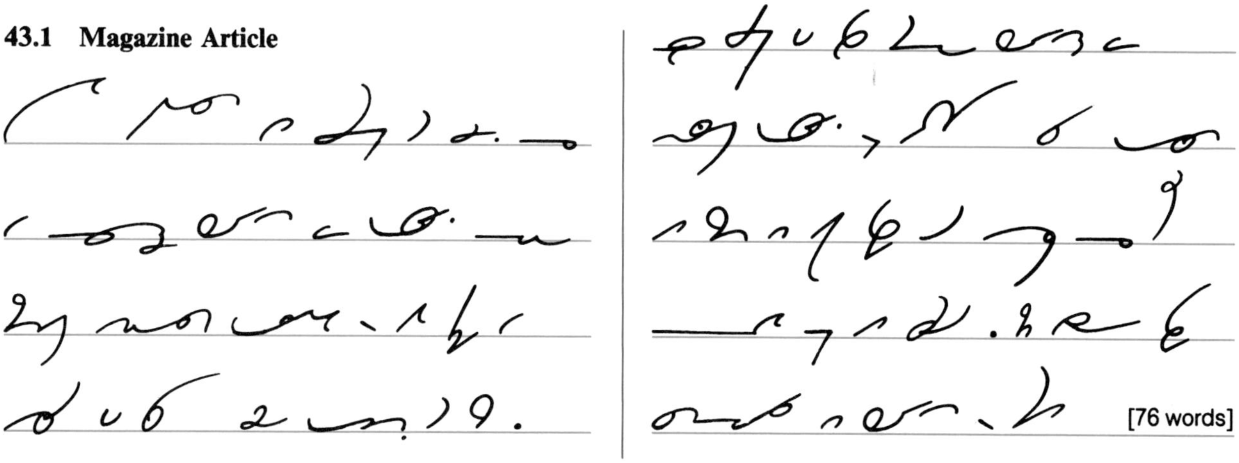

[76 words]

TRANSCRIPTION SKILL DEVELOPMENT

Transcribe the following words and phrases, noting spelling and capitalization. Then transcribe the transcription letter which follows.

Transcription Warmup

43.2

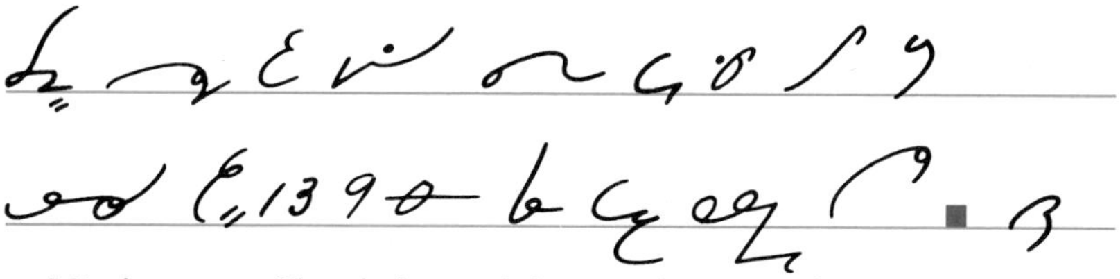

[shorthand symbols]

■ *Miss* is not an abbreviation and does not have a period.

Transcription Practice

43.3 Speaker Presentation

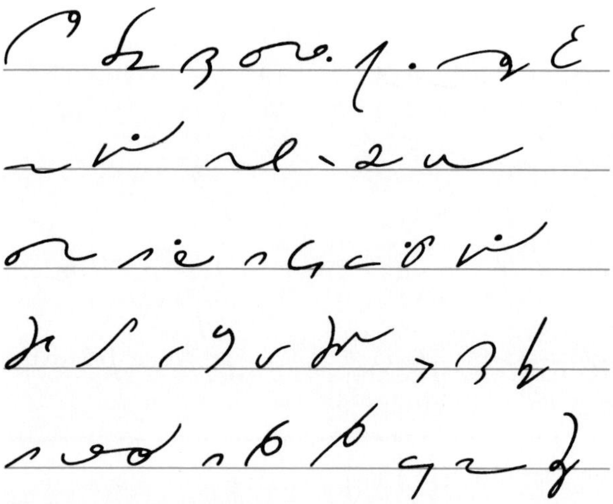

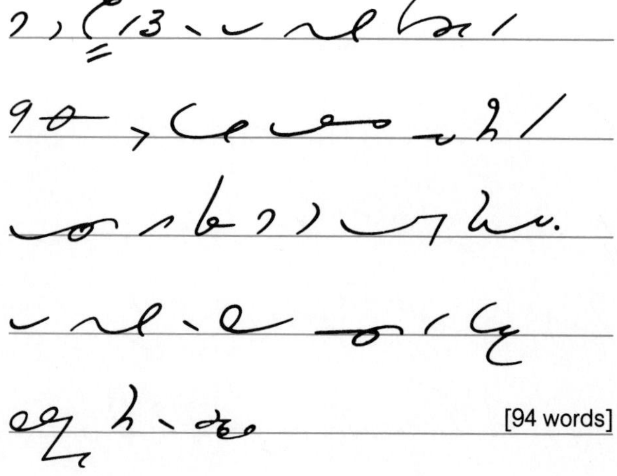

[Shorthand outlines]

[94 words]

Communication Skill Builder

Similar Words: stationary, stationery

stationary: fixed; not movable
stationery: writing materials

[Shorthand outline]

The price index is *stationary*.

[Shorthand outline]

I have ordered *stationery* with our new address.

43.4 Investment Planning

(shorthand outline)

[95 words]

43.5 Telephone Techniques

(shorthand outline)

[114 words]

1 research 2 enable 3 holdings 4 unique
5 New York

6 seminar 7 sessions 8 result 9 concerns

LESSON

NEW IN LESSON 44

- Dictation speed building
- Transcription skill development
- Punctuation: *as*, *if*, and *when* clauses

DICTATION SPEED BUILDING

The shorthand outlines below appear in the speed dictation practice which follows. Practice writing these words using the shorthand outlines. Then, using the key which follows, dictate the words to yourself.

Theory Words

Brief Forms

Phrases

Key *Theory*: Personnel Committee, Myers, 3 p.m., agenda,
              items, discussed, whether, response, attendance,
              greatly, appreciated
     Brief Forms: from, subject, enclosed, immediate, regarding
     Phrases: there will be, of the, for the, let me, if you have, to
              have, you will be able

Speed Dictation Practice

44.1 Memo

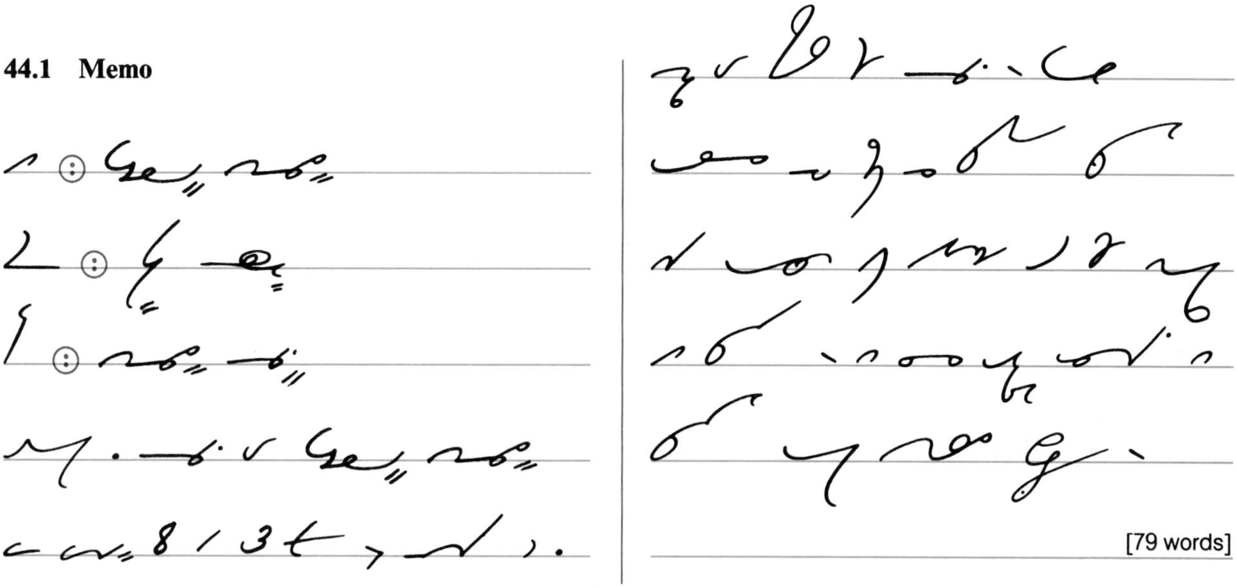

[shorthand outlines]

[79 words]

TRANSCRIPTION SKILL DEVELOPMENT

Transcribe the following words and phrases, noting spelling and capitalization. Then transcribe the letter which follows.

Transcription Warmup

44.2

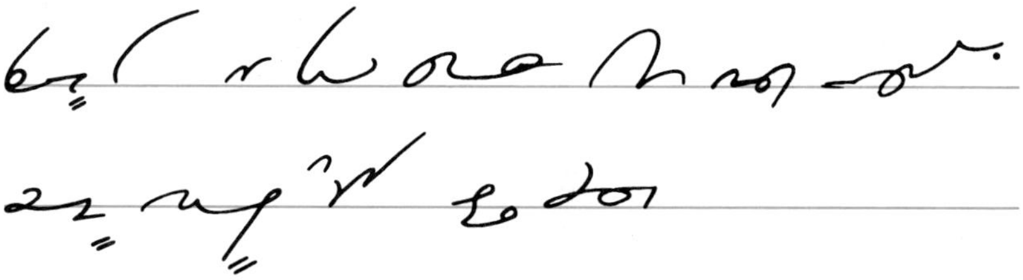

[shorthand outlines]

Transcription Practice

44.3 Wilson College

[Shorthand outlines]

[67 words]

Punctuation: *As, If, When* Clauses

A group of words that begin a sentence with *as*, *if*, or *when* followed by a subject and a predicate is an introductory clause. An introductory clause is dependent on the remaining part of the sentence and should have a comma to set it aside from the rest of the sentence. Be sure the comma is placed at the end of the clause that is introduced by *as*, *if*, or *when*.

The *as clause comma* is indicated by *[symbol]* as

The *if clause comma* is indicated by *[symbol]* if

The *when clause comma* is indicated by *[symbol]* when

[Shorthand outline]

As you know, we will be open Monday through Saturday.

[Shorthand outline]

If you need additional assistance, let me know.

[Shorthand outline]

When the shipment is received, I will notify you.

278 ■■■ LESSON 44

44.4 New Office

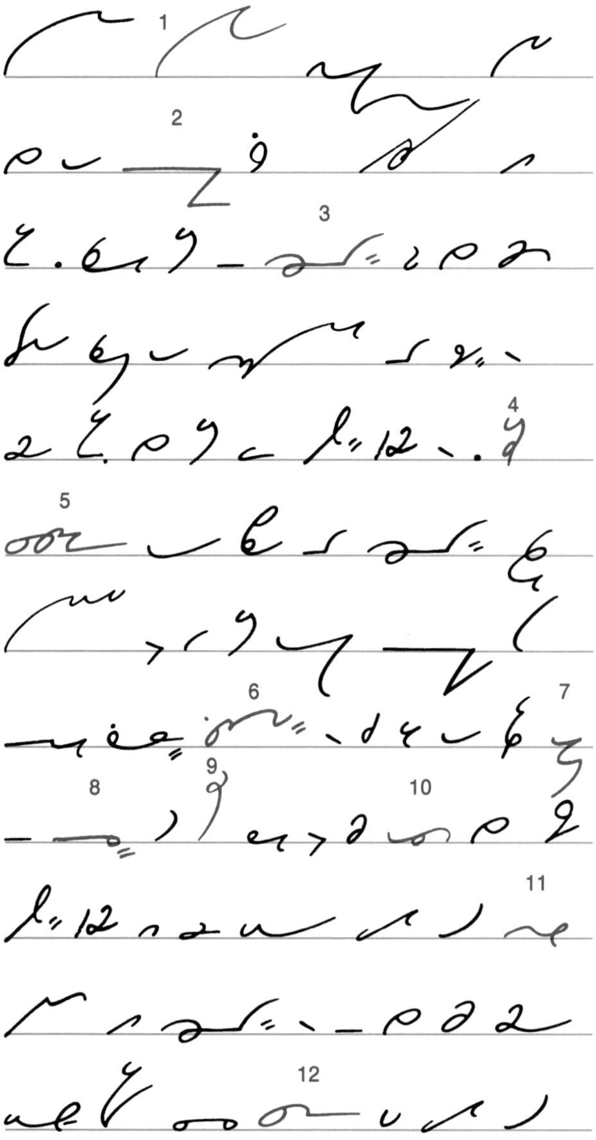

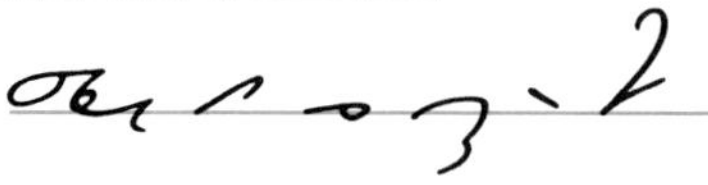

(shorthand outline, numbered 1-12)

[100 words]

44.5 Book Exhibition

(shorthand outline, numbered 13-18)

[91 words]

1 Temple   2 management   3 Camden
4 official   5 announcement   6 Hugo
7 representative   8 Maine   9 several
10 recommend   11 correspondence
12 acknowledgment

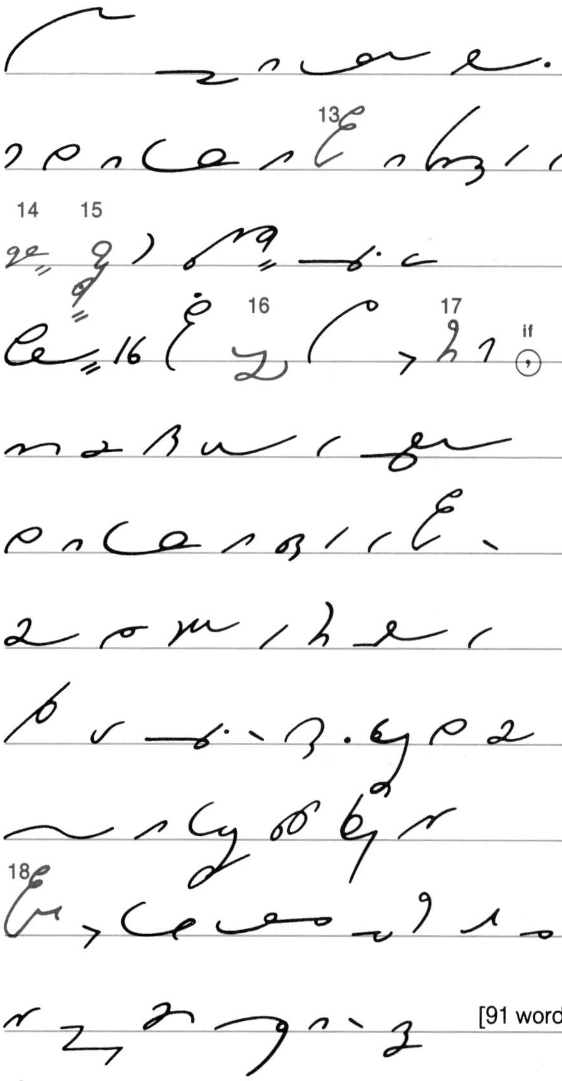

13 exhibit   14 Eastern   15 Association
16 referred   17 if you   18 exhibitors

U N I T

XII

LESSON 45

NEW IN LESSON 45

- Dictation speed building
- Transcription skill development
- Differentiating between *past* and *passed*

DICTATION SPEED BUILDING

The shorthand outlines below appear in the speed dictation practice which follows. Practice writing these words using the shorthand outlines. Then, using the key which follows, dictate the words to yourself.

Theory Words

Brief Forms

Phrases

Theory: bond, supplies, delighted, first, received, firm,
                processed, sincere, also, lowest, industry
       Brief Forms: Gentlemen, order, yesterday, were, one, soon,
                manufacture, products
       Phrases: thank you for the, it was, has been, this will be,
                Yours very truly

Speed Dictation Practice

45.1 Purchase Order

[shorthand outlines]

[84 words]

TRANSCRIPTION SKILL DEVELOPMENT

Transcribe the following words and phrases, noting spelling and capitalization. Then transcribe the transcription letter which follows.

Transcription Warmup

45.2

[shorthand outlines]

Transcription Practice

45.3 Credit Account

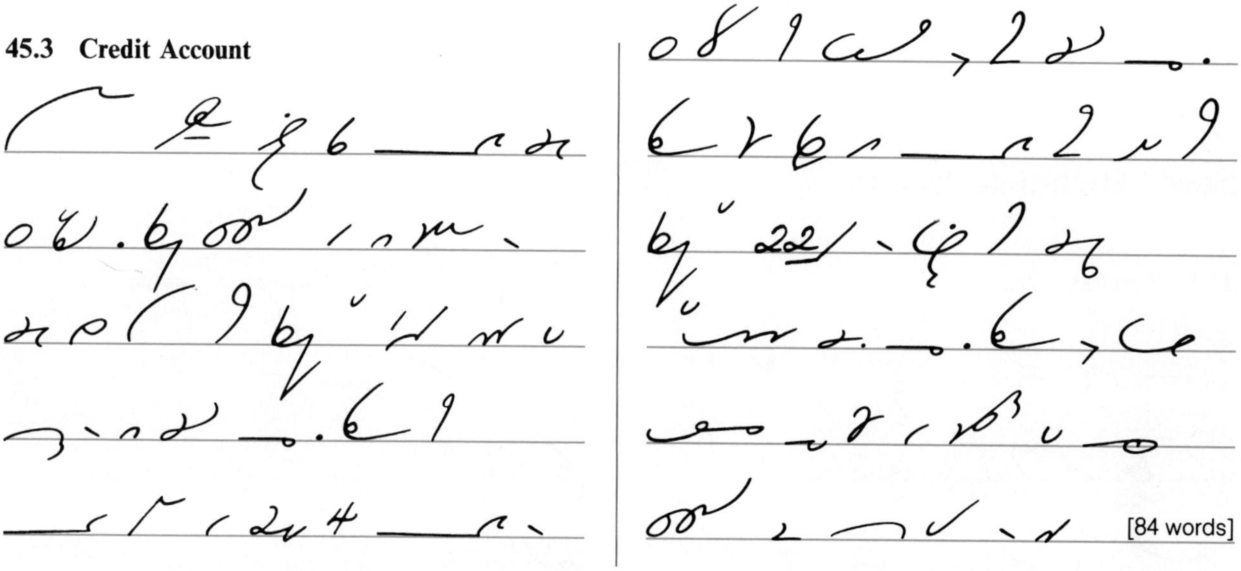

[shorthand outlines] [84 words]

Communication Skill Builder

Similar Words: past, passed

past: (n.) time gone by

passed: (v.) moved from one point to another (past tense of *pass*)

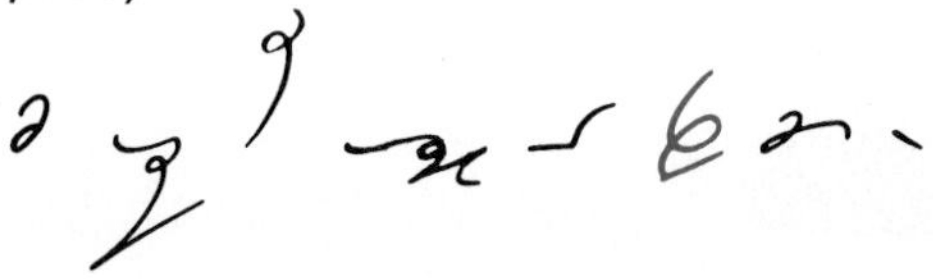

[shorthand outline]

We received several requests in the *past* week.

[shorthand outline]

We *passed* this building several times.

45.4 Credit Reference

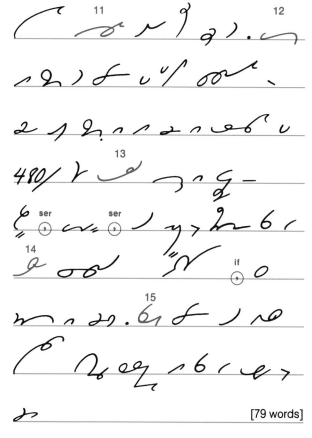

[94 words]

45.5 Credit Collection

[79 words]

1 Baker   2 payment   3 items   4 purchased
5 There was   6 time   7 sent   8 excellent
9 record

10 reference   11 Gates   12 organization
13 leather   14 entire   15 partial

LESSON

46

NEW IN LESSON 46

- Dictation speed building
- Transcription skill development
- Differentiating between *council* and *counsel*

DICTATION SPEED BUILDING

The shorthand outlines below appear in the speed dictation practice which follows. Practice writing these words using the shorthand outlines. Then, using the key which follows, dictate the words to yourself.

Theory Words

[shorthand outlines]

Brief Forms

[shorthand outlines]

Phrases

[shorthand outlines]

Key *Theory*: Hanson, announce, Westport, better, customers, area, November 10, official, address, letterhead
   Brief Forms: office, after, orders, correspondence, direct
   Phrases: we are, we will, we can, in the, which is, in this, Yours very truly

Speed Dictation Practice

46.1 New Sales Office

[78 words]

TRANSCRIPTION SKILL DEVELOPMENT

Transcribe the following words and phrases, noting spelling and capitalization. Then transcribe the letter which follows.

Transcription Warmup

46.2

Transcription Practice

46.3 Adult Education Program

[Shorthand notes for the Adult Education Program transcription practice]

[81 words]

Communication Skill Builder

Similar Words: council, counsel

council: (n.) an assembly

counsel: (v.) to give advice

[Shorthand outline]

The meeting of the city *council* will be held in February.

[Shorthand outline]

Dr. Jennings will *counsel* my daughter.

46.4 Credit Card

[shorthand outlines]

[82 words]

1 application 2 Worth Ladies 3 accessories
4 quickly

46.5 Public Relations

[shorthand outlines]

[86 words]

5 Ron 6 pleasure 7 appreciated 8 regularly
9 executives 10 taught 11 communications
12 San Francisco

LESSON 47

NEW IN LESSON 47

- Dictation speed building
- Transcription skill development
- Punctuation: words or phrases in apposition (apposition comma)

DICTATION SPEED BUILDING

The shorthand outlines below appear in the speed dictation practice which follows. Practice writing these words using the shorthand outlines. Then, using the key which follows, dictate the words to yourself.

Theory Words

Brief Forms

Phrases

Theory: minute, answer, determine, improve, services,
             renew, membership, expire, few, responding,
             Sincerely
     Brief Forms: questionnaire, short, questions, where,
                   nevertheless, idea, requests
     Phrases: will you please, to the, we need, will not, it is, you
               will be

Speed Dictation Practice

47.1   Membership Survey

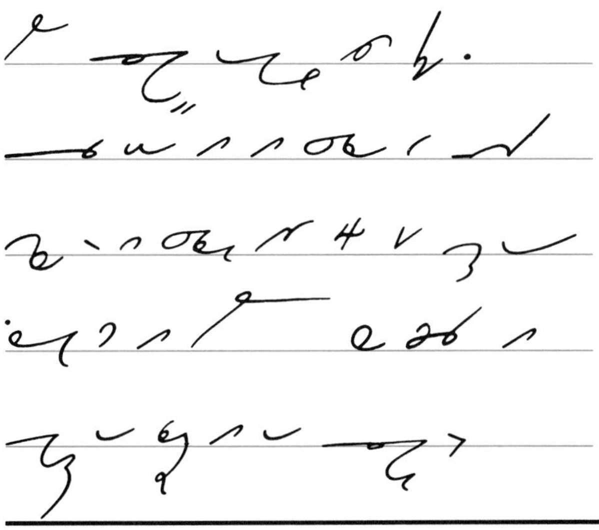

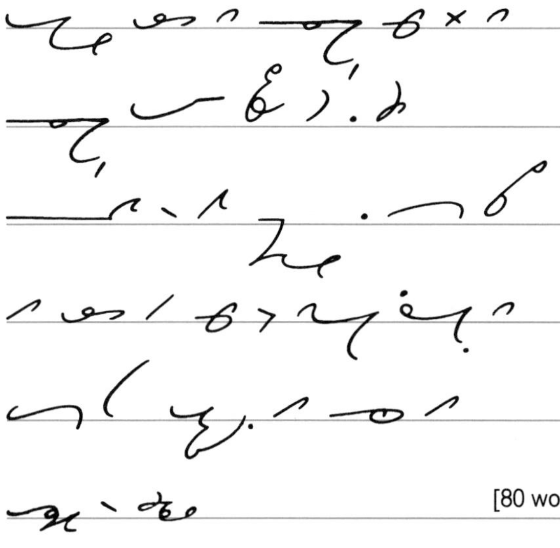

[80 words]

TRANSCRIPTION SKILL DEVELOPMENT

Transcribe the following words and phrases, noting spelling and capitalization. Then transcribe the transcription letter which follows.

Transcription Warmup

47.2

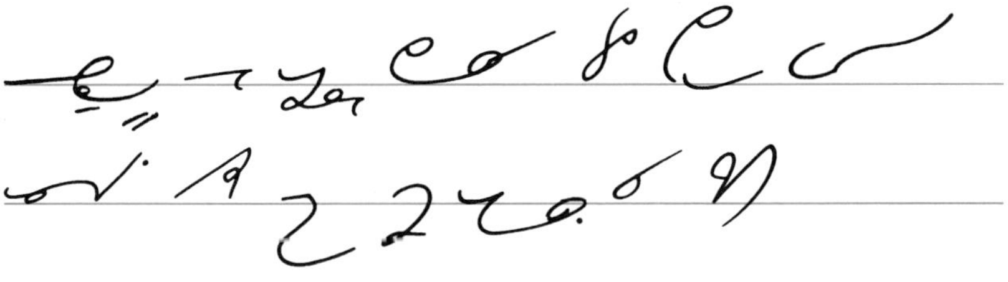

Transcription Practice

47.3 Reference Request

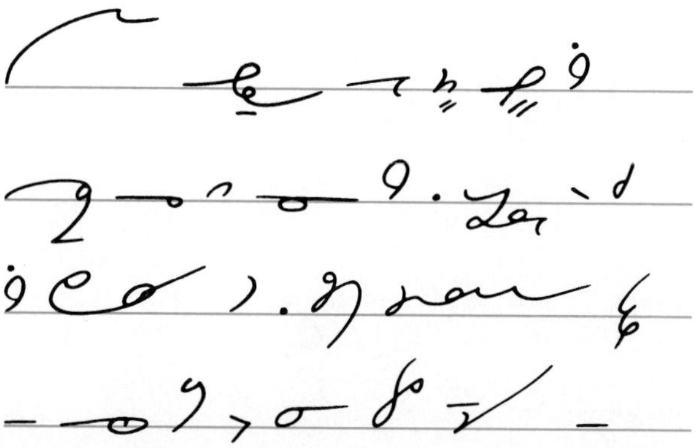

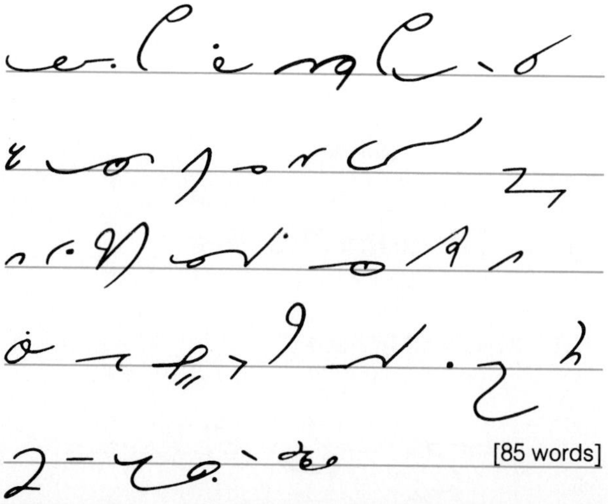

(shorthand outlines)

[85 words]

Punctuation: Words or Phrases in Apposition

A word or phrase used in apposition is one that explains or identifies other terms. When it occurs within a sentence, it is set off by two commas. When it occurs at the end of a sentence, only one comma is used.

The *apposition comma* is indicated by ⊙ (ap)

(shorthand outline)

Our auditor, *Ms. Santiago*, is ill.

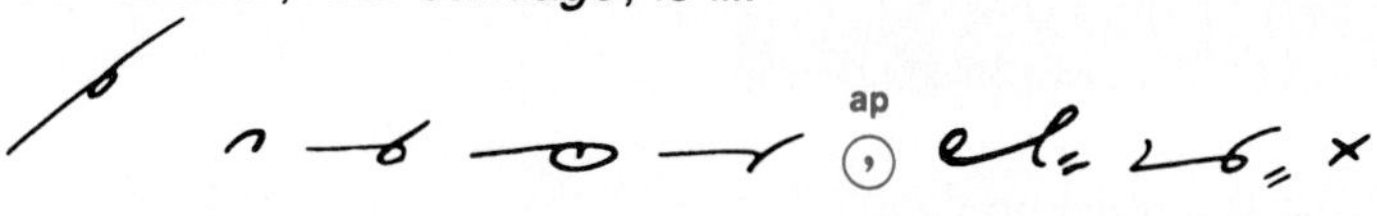

(shorthand outline)

Did you meet my mother, *Elise Smith*?

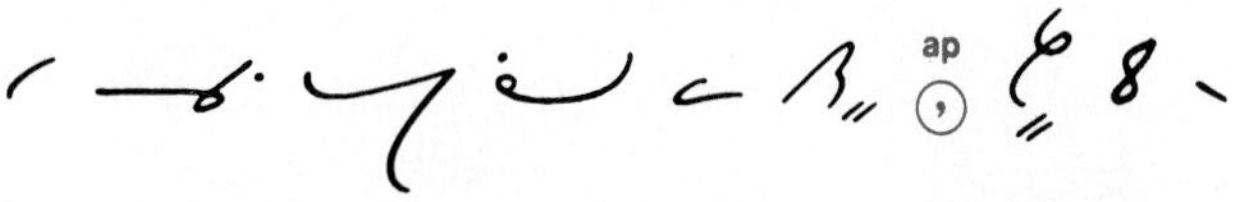

(shorthand outline)

The meeting will be held on Tuesday, *September 8*.

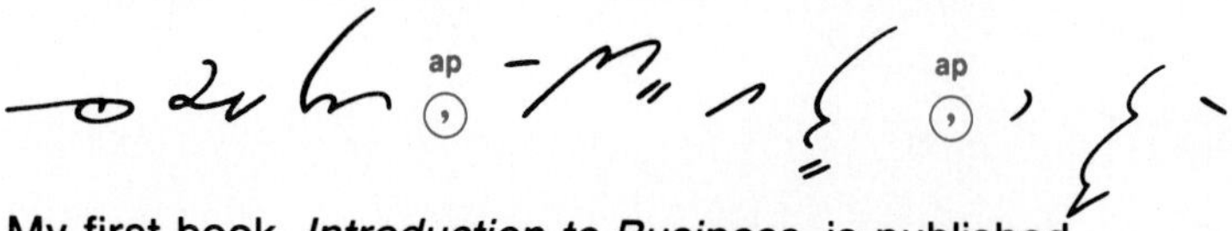

(shorthand outline)

My first book, *Introduction to Business*, is published.

47.4 United Way

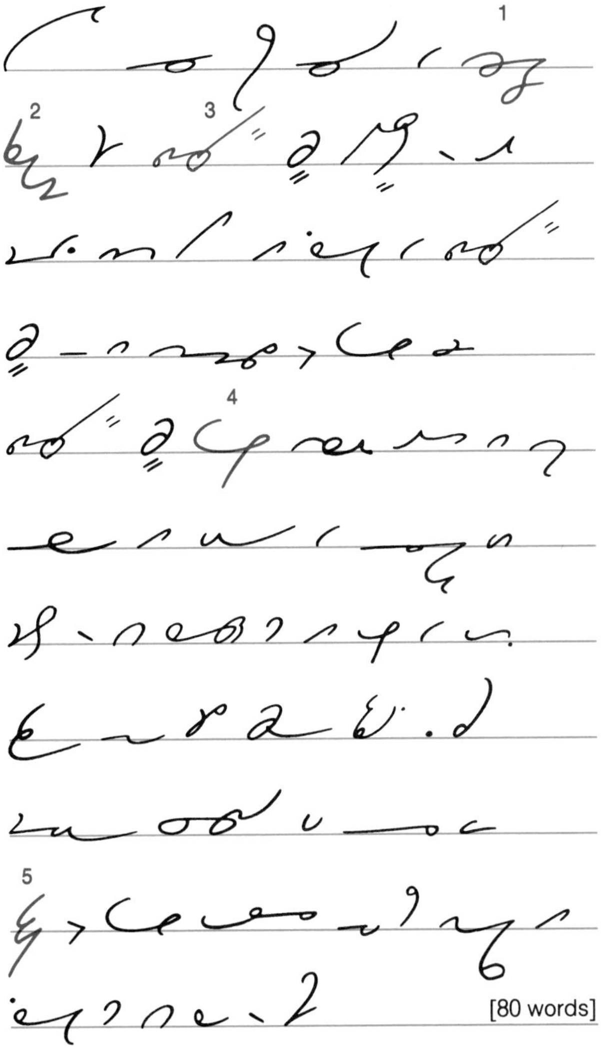

[shorthand]

[80 words]

1 campaign   2 chairperson   3 United   4 pledge
5 postage

47.5 Business Memo

[shorthand]

[82 words]

6 Jack Lopez   7 Vacancies   8 territories
9 includes   10 Dallas   11 Boston
12 Lexington

LESSON 48

NEW IN LESSON 48

- Dictation speed building
- Transcription skill development
- Differentiating between *lose*, *loose*, and *loss*

DICTATION SPEED BUILDING

The shorthand outlines below appear in the speed dictation practice which follows. Practice writing these words using the shorthand outlines. Then, using the key which follows, dictate the words to yourself.

Theory Words

Brief Forms

Phrases

Key   *Theory*:   Adams, determined, legally, obligated, expenses, Philip, injured, Washington, total, medical, $3,800, issue, additional
       Brief Forms: department, company, was, questions
       Phrases: Dear Mrs., on the, as soon as possible, if you have, Very truly yours

Speed Dictation Practice

48.1 Insurance Payment

[86 words]

TRANSCRIPTION SKILL DEVELOPMENT

Transcribe the following words and phrases, noting spelling and capitalization. Then transcribe the transcription letter which follows.

Transcription Warmup

48.2

Transcription Practice

48.3 **Magazine Subscription**

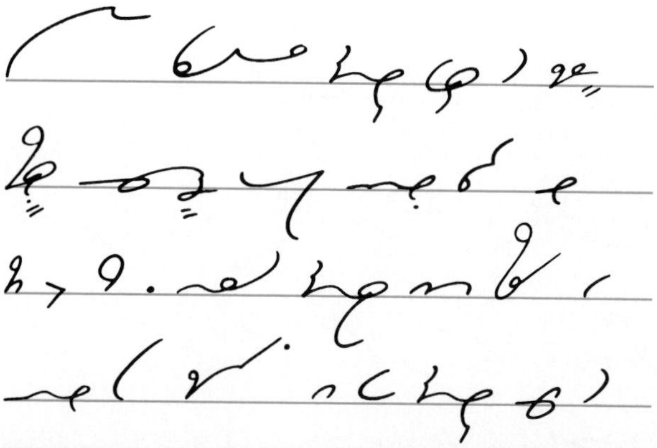

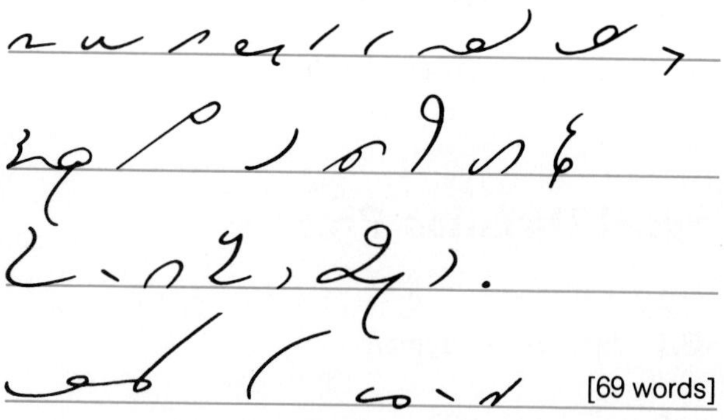

[shorthand outlines]

[69 words]

Communication Skill Builder

Similar Words: lose, loose, loss

lose: (v.) to part with unintentionally
loose: (adj.) not tight
loss: (n.) something lost

[shorthand outlines]

Miss Martin did not *lose* the report.

[shorthand outlines]

The coat is too *loose* for me to wear.

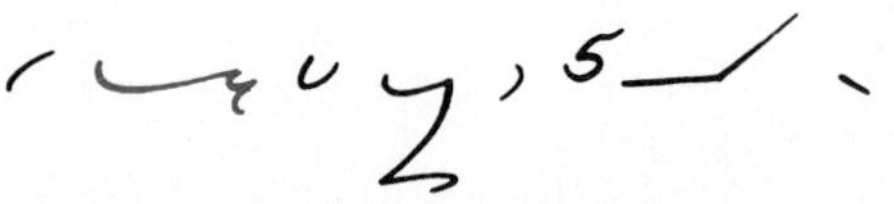

[shorthand outlines]

The *loss* of revenue is $5 million.

48.4 Communications System

[88 words]

1 appreciation   2 assistance   3 reorganizing
4 worldwide   5 solution   6 assistance
7 valuable

48.5 Publishing Opportunities

[102 words]

8 relations   9 Worth   10 unusual
11 responsible   12 industry   13 ordinarily

U N I T

XIII

LESSON 49

- Dictation speed building
- Transcription skill development
- Punctuation: commas with conjunctions (conjunction comma)

DICTATION SPEED BUILDING

The shorthand outlines below appear in the speed dictation practice which follows. Practice writing these words using the shorthand outlines. Then, using the key below, dictate the words to yourself.

Theory Words

Brief Forms

Phrases

Key *Theory*: agreement, opened, reasonable, records, purchases, $250, yet, received

Brief Forms: State Street, part, when, after, during, envelope

Phrases: for you/for your, of our, you would, we have not, send us

Speed Dictation Practice

49.1 Late Payment

[shorthand notation]

[81 words]

Transcribe the following words and phrases, noting spelling and capitalization. Then transcribe the transcription letter which follows.

Transcription Warmup

49.2

[shorthand notation]

Transcription Practice

49.3 Public Relations Visit

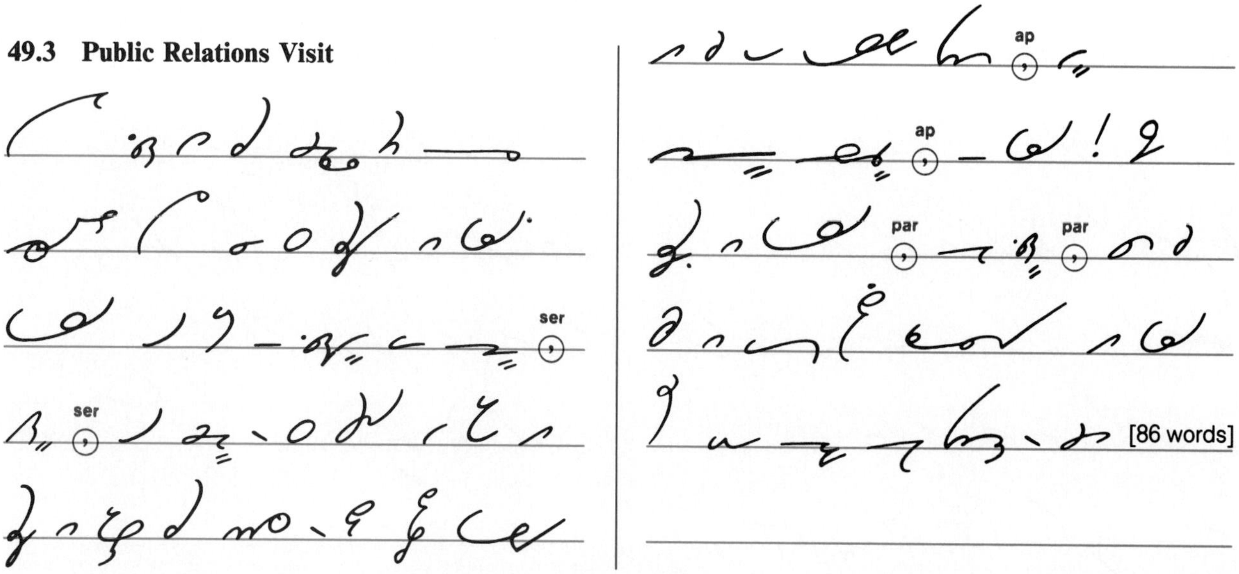
ser
ap
par
[86 words]

Punctuation: Commas With Conjunctions

Sometimes two simple sentences are joined together. Usually the sentences are joined by a conjunction such as *and*, *or*, or *but*. This type of sentence is called a compound sentence, and the conjunction is preceded by a comma.

The *conjunction comma* is indicated by (,) conj

conj

Today the weather is stormy, *and* I want to stay home.

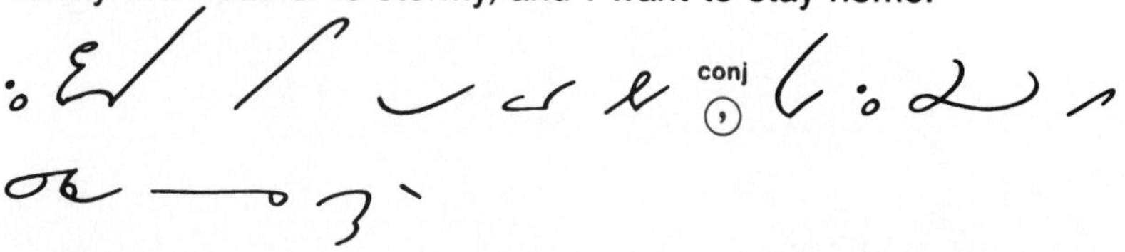
conj

He expected to do well on the test, *but* he failed to answer many questions.

49.4 Guest Speaker

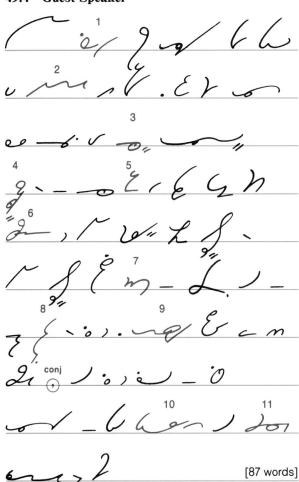

[87 words]

49.5 Time Management

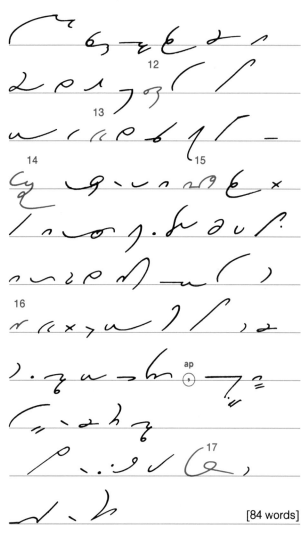

[84 words]

1	Harrington	2	directors	3	New York
4	Association	5	opinion	6	assignment
7	successful	8	publishing	9	recognized
10	political	11	financial		

12	enough	13	things	14	professional	15	one
of these	16	other	17	blank		

LESSON 50

- Dictation speed building
- Transcription skill development
- Punctuation: introductory expressions (introductory comma)

DICTATION SPEED BUILDING

The shorthand outlines below appear in the speed dictation practice which follows. Practice writing these words using the shorthand outlines. Then, using the key which follows, dictate the words to yourself.

Theory Words

Brief Forms

Phrases

Key *Theory*:   editor, magazine, Janice Hastings, asked, article, technical, appear, done, job, reporting, computer, printers
Brief Forms: inform, that, published, publish/publication, thinking, time, very, glad
Phrases: will be, I have been, of this, thank you for, Yours truly

Speed Dictation Practice

50.1   Article Publication

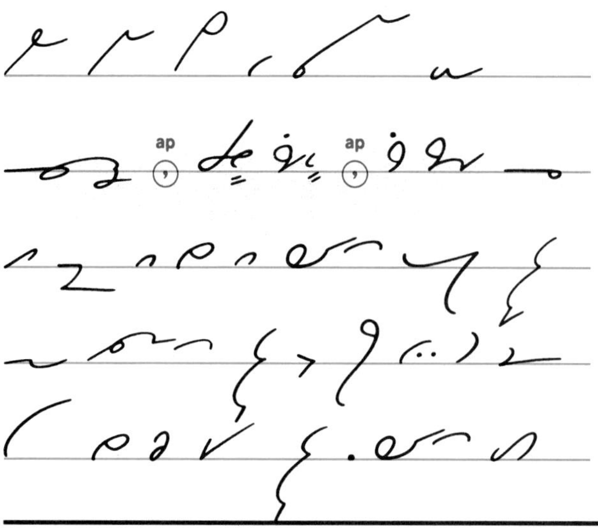

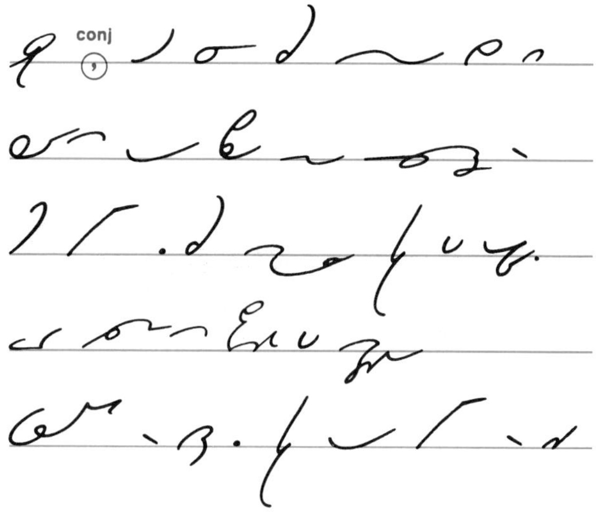

[83 words]

TRANSCRIPTION SKILL DEVELOPMENT

Transcribe the following words and phrases, noting spelling and capitalization. Then transcribe the transcription letter which follows.

Transcription Warmup

50.2

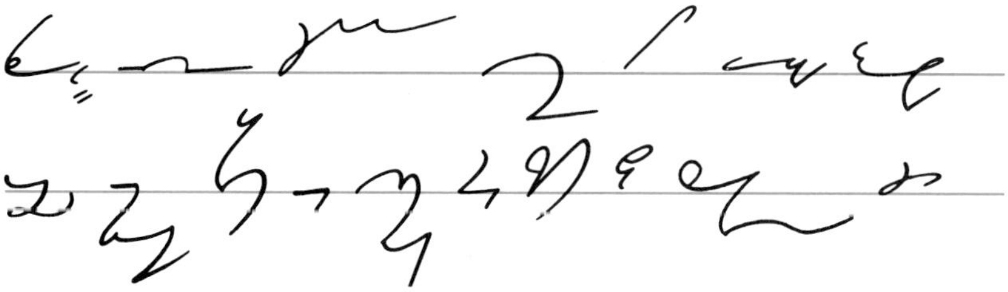

Transcription Practice

50.3 Tax Report

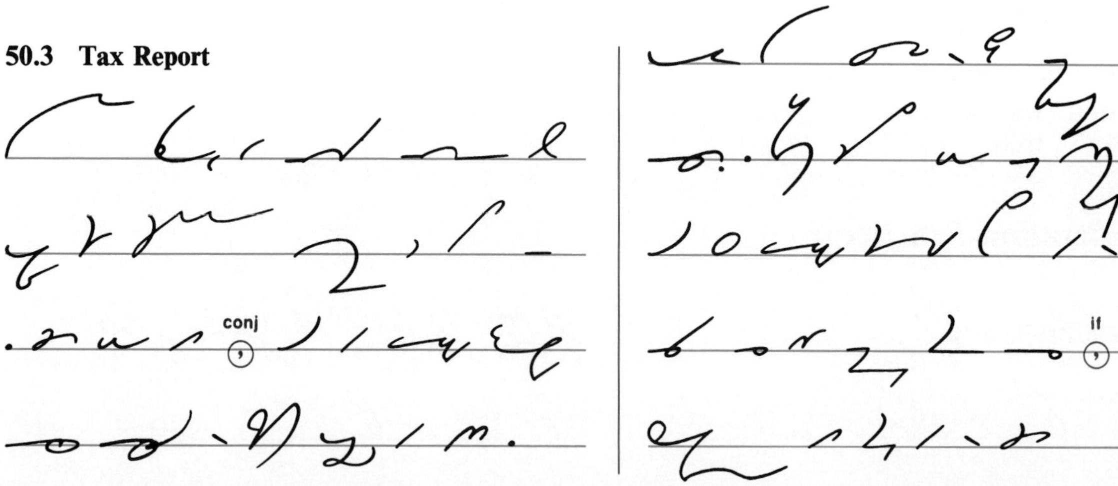

[shorthand outlines]

[71 words]

Punctuation: Introductory Expressions

Introductory expressions are elements such as single words, phrases, or clauses that begin a sentence and come before the subject and verb of the main clause. The comma is placed after the introductory expression.

An *introductory comma* is indicated by ⊙ (intro)

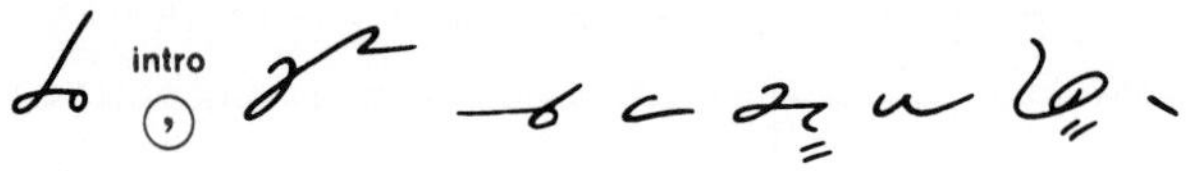

[shorthand outlines]

Generally, we do not meet on Wednesday or Friday.

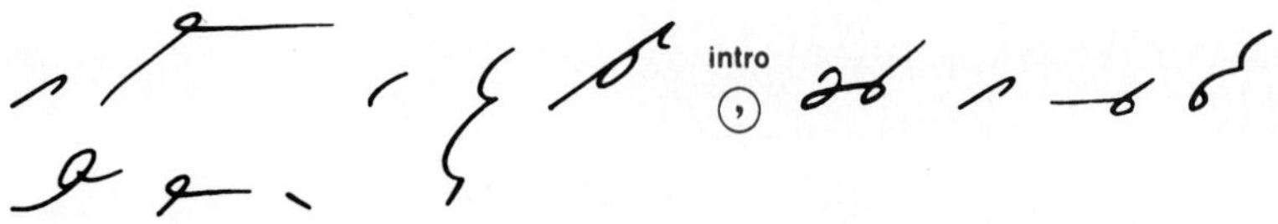

[shorthand outlines]

To determine the publication dates, we need to meet with the entire team.

[shorthand outlines]

Before we make the final collection, check with the advertising department.

Reading and Writing Practice

50.4 Equipment Needs

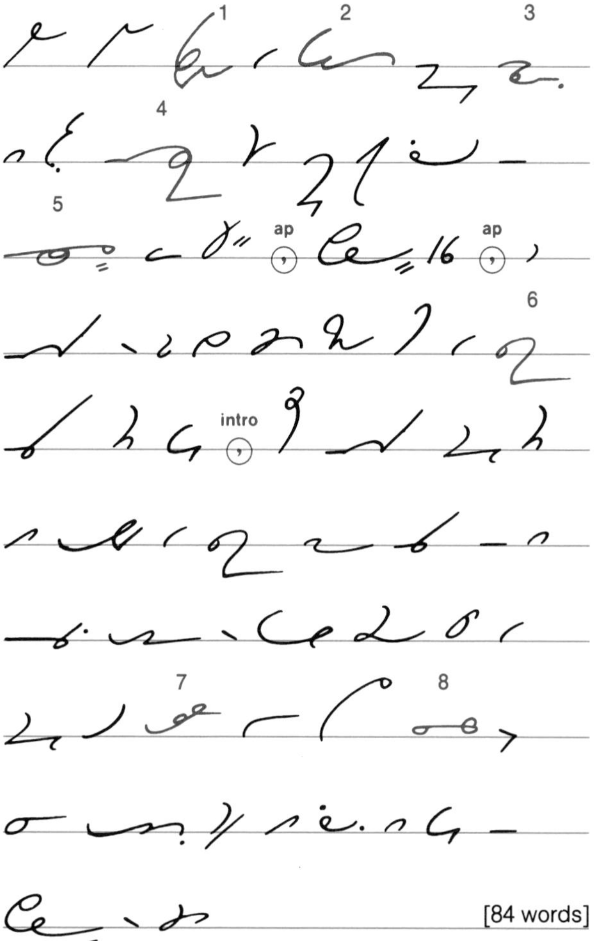

[Shorthand outlines]

[84 words]

1 Baxter   2 program   3 concerning
4 engagement   5 Miami   6 equipment   7 return
8 immediately

50.5 Presentation Preparation

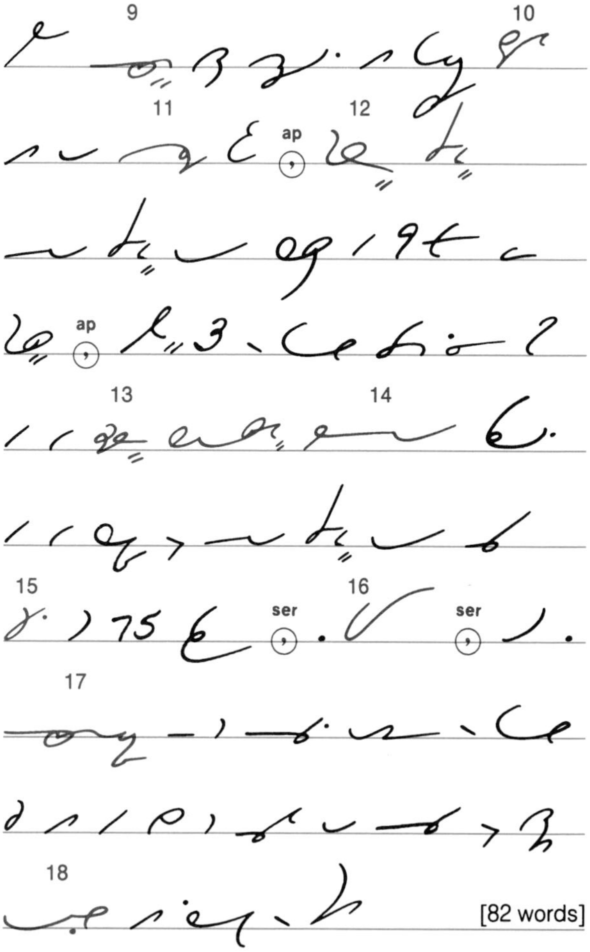

[Shorthand outlines]

[82 words]

9 Mike   10 assistance   11 guest   12 Frank
Jennings   13 Western Airlines   14 terminal
15 seating   16 podium   17 microphone
18 willingness

NEW IN LESSON 51

- Dictation speed building
- Transcription skill development
- Punctuation: commas with parenthetical expressions (parenthetical comma)

DICTATION SPEED BUILDING

The shorthand outlines below appear in the speed dictation letter which follows. Practice writing these words using the shorthand outlines. Then, using the key which follows, dictate the words to yourself.

Theory Words

Brief Forms

Phrases

Key *Theory*: Parker, increased, adequately, rebuilding, agents, policy, reviewed, years

Brief Forms: insurance, property, probably, insured, part, opportunity

Phrases: you have not, you will have, to have, one of our, if your, has not been, in the

Speed Dictation Practice

51.1 Insurance Renewal

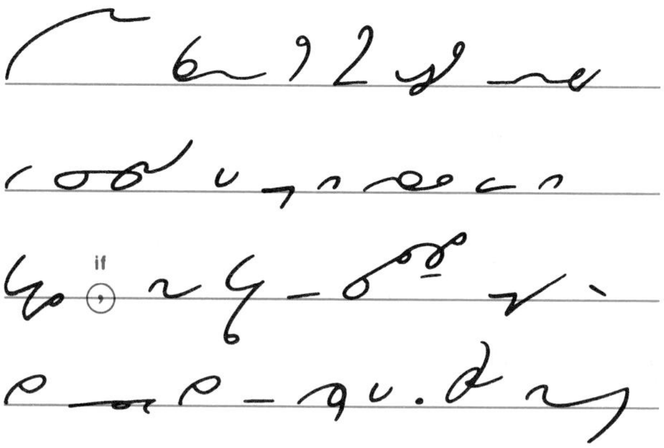

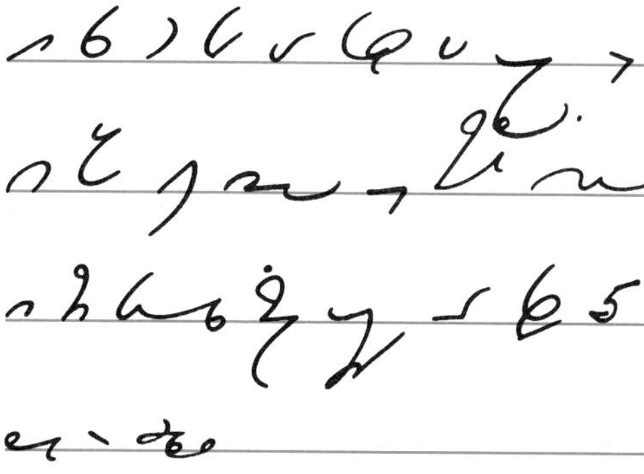

[72 words]

TRANSCRIPTION SKILL DEVELOPMENT

Transcription Warmup

51.2

Transcribe the following words and phrases, noting spelling and capitalization. Then transcribe the transcription letter which follows.

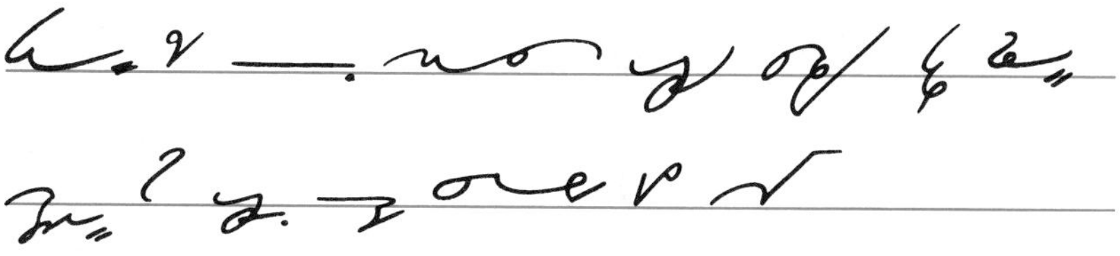

Transcription Practice

51.3   Available Employment

[shorthand notation]

[69 words]

Punctuation: Commas With Parenthetical Expressions

Parenthetical expressions are words or phrases that are not needed for the meaning or the grammatical completeness of the sentence. They are set off by commas. A parenthetical expression occurring at the end of a sentence needs only one comma.

A *parenthetical comma* is indicated by ⊙̸ (par)

[shorthand notation]

Today is, *of course*, a holiday.

[shorthand notation]

Tell me, *Tom*, what time you will arrive.

[shorthand notation]

It is too cold for swimming, *as you know*.

Reading and Writing Practice

51.4 Finance Committee

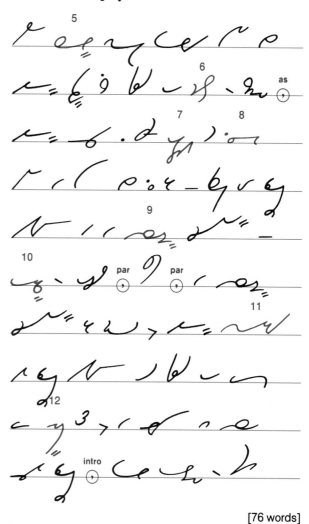

[86 words]

1 I will be glad   2 begin   3 budgets   4 recent

51.5 New Employee

[76 words]

5 Alice   6 staff   7 reputation   8 himself
9 Carson   10 Los Angeles   11 closed
12 November

NEW IN LESSON 52

- Dictation speed building
- Transcription skill development
- Geographic references

DICTATION SPEED BUILDING

The shorthand outlines below appear in the speed dictation practice which follows. Practice writing these words using the shorthand outlines. Then, using the key which follows, dictate the words to yourself.

Theory Words

Brief Forms

Phrases

Key   *Theory*:   Jackson, agreeing, Chicago, Western, Flight, 3 p.m.
      Brief Forms: office, presenting, which, company, with,
                       what, after
      Phrases: thank you for, I will be, I am, I have, I know, I
                   hope, to be

Speed Dictation Practice

52.1 Business Meeting

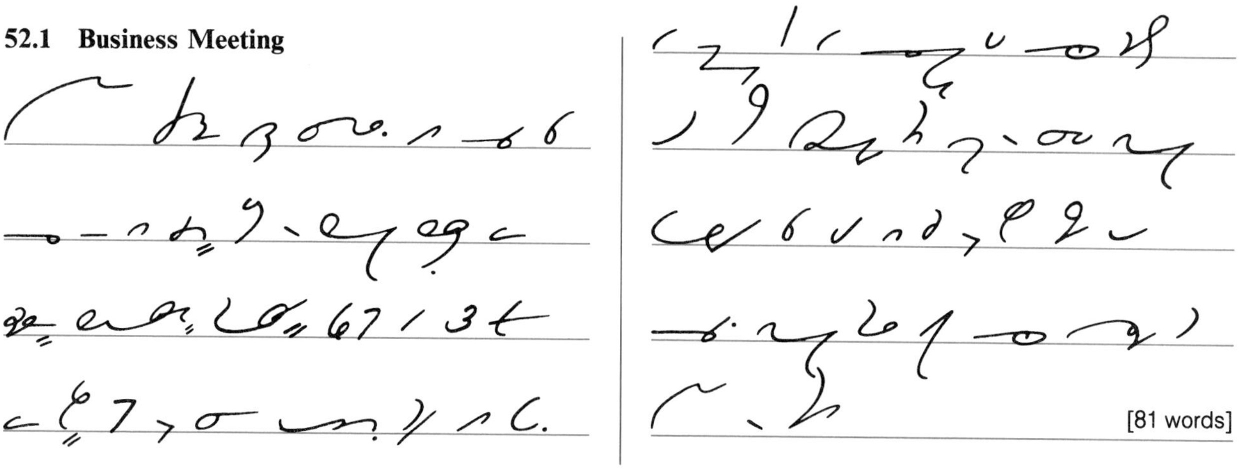

[81 words]

TRANSCRIPTION SKILL DEVELOPMENT

Transcribe the following words and phrases, noting spelling and capitalization. Then transcribe the transcription letter which follows.

Transcription Warmup

52.2

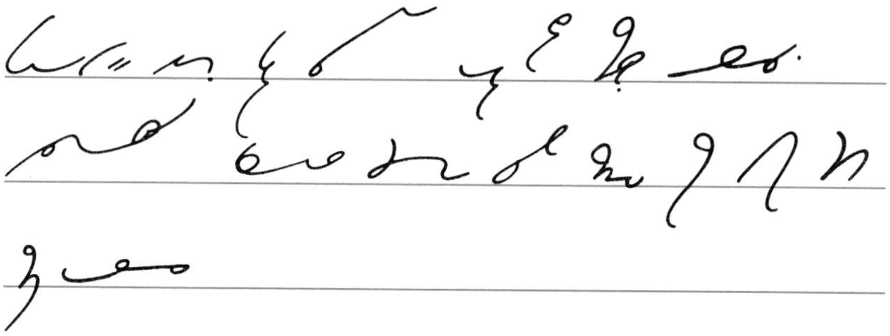

Transcription Practice

52.3 Job Vacancy

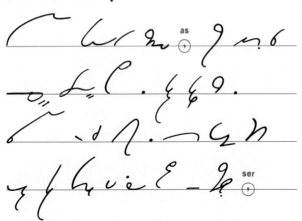

[72 words]

Geographic References

A comma is used to separate a city and a state. If the name of the state does not end the sentence, place a comma after the state also.

A *geographic comma* is indicated by ⊙ (geo)

We will meet in *Dallas, Texas.*

We will meet in *Dallas, Texas,* on Wednesday.

52.4 Transportation Costs

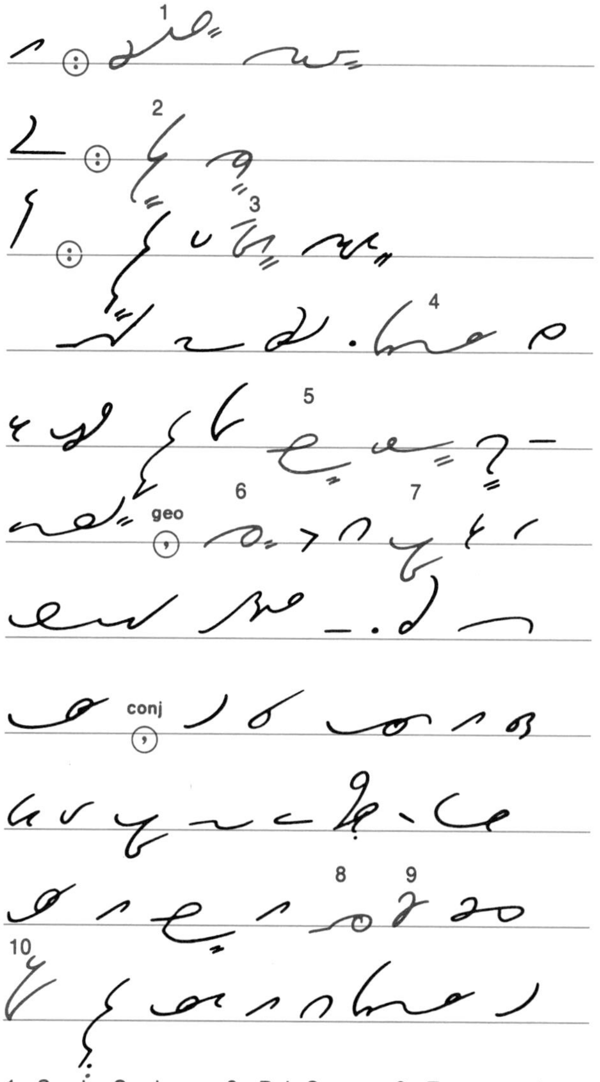

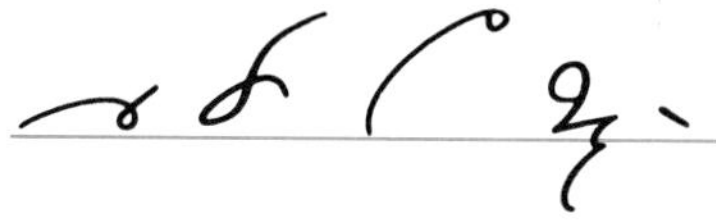

(shorthand outlines)

[86 words]

52.5 Business Letter

(shorthand outlines)

[78 words]

1 Sandra Gordon   2 Bob Case   3 Transportation
4 booklet   5 National Oil   6 California   7 report
8 inquire   9 whether   10 obtain

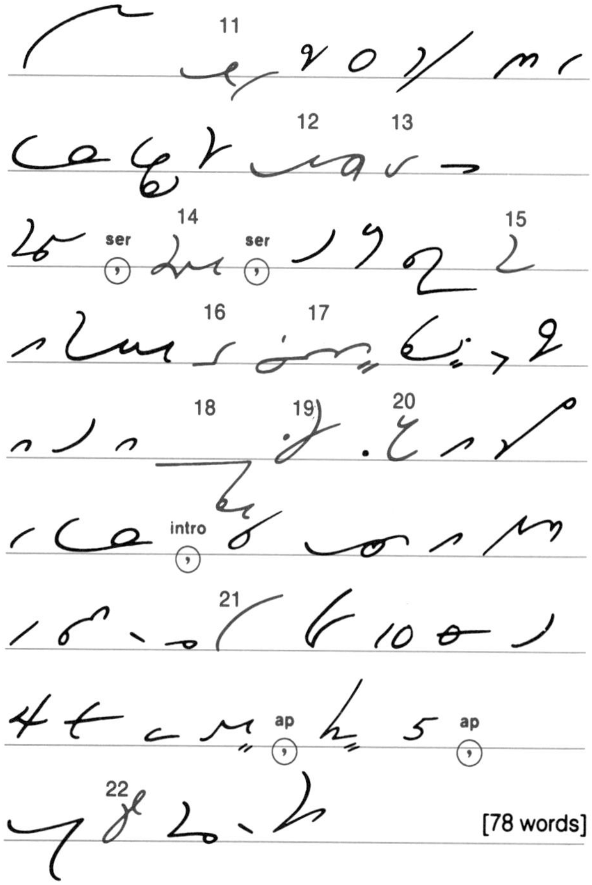

11 Lexington   12 location   13 of the
14 fixtures   15 for our   16 in the   17 Hancock
18 managers   19 have had   20 opportunity
21 time   22 satisfactory

TRANSCRIPT

The material is counted in groups of 20 standard words or 28 syllables
for convenience in timing the reading or dictation.

LESSON 1

1.1

1 I aim to please.
2 She may go to the game.
3 My knee hurts.
4 He did not meet me.
5 What is her name?
6 Meet me at 3 o'clock.
7 The main gate is open.
8 His name is Jim.
9 He is not mean.
10 I may name the dog.

1.2

1 The dog is tame.
2 The date has been decided.
3 My sister made tea.
4 Jeff will meet my father.
5 The deed is signed.
6 Check the date on the calendar.
7 Our team won!
8 When will you eat dinner?
9 Kathy is a nurse's aide.
10 We ate lunch late.

1.3

1 Dean won the track meet for his team.
2 Put your name on the deed next to the date.

3 Amy ate meat.
4 Nate made a date with May.
5 Our friend, Amy Dean, made the team.
6 Dean made the team.
7 Meet me for a day in May.
8 Can Dean meet me too?
9 Amy is mean.
10 What made Amy mean?

1.4

1 My knee may stop me from going.
2 Nate will meet me any day.
3 Meet me at 4 o'clock for tea.
4 Amy may meet me.
5 Dean may be on the team.
6 Amy may sign the deed in May.
7 He will need the date of the track meet.
8 Nate made tea for the team.
9 Meet me on East Main to sign the deed.
10 Mark the date on the deed.

LESSON 2

2.1

1 I hate missing the meeting with Amy.
2 A team meeting was held in May.
3 He may be meeting me that day.
4 Dean is dating Amy.
5 Nate enjoys taming animals all day.

6 He may hate the meeting.
7 May is not heeding our warning about Dean.
8 The date for the meeting is in May.
9 Who is naming the team?
10 He may repair the heating.

2.2

1 My team ended the game in a tie.
2 The date is in May.
3 Amy might go out at night.
4 He did not dye my tie before the meeting.
5 He might learn to tie his tie.
6 The rate on my deed might be high.
7 He might write Dean at night.
8 My deed is in the safe at night.
9 Nate tied my tie.
10 The price of my deed is too high.

2.3

1 May tied her tie.
2 The tie is not mine.
3 Amy will name the team.
4 Amy might be at the team meeting.
5 The meeting will be held with Dean.
6 My team may meet me at 10 at night.
7 We need heat in the room at night.
8 Dean will heed the warning of Nate.
9 The rate Dean gave me is high.
10 The price of the tie is too high.

LESSON 3

3.1

1 Lee wrote a note home.
2 He may mail the note.
3 Dale may read without a light.
4 Do not try reading without a light.
5 Dale made a deal with Ray.
6 He will trade the team in May.
7 Lee may write a note about the low rate.
8 At night Dale rode the train to his home.
9 Nate was late in writing the note.
10 Leo was late for the meeting.

3.2

1 Dale will write Amy later in the day.
2 Will Mary make a trade with a car dealer?

3 Lee is known as a leader.
4 A delay will make Amy even later.
5 Lee set a low rate.
6 Do you know the leader of the team?
7 Lee tried to speak to the dealer about the low rate.
8 Ray may delight in reading the title.
9 He will try to trade the car for a trailer.
10 The total of the account is not known.

3.3

1 Lee did knit a sweater for Mary.
2 The team is hitting a little better.
3 The baseball hit him on the ankle.
4 Lee did better than Tim.
5 Did Tim pick up the litter on the train?
6 Did the team choose him?
7 He did not try to trade the trailer.
8 Is Ray eating at home?
9 Tim did not write the note.
10 A little light is needed to write.

3.4

1 Ray is mailing his writing to me late.
2 He will delay the leader at the train.
3 We are deciding the title of the book in May.
4 The total price is not known.
5 We will need the date of the meeting.
6 Lee may write a new title.
7 Do you know who will own the home?
8 The leader will delay the meeting.
9 Lee rode the train at night.
10 Mary may try to write a report.

LESSON 4

4.1

1 Lee will meet me in an hour.
2 Will Leo Dean lead our team?
3 You and I are doing well at reading.
4 I am the leader of a meeting.
5 I would not miss it.
6 Ray is willing to lead the meeting in an hour.
7 Would Leo meet me in an hour?
8 Will Lee read our note?
9 Our train will leave in an hour.
10 We are trading in our car.

4.2

1 Leo ran home to get a ladder.
2 My dad bought a new hammer for me.
3 Is something the matter with his arm?
4 Matt ran to strengthen his heart.
5 She had an old hat from the Army.
6 A man will write the story.
7 Matt had a low reading rate.
8 Will my dad go to the meeting at night?
9 The matter will be settled in May.
10 Dad had a leading role in a play.

4.3

1 Her dad was in the Army.
2 Let Amy have the red ladder.
3 Matt hurt his head on the ladder.
4 Mary read her letter.
5 He met her dad, Matt Dean.
6 Let Tim meet the leader.
7 He will mail a letter to Leo.
8 A letter was sent to my home.
9 My red tie is missing.
10 What will be the net rate on the loan?

4.4

1 Lee will meet Dean in an hour.
2 Will Leo read our note?
3 Would Lee Dean meet me at the train?
4 Is the leader willing to hold a meeting in May?
5 Ray and I are writing a story.
6 We will trade our car in at the sale in May.
7 A letter did arrive in the mail.
8 A man in a red hat will mail our letter.
9 Matt would be willing to read the letter.
10 Mary will hold a meeting in May at her home.

LESSON 5

5.1

1 I am not well.
2 Meet me in our home.
3 I will not try writing in our trailer.
4 It will delay my meeting. It will not matter.
5 I would not try reading in low light.

¶ Paragraph

I will trade Matt my trailer. Matt will not need a deed in our trade. He wrote it will not matter. I will not try[1] writing a deed. [23 words]

5.2

1 Fay has seen Lee.
2 Steven ran as fast as Dave.
3 Did I say Steven will see Lee?
4 Our team has faced a Navy team.
5 Dave will not even say if Amy will sign a deed.

¶ Note

Dale wrote to Steven. Her letter made him laugh as he read it. Her fame will not make her vain. Steven will save her[1] letter. Steven will even save her letter in a safe. [29 words]

5.3

1 Dave has a flight at noon.
2 Fred will fly home in a day or so.
3 Has Fred flown free at night?
4 I am afraid of flying at night.
5 He may own a frame home.

¶ Phone Message

To: Fred Hill
From: Mary Lowe
Date: May 6
Time: 12:15
I am afraid I will not see Dave in Reno. I had a flat tire.[1] Dave's flight leaves in an hour or so. I may see him at a later date. [32 words]

5.4

1 I saw Tom at home.
2 He met Tom on a rainy day.
3 He saw a small tame deer.
4 I hear a lot of laughter in our home.
5 Tom taught in a small city.

¶ Letter

Dear Dave   I hear Tom will own a small farm near our city. I will need a site. Will Tom save me a small lot? Write me in a[1] day or so. Dale [23 words]

5.5 Agenda for Yearbook Staff Meeting

1. Start staff meeting at three.
2. Vote on title of scene.
3. Will late photo mailing hurt final date?

4. See if Steven or Dave[1] will lead May meeting.
5. Decide on date of staff meeting in May.

[28 words]

5.6 "To Do" List

Write Steve in Army.
Decide on meeting site.
Tell Mary I will see her in Reno.
Tell her I am not[1] afraid of flying.   [23 words]

LESSON 6

6.1

1 I will invest in a motor home.
2 If Fred arrives, invite him in.
3 Rain has made our river high indeed.
4 Light a fire inside our stove.
5 Dave will invite him in an hour.

¶ Phone Message

To: David Lane
From: Ann Cline
Date: May 13
Time: 11:30
Dale will invest in a hotel in Reno. He said I will
learn more in May.   [15 words]

6.2

1 Gary will move to Reno.
2 Sue will clean her car.
3 I may move to a new room.
4 Mike may make a cake.
5 Greg will take care of our legal file.

¶ Note

Dear Greg   I regret to say a rainstorm hit our farm.
It moved a great deal of dirt in our lane. A road
grader[1] will need to clear our lane.

   I am eager to get our lane clear again. Mike

[33 words]

6.3

1 We may not waste food.
2 Why are we waiting so late?
3 Our hot fire has a white flame.
4 Her hurt arm may swell.
5 Will Mike read while waiting?

¶ Note

Dear Sue   Dave White has asked why it has taken
two weeks to get a rail car to him ready to load. Tell
him[1] we had to wait while we got legal title to our
new rail car fleet. Mike   [32 words]

6.4 List of Points for Phone Call

1. Why did Dave leave school at noon?
2. I got a new white suit. I hate my green suit.
3. Give my history note to[1] Sue.
4. I got a lot of filing.   [26 words]

6.5 Army-Navy Game

Dear Mike   I am eager to go to an Army-Navy
game in May. I will get a free ticket if I see Fred[1]
White. Will Sue go if I get her a free ticket?

   I will not decide to go till I hear if Sue will go too.
Dean[2]   [40 words]

6.6 Memo

To Our Staff   Green Airline will not start flying to
Reno in a week. We regret making a delay.

   I am[1] eager to take care of our legal matter so we
may start flying to Reno in May.   [36 words]

LESSON 7

7.1

1 My neighbor may buy my boat.
2 Most people hope to please.
3 Please place a piece of paper on my desk.
4 It pays most of our readers to lease floor space.
5 Our sale price beats our best list price.

¶ Note to a Sales Manager

In May we raised our base price of our leading suit
label.[1] Despite our price increase, our suits are still
sales leaders. Our high sales are based on our sales
people.

   Please write nice brief[2] letters to all sales staff
people who made our May sales great. [49 words]

7.2

1 Sue took her new plan up to our boss.
2 May we increase sales of our cookbook?
3 Not enough people seem to like our high rates.

4 Please put us on a new list.

5 We put a number of new books in our store.

¶ Memo

To Our Staff   Our book sales are off again in May. We need new books to increase our sales. We must locate a number[1] of new writers who will put us back in a leading role in selling books.

If all of us would try to locate two[2] new writers, it would make enough of an increase in book sales to keep us a market leader.   [56 words]

7.3   Sales Letter

Dear David   Last night I read my copy of our new sales letter. We plan to mail it to our book dealers in May.[1]

I am pleased to read of our new low base price. May we mail our sales letter in a day or so? Myra
[39 words]

7.4   Notes From a Meeting

Sales Staff Meeting on 9-30

1. We need names of a number of people to hire in Dallas.
2. Most people[1] seem to hate our new labels.
3. Most people still like our paper labels.
4. Fred has sales leads in Erie.[2]
5. People still like our books best; price will not matter.   [51 words]

LESSON 8

8.1

1 Mr. Lee believes he can sell his goods for a good price.
2 Mr. Lee cannot forget his trip.
3 Tom can go to Dallas before May.
4 Mr. Baker believes in having a good sales force.
5 Please call me before 10 if Dave cannot afford to buy goods.

¶ Travel Plans

Dear Fay   Please forgive my delay in writing you. Because of my class load, I will not[1] go to Dallas before May.

I will inform you of my travel plans later. I will not forget our plans for a good[2] visit. Paul
[42 words]

8.2

1 I will be reading a book while I wait for you.
2 You can have my spare tire if you would like it.
3 I will be happy if I can meet our new neighbor.
4 You will not have a meeting at your home.
5 I have an airline ticket for you.

¶ Note

Dear Sue   I have good news for you. I will be moving to Erie in May. I will be looking for a place to live[1] in Erie. May I stay at your home for two days while I am looking for a place?

I will not be[2] in Erie before April 16. Please tell me if I can stay at your home. Ellen   [52 words]

8.3   Changing Jobs

Dear Carol   Last evening Dave White made a phone call to tell me he will leave our staff in April. He said he[1] is leaving because his salary is too low. I believe he will be happy if he has a new start on a[2] smaller sales staff.

May I begin looking for new people to hire? Robert Moreno   [57 words]

8.4   Personal Note

Mr. Stein   It will be three weeks since you wrote us to say you would buy our sailboat. It is a great boat. Its price[1] is low.

Please tell us if you plan to buy our boat. Amy Bailey   [32 words]

LESSON 9

9.1

1 We will be flying to Reno in May.
2 We cannot see people in our rooms.
3 Do you have a legal problem for our staff?
4 We will not be in our home, so we will have our heat off.
5 We are afraid we cannot be of help to you.

¶ List of Points to Discuss With the Boss

1. We have a legal problem on our copyright for our new magazine title.
2. We might have to delay[1] our sales meeting till May.
3. We might have a price increase on our mailing labels.   [36 words]

9.2

1 Beth took these notes in her math class.
2 Our sales staff has faith in our math book.
3 Keith has Mr. Smith for math.
4 Ruth will read her book, then go to class.
5 Mr. Smith writes in thin, smooth lines.

¶ Personal Note

Dear Beth   I know you are taking a math course in school. Do you have Mr. Keith for math? We have five math problems Mr.[1] Keith gave us.

Can you help me do these problems? Ruth
[29 words]

9.3

1 Janet showed me her new chair.
2 James changed jobs in search of higher pay.
3 She teaches in a large college.
4 Check each page of our math papers.
5 June showed up late each day for her college class.

¶ Evening Class

Dear George   A Smith College evening class in French will start in March. Are you willing to teach our French class again?[1]

Please call if you will teach our class. James
[27 words]

9.4   French Teacher

Dear Keith   I know your high school will need a new teacher of French. I urge you to write to Mr. Dave James.

Mr. James[1] is a French major here at Page College. He did his practice teaching at Smith High School.

If you hire Dave James,[2] I know he will do a great job for you. Kathy Briggs   [51 words]

9.5   Personal Note

Dear Ruth   My math teacher, Janet Jones, plans to leave her teaching job here at Keith High School. She will open a store in[1] Great Falls in March or April.

Since you are so good in math, you might really like a[2] job in her store. Beth   [45 words]

10.1

1 I had a delay in writing this paper.
2 Ann forgot which book is mine.
3 The school is small, but the class is good.
4 Our team should beat them in football.
5 Did you know that Jean could fly a plane?

¶ Agenda for a Meeting

Begin the meeting at two.
Take the roll call of members.
Read the letter which Dale Baker wrote us.
Ask the members:
    Should[1] we increase our fees?
    Could a member write a newsletter?
    Could a member make copies of our newsletter?
    Could a[2] member mail them?
Tell them that this meeting is our last meeting before fall.   [53 words]

10.2

1 By the way, this will be the first test of our new factory.
2 You have the same chance as the best member of the class.
3 This is the first day of our new French course.
4 Will the airline increase the number of flights to the East?
5 Is this the paper that you will give to the teacher?

¶ Business Letter

Miss Ruth   This is a hard letter for me to write. Your March bill arrived in the mail last week. I wrote a check to you[1] on the same day.

I noticed I forgot to mail the check. I will mail the check in this letter. Please accept my[2] regrets. Dean Goodman   [45 words]

10.3

1 Beth is likely to finish the job properly.
2 I am highly pleased by the totally new look of our store.
3 In only five weeks we will begin meeting daily.
4 If you are really early, go to the meeting room.
5 Sales have finally increased.

¶ **Interoffice Note**

Ann In only two days our weekly meeting will take place. All members of our staff who will be involved in our project[1] will be at the meeting.

If we are totally ready for this meeting, we can greatly increase the chance that our[2] plan will succeed.

Please arrive at the meeting room early on the day of the meeting so that we can plan our approach.[3] Beth   [61 words]

10.4 Travel Note

To: James Cook Attached are the travel plans of the members of the sales staff. As you can see, all of them plan to[1] travel to the meeting by airline. This will make it easy for you to get all of our people to the hotel.[2] The attached plans are the best we could make. Ray   [48 words]

10.5 Notes About Accident

Car Crash of Dave Jones
    Dave Jones owns the car.
    The car crash took place at noon on May 7.
    Mr. Jones is clearly at[1] fault.
    He got a ticket for driving too fast.
    He drove at 65 miles an hour. The speed limit on this road is[2] 45 miles an hour.
    The Jones car is totally wrecked.
    Mr. Jones did not have injuries.   [58 words]

LESSON 11

11.1

1 I made the decision to accept the position.
2 Occasionally, we do receive promotion on the art collection.
3 The National Corporation will move to a new location.
4 Can the patient have the operation?
5 Typing proficiency makes her an efficient staff member.

¶ **Vacation Photos**

Mr. James Attached is a collection of photos that I took on vacation. A portion of the photos shows[1] the normal vacation spots. Most of the photos show locations that most people on vacation do not[2] see.

If these photos appear in your national paper, it will help promote travel.

Please tell me if you have a[3] sufficient number of photos. I will be waiting your decision. Sincerely   [76 words]

11.2

1 Only 500 people bought a ticket.
2 Fred paid a dollar for my book.
3 The check is for $7,000.
4 His nation has only 900,000 people.
5 Beth will sell a book for $7.50.

¶ **Art Collection**

Mr. Jones We are pleased that you asked us for facts on the cost of selling your art collection. Our rates are[1] $10 for each $1,000 of the cost of your collection. If your collection would cost $3,000,[2] then our fee would be $30.

Please call if we can sell your art collection. Sincerely   [59 words]

11.3

1 We have to be sure we are right.
2 Gary has to have $8 for the book.
3 If you have been in class lately, you know we will have a test in a week.
4 You have been late for each class, so you have not been able to take good notes.
5 People have not been able to be in class.

¶ **French Grade**

Dear Jean I am afraid you have not been easy to reach. I am eager to tell you the grade I got in my French[1] class. I have not been able to talk to the French professor. I will not be able to talk to her for a day[2] or so.

I suppose you have not been able to get your grade in math this early. In a day or so we will have[3] all of our grades. Mike   [64 words]

11.4 Collection Letter

Mr. Brooks We have not had a check or even a letter in 15 weeks. I must have your check for[1] $1,000 in my possession by June 7.

If I do not have your check in my possession by June 7,[2] I will have to take this matter to a collection firm.

I am waiting for it patiently. Sincerely[3]
                                      [60 words]

11.5 News Reporter's Notes

A robbery took place at the James Food Store at eight in the evening on June 18. Only three members of the[1] staff of the store saw the robber. The names of these three people are not being made known.

The robber took nearly[2] $3,000 in cash. The robber left the scene on foot. The police will have a news release in an hour. [58 words]

LESSON 12

12.1

1 I am glad to have a letter from Mrs. Bates.
2 After all these weeks, it is good to hear from Mr. Jones.
3 I will not be able to talk with you about the answers to the test.
4 Please get the facts about the game from the team.
5 I have not had a call from you.

¶ Staff Meeting

Dear Jody   I am writing about the meeting of the sales staff starting on April 14. We will be meeting[1] with our sales staff about the plans for selling our latest fashions.

I am glad to hear you will be able to talk[2] with our staff. I will be glad to be with you in Dallas on the day we meet with the sales staff. Betty
[57 words]

12.2

1 Dean lost his temper because of the damage to his car.
2 Our customers seldom arrive at our store by automobile.
3 Ann will attempt to have a cost estimate for us tomorrow.
4 Each item for sale in our store is in the medium price range.
5 We need an estimate for the items.

¶ Damage Estimate

Mrs. Adams   We are glad to have the estimate of $350 to take care of the damage to[1] your car. I am happy with the low cost of the estimate.

Your cost estimate is low enough that we do not have[2] to have an itemized estimate. I will have a check in the mail to you by tomorrow at the latest. Keith Temple[3] [60 words]

12.3

1 Dear Mr. Jones   I will mail you the estimate for the damage. Very truly yours
2 Dear Mrs. Black   We are glad to learn about the new items. Cordially yours
3 Dear Madam   The demonstration will be on April 15. Yours very truly
4 Dear Sir   We have two new staff members. Very truly yours
5 Dear Miss Dempsey   We are pleased to have you as a customer. Cordially yours

12.4   A Student's "To Do" List

Do June 10
1. Prepare for history test tomorrow.
2. Get gas for the automobile.
3. Go to physics class demonstration.
4. Try to get news items for the school paper.
5. Agree to be a temporary helper in the library.
[45 words]

12.5   Store Opening

Dear Mrs. Dempsey   We are happy to tell you that we are opening a new store on March 17. Our new[1] store will be on Main Street here in Mason City.

We are inviting you to a demonstration of our new line even before our[2] new store is open. Show this letter to the member of our staff who will greet you at the door.

I will be glad to[3] see you at the opening of our new store. Cordially yours [71 words]

LESSON 13

13.1

1 Following our conversation, we will compare the contract.
2 Compile complete data for the committee.
3 The committee considers the contract to be complete.
4 Elaine will control the committee completely.
5 Do not complain about his conduct.

¶ Personnel Problem

To: Nancy Robbins
From: Fred Rice

This note is to tell you about my concern for Judy Page. She does not seem[1] to have consideration for people. She has completely lost her temper with good customers. She complains[2] about the rest of the people on our staff.

On two occasions I had a conference with her. These conversations[3] have not helped matters.

Do you agree that we should release her from her contract completely?   [74 words]

13.2

1 The cost of health care is high.
2 Our clothing factory will be closed through July.
3 It is a great book, though it takes a while to read.
4 George thought the clothes had a high price.
5 We will mail a pamphlet to all those on our mailing list.

¶ Memo

To: June Day
From: James Casey

I have thought through the problem of increasing health care costs. I would like to share[1] my thoughts with the members of our planning committee early in March.

Attached is a list of those people who should be[2] at the meeting to hear my thoughts on health care.   [49 words]

13.3

1 Replace Bob on the research committee.
2 I need to reply to the letters I received.
3 Can you refer me to a place which will repair my car?
4 Robin will receive a good letter of reference from Mrs. Smith.
5 Can you tell me the reason Dave will retire early?

¶ Reference Letter

Dear Mr. Brooks   It is a delight for me to provide a reference letter for June Johnson. June had been[1] in charge of the research in our new data control lab. She received a large number of honors for her[2] research projects.

I am sure June will do a fine job. Very truly yours   [53 words]

13.4   Dictation Speed Letter

Dear Mrs. Steiner   I have been calling you since May 17, but I have not been able to reach you.

I would like[1] to have about 500 copies of our research paper by June 12. I need these copies for a research[2] conference which will be taking place early in July. The members of our research committee need to have a[3] copy of the paper before our conference begins. Please mail the copies to my research lab. Very truly yours[4]   [80 words]

13.5   Car Leasing

Dear Mrs. Green   If you would like to save cash, you should consider leasing a new car from us. Leasing a car saves[1] you the cost of car repairs. If you have a problem on the road, simply call us. A member of our repair staff[2] will arrive to take care of the problem. If your car is damaged, we will pay the cost of repairing it.

After[3] you have thought through the reasons why it makes sense to lease a car, give us a call. We will write a contract which completely[4] frees you from worries about automobile repair. Yours very truly   [93 words]

LESSON 14

14.1

1 The doctor has a meeting in our office during the afternoon.
2 There is a place where one can get more office space.
3 There was a meeting of our office staff yesterday.
4 There are one or two problems.
5 Dr. Day had hoped to open her new office yesterday afternoon.

¶ Research Project

Dear Dr. Blair   Will you be willing to have a brief meeting in my office on April 15? I would like to talk to you[1] about a research project which we need to finish during July.

The research project will ask our customers[2] where they prefer to shop.

Please call me concerning our proposed meeting. Very truly yours   [59 words]

14.2

1 One of the reference books was not up to date.
2 This is one of our reference books; it is up to date.
3 One of our customers often complains about our service.
4 One of them complains about his temper.
5 Our staff receives health care that is up to date.

¶ Memo

To: Albert Wilson
From: Mary James
I was pleased to hear that you received one of the top honors at the research[1] convention last week.

You have been in charge of one of our best research projects. Because of your efforts, our research[2] is sure to stay up to date.   [45 words]

14.3

1 Our editor drafted a list of needed books.
2 The editor omitted a price deduction from the listed retail price.
3 We will be tested in great detail today.
4 Judy has been accepted by the editor of our local paper.
5 My credit application has been accepted.

¶ Sales Promotion

Dear Mr. Sanchez   The pamphlet you drafted for the sales promotion of our books is great! Our team of editors[1] is as happy with it as I am. They have accepted all its details.

When you accepted this project, you[2] listed a price of $1,000. I am asking that our check to you be drafted this afternoon. Very truly yours[3]
[60 words]

14.4   Dictation Speed Letter

Dear Sir   You may remember me as a salesman who often waited on you at the Adams Clothing Store. I waited[1] on you often during the time I was there.

During June I began setting up my own shop at 721[2] Bates Street. My new shop opens today.

I will be glad to have you as one of our customers at our new store.[3] Very truly yours   [64 words]

14.5   A Page From a Real Estate Agent's Notebook

Notes about the Smith home on Adams Street here in James Lake
The home was listed with us on May 4.
The first offer[1] was made on June 7.
The offer was made by Mr. David Stone.
The original price was $75,000.[2]
The Stone offer was $73,000.
The offer was accepted on June 15.
The contract was drafted[3] on June 18.
The closing meeting will be July 1 in the afternoon.   [73 words]

LESSON 15

15.1

1 I gather that you would rather get together on another day.
2 I would rather not bother my mother.
3 Give my bill to either my brother or my father.
4 We will get together on another day when the weather is better.
5 Paul likes to get together with other authors.

¶ Book Idea

Dear Mr. Perez   I am gathering the facts for another book about predicting the weather. Most other books[1] about the weather are college books.

The book I am proposing will be for all people who would like to learn[2] more about the weather.

When may we get together to talk about my proposed weather book?[3] Very truly yours
[62 words]

15.2

1 Furthermore, we are pleased with the new furnace.
2 Her writing will further the cause of freedom.
3 Kathy is furnishing her new home.
4 Our home is heated with a gas furnace.
5 We furnish our authors the service of good editors.

¶ Service Contract

Dear Mr. Reed   On June 16 you came to my home to repair the gas furnace. After the repairs were completed,[1] you convinced me to buy a service contract from you.

I wrote you a check for the contract. You said your office[2] would furnish me with a copy of the contract. It has been four weeks. I would like to hear from you.[3] Yours very truly   [62 words]

15.3

1 Do you know how to go to town?
2 Jack will announce that the crowd is large.
3 He announced our new house is south of town.
4 Mr. Brown felt like shopping in town even though it is crowded.
5 Fred really doubts that Mark will make a good decision.

¶ Rough Draft for a School News Release

The South Side High School gave the play <u>Our Town</u> each evening from April 12 through 15. We are pleased to announce that the[1] cast played to a full house each evening.

People in the crowds said how well they liked the play. Mrs. Edith Brown,[2] principal of South Side High School, said, "There is no doubt that this is one of the best plays in the history of our school!"[3]
[60 words]

15.4   Dictation Speed Letter

Mr. Day   I am glad you wrote me about the job you have in your sales office. I will be able to go to your[1] office on May 7 at about two in the afternoon.

When I arrive at your office, I will have with me[2] the list of grades I received in school. I will be ready to talk about the job you have open. Very truly yours[3]   [60 words]

15.5   Letter of Application

Dear Mr. Lopez   I just noticed in the afternoon paper that you are announcing the opening of a[1] new sales territory here in the South. I would like to apply for this position.

The job I have right now is[2] in the customer sales office of Brown Brothers. I have had this job since completing my studies at South High School.[3] Please tell me whether I may talk with you about this sales position. Yours very truly   [77 words]

LESSON 16

16.1

1 Our communications teacher will direct our sales campaign.
2 Every communications worker in the state is needed.
3 We need new direction for our company.
4 I recommend that we meet soon.
5 Laura works for a company in town.

¶ Notes for a News Story

The communications workers in our state may go on strike soon. They have voted to reject the contract[1] recommendation which was made by their own directors. One of the[2] directors of the communications workers stated that whenever the strike might begin, it will affect telephone[3] service everywhere in the state.   [65 words]

16.2

1 Please mail it to me at home to make sure I get it.
2 The news came as a surprise to us, of course.
3 Please communicate with us as soon as possible.
4 We will reply as soon as we hear from you.
5 I will give it to my brother to do tomorrow.

¶ Note to Secretary

I need to make airplane reservations so that I can go to Dallas on May 12 to do research. I need to[1] fly back on the afternoon of May 14.

I will, of course, have a check ready for the tickets as soon as I[2] receive them.

Please try to get the tickets to me at my office as soon as possible.   [58 words]

16.3

1 They will share equally in the failure of their latest motion picture.
2 Annually we prepare a factual credit list.
3 There is pressure to follow contractual procedure.
4 Is there actually a procedure for writing contractual matters?
5 Tim likes the natural features of the scenery.

¶ Class Notes From a Marketing Course

Market Change

1. Change is one of the natural features of the marketplace. It takes place gradually.
   a. It[1] may be so slow it cannot be seen from day to day or annually.
   b. Change is still[2] taking place.
2. Failure to notice gradual change can mean that items gradually lose their appeal.
3. There are[3] procedures for getting an accurate picture of the market change.   [70 words]

16.4   Phone Message

To: Mrs. Brown
From: Lee Smith
Date: April 18
Time: 12:15

He said work will begin on our communications lab[1] tomorrow. Every detail of the planning seems to be complete. Lee will be directing the work. All[2] communications about the project should be directed to him.   [53 words]

16.5   Hotel Reservation

Dear Mr. Carson   Your letter confirming my reservation at your hotel has arrived. You will recall that when[1] I made this reservation, it was for the night of August 11

Because of my work schedule, I will not be able[2] to leave for Reno on August 11. I will be arriving in Reno on August 12. Therefore, I need to have my[3] reservation changed for that day.

Please write to me as soon as possible to tell me if my reservation may be[4] changed. Very truly yours   [85 words]

LESSON 17

17.1

1 Apparently, the accountant planned to spend the entire amount.
2 The agent is currently assigned to Dallas.
3 It is apparent that our entire stock of accounting books is not currently in print.
4 Would you please remind me to print a copy for my friend.

5 I spent entirely too much time checking the account numbers.

¶ Memo

To: Charles Smith
From: Judy Chase

Can you be at my office on July 25 in the afternoon for a brief meeting? Currently, there are three people[1] I would like you to meet. They seem to have the kind of accounting training we need for the positions we have open.[2] They sent me their data sheets; you will find them attached.   [49 words]

17.2

1 We will have much fun when summer comes.
2 They have begun to eat some lunch.
3 He was in such a rush to get work done on this budget.
4 Some people say summer is their favorite season.
5 The cash refund is a welcome help to my budget.

¶ Student Meeting

Agenda for Annual Staff Meeting
Announce to the staff the following:
1. The editing of the entire book[1] is done.
2. We have begun to receive pages from the printer.
3. Some changes will have to be done.[2]
4. The color pictures add a touch of class; they did not increase the budget.
5. We need to rush our advance[3] selling to make sure that we will have the income we need.   [69 words]

17.3

1 The personnel agency had a job description for a secretary.
2 Please describe your problem to the person at the courtesy desk.
3 Perhaps another personnel agency can handle your account.
4 It is common courtesy not to disturb a person while taking a final test.
5 Please pursue the purchase of a display typewriter.

¶ Memo

To: Mike Farrell
From: Lynn Charles

I am asking that the personnel office find a

secretary[1] for me. I prefer a person with some work background in a claims agency. I would describe the ideal[2] secretary as a person who not only makes rapid decisions but displays courtesy.   [56 words]

17.4   Dictation Speed Memo

To: Personnel Staff
From: Joe Jefferson
The staff of the Personnel Office will have a luncheon meeting at noon[1] tomorrow. We will meet in the conference room to discuss some of the personnel problems which have come up in[2] recent weeks. A problem that is currently severe is absence caused by personal illness.

Please do not miss this[3] meeting as we have much to discuss.   [66 words]

17.5   Sales Letter

Dear Mr. Kennedy Have you found a perfect place where you would like to go this coming summer for your vacation?[1] If you have found the perfect vacation spot, perhaps you have decided that such a vacation trip will cost[2] too much. If this is your problem, you should come to us. We are the National Credit Company. Some 2,000[3] people borrowed vacation funds from us last year.

Find out how easy it is to become a customer of our[4] credit company. Stop in for a visit. Very truly yours   [91 words]

LESSON 18

18.1

1 There were several advantages to advertising with them.
2 One immediate advantage is value.
3 My partner will depart immediately after this party.
4 There is a disadvantage to the advertising plan.
5 Keith and Judy were several hours late to the party.

¶ Rough Draft of an Idea for a Term Paper

Part of the value of advertising is that it may increase the sale of a line of goods. The more items that[1] sell, the less each item costs to produce. This advantage of decreased cost of making goods is passed to the customer[2] in the form of good market values.   [47 words]

18.2

1 Is it sensible to leave this valuable table?
2 Is it possible to find a suitable home at a reasonable price?
3 Greg is considerably troubled that he is not suitable for the accounting job.
4 Our furniture is available at a considerably reasonable price.
5 My accountant is highly reliable and capable.

¶ Car Sale

Dear Ellen I am sorry to hear that you have had considerable trouble selling your car. Perhaps I can be[1] of some help to you. I have a friend who is willing to pay a favorable price for a suitable[2] car. He needs a car that is reliable that is available soon.

I will have him call[3] you today, if possible. Charles   [64 words]

18.3

1 Her assignments are completed with fair judgment and commitment to the company.
2 Our investment department needs a replacement.
3 I have received your agreement to make installment payments on your account.
4 The new shipment of supplies is in the basement.
5 An advertisement should increase the number of people in our private school.

¶ Memo

To: Staff
From: Director of Marketing
At the end of March, Mary Benson will be retiring from our advertising[1] department. She became a member of our advertising department in 1962.[2] In my judgment, Mrs. Benson wrote a number of our best advertisements. It will not be easy to find a replacement[3] for her.   [61 words]

18.4   Dictation Speed Letter

Dear Mr. White Can you tell me the advantage of advertising in your paper? My partner and I are trying[1] to find the best advertising value in town for our limited advertising budget. If you could list[2] several advantages of advertising in your paper, we would be happy to consider becoming[3] one of your customers. Very truly yours   [68 words]

18.5 Urgent Request

Dear Mr. Grant   Please send me immediately a shipment of 20,000 copies of the attached form.[1] This form is a copy of our company billing statement.

It is urgent that we receive this shipment by July[2] 15. If we receive the shipment after July 15, we will have a delay in receiving several payments.[3]

Please let me know if it is possible to meet our schedule. Very truly yours   [75 words]

LESSON 19

19.1

1 I hope to meet some of the staff.
2 I hope that you will use some of our recommendations.
3 I hope that the office assigned to you is acceptable.
4 I hope the decision is correct.
5 I hope that you have decided to accept the price.

¶ Office Note

Mr. Tracy   I hope that you can help me. My secretary tells me that the current issue of The Automobile[1] Guide is not in the library.

I hope you can tell me who has[2] this issue. It has a list of car rental firms, and we hope to mail our latest catalog to them. Bill Smith   [59 words]

19.2

1 We will build the house toward the south end of the street.
2 I have prepared a record of children who have failed their vision test.
3 Our older records are stored in the basement of the records center.
4 I told Edith that we need to be billed for the file folders.
5 My children have sold their old record player.

¶ Lost Luggage

Dear Sir   On July 18 my wife and I were on a flight from Grand Falls to Dallas. When we arrived in Dallas,[1] I could not find my briefcase, I called your baggage claim department and Mrs. Neal assured me that she would search for[2] the briefcase. Two hours later she called to tell me that my briefcase would be sent to my hotel.

I am pleased with the[3] efficient service your airline provided through the office of Mrs. Neal. Very truly yours   [77 words]

19.3

1 I insist that you assist with the necessary system analysis.
2 I suspect we will have to suspend telephone services to your offices for a week.
3 On the basis of your analysis I agree that our office faces a problem with filing space.
4 Our office services staff can assist you with word processing.
5 I suspect he makes promises only when necessary.

¶ Note

Barbara   According to Fred the biggest problem our offices face is in word processing services. He[1] suspects it will be necessary for us to train some of our own staff people. His analysis reveals that there[2] are not enough people available with the necessary office skills.

We will have to do an analysis[3] of the steps that will be necessary for us to begin an office training department. Janice   [78 words]

19.4   Dictation Speed Letter

Dear William   On April 7 Robert Brady called on me and applied for a position on our staff. I would[1] like to hire him, but before I do so, I need more facts which I hope you will be able to supply.

1. Would you[2] hire him again if you had an opening?
2. Why is he planning to leave you?

Your answers will help me[3] greatly. Very truly yours   [66 words]

19.5   Memo

To: Ruth Temple
From: Brady Taylor
When I called at the Barker Clothing Store in Flint on West Street this afternoon,[1] the owners told me that they are not pleased with the services they have been getting from our salesman, Mr. Childs.[2] He has not been in to see them for weeks. In fact, he failed to mail them the samples they asked for after his last visit.[3]

Could you talk to Mr. Childs one day soon and get his side of this latest story for me? [76 words]

LESSON 20

20.1

1 You will acknowledge that an opportunity was not present.
2 Generally, however, there are many opportunities in this organization.
3 The representative had an opportunity to organize.
4 A committee for good government has been organized.
5 Our organization did not acknowledge the present.

¶ Good Government

Dear Mrs. Keller   I am glad to hear that you are organizing a committee for good government in our[1] city. Generally, I feel that most people are happy with the present government. However, people should[2] be concerned about their government.

May I have the opportunity to be of service to your committee?[3] Very truly yours   [64 words]

20.2

1 We may differ on some issues, but we will not let these differences divide us.
2 We will devote $200,000 to the development of a different item.
3 We definitely need to divide our marketing division into two divisions.
4 Our development division will definitely have an answer.
5 They need a different device than the one you devised.

¶ Product Development

Dear Dr. Michaels   There are different sizes and different types and different costs of word processing printers.[1] Our industry needs to develop a new word processing printer that will print at a high speed and still produce[2] suitable copy.

Are you available to assist us in the development of a new printer that is[3] totally different from those now on the market? Cordially yours   [74 words]

20.3

1 We need to review the unit plan.
2 Do not refuse to use a unique plan we have just developed.
3 We need to review the policy which we have just developed.
4 Mrs. Hughes developed one new unit on the history of government.
5 Our word processing unit will unite with our data processing unit.

¶ History Book

Dear Mrs. Hughes   The new unit you developed for your history book is unique, and it should help to increase[1] the sales of your book.

I will have your new unit sent to be reviewed by a teacher who has used the old copy of[2] your book.

When you have the opportunity to do so, please provide us with a few pictures you will want to use[3] with the new unit. Very truly yours   [67 words]

20.4   Dictation Speed Letter

Dear Mr. Day   I am glad you invited me to apply for a job with your organization. I will be able[1] to go to your office to meet with you during the first week in May. The afternoon of May 6[2] would be good for our meeting.

Please let me know if you will be available to meet with me then. I am eager[3] to meet you and learn more about your company. Very truly yours   [72 words]

20.5   Job Opportunity

Dear Miss Jensen   Our organization currently needs to hire a new film editor for our film division.[1] We have recently developed some unique editing techniques. We need to hire a person who is familiar[2] with different editing techniques.

If you know a few people who might like this job, please mail their names to me. Tell them[3] that working for our organization represents a unique opportunity. Yours very truly   [79 words]

LESSON 21

21.1

1 She certainly attained the presidency of the company at an early age.
2 One other student gave Philip assistance on the paper he has written on the presidents.
3 We intend to maintain the market position we attained.
4 I am sure that the bulletin will get their attention.
5 This letter contains a maintenance contract.

¶ Visitor to the Office

Mr. Fulton stopped at the office to see you. He came to town suddenly and did not have an opportunity[1] to call before arriving. He would like to take you to dinner tonight and maybe attend a play. He will[2] give you a phone call after three today. David [49 words]

21.2

1 The medical article described the technical aspects of chemical injuries.
2 His political position is radical and not logical.
3 Technical and medical articles are typically written in a dry style.
4 The medical bills at that hospital are typically high.
5 We will take a physical inventory of the articles in the warehouse.

¶ Library Orientation

Proceed logically when searching for an article. The article typically will be found in several[1] places in the card catalog. An article can be found by its author[2] or by its title. An article should not be physically removed from the library. A copy should be made at[3] a copy machine. [63 words]

21.3

1 Do you need to know the price of the article?
2 Mr. Davis needs to know when the bulletins will be printed.
3 I would like to know the catalog number.
4 I want to know when you will call.
5 Harvey has to know his grade.

¶ Holiday Schedule

John Mrs. Green just called. She needs to know if our office will be open during the holidays.[1] Such a large number of people want to know our schedule. I believe we should advertise it. David [35 words]

21.4 Dictation Speed Letter

Dear Madam We have written you several letters asking you to mail us your remittance for the advertisements[1] we printed for you last July. However, we have not received a remittance from you.

It is to the[2] advantage of your company to maintain a good credit standing with its creditors. I ask, therefore, that you[3] mail us a check for $2,200. Yours very truly [73 words]

21.5 Dictation Speed Letter

Dear Mrs. Brandon We are sorry that we cannot mail you 50 copies of our bulletin entitled "Tennis[1] for Beginners." This bulletin has been out of print since April, and we have no immediate plans to have[2] more copies printed.

However, I have several file copies. I will be glad to loan you a copy to[3] duplicate. All we ask is that you place a credit line on your copies saying that you made the copies with our[4] approval. Sincerely [85 words]

LESSON 22

22.1

1 Did you overlook the difficulties we had with Ms. Adams?
2 We can make a profit without high overhead costs.
3 What difficulty did you have with our overnight mail service?
4 What was the outcome of the business meeting?
5 Ms. Fields has overcome several difficulties.

¶ Thank-You Letter

Dear Miss Adams It was a pleasure to have you visit our business last week. It is good to have a person from the outside[1] look over the operations of a business.

We are glad to have whatever recommendations you[2] developed. You can be sure you will have your payment no later than March 10. Very truly yours [57 words]

22.2

1 Mary had difficulty applying for student financial assistance.
2 We will attend a special social event for Dr. Davis.
3 It is essential that our financial officer be present.
4 It is essential that all of our officials initial the financial papers they approve.
5 The special dinner is partially ready.

¶ Business Letter

Dear Miss Crane Your letter referring me to Ms. Smith was especially valuable. Ms. Smith is in charge of the[1] Financial Department of our college. She was able to tell me officially that I will be able to[2] receive financial aid.

This visit has certainly removed my initial fears about not being able to[3] attend college. Very truly yours   [66 words]

22.3

1 He wants to avoid the appointment with the toy company.
2 Ray tried to avoid getting oil on his royal blue shirt.
3 I made an appointment with an accountant to check the void invoice.
4 Ms. Roy has been appointed to the board.
5 I cannot work on invoices if there is too much noise in the office.

¶ Insurance

Dear Miss Roy When you need financial advice, what do you do? You go to Royal Financial Services.

Royal[1] Financial Services has been in business for over half a century. Recently, Ms. Sara[2] Evans joined our organization.

If you need advice on financial matters, make an appointment with Ms. Evans.[3] Yours very truly
                                    [62 words]

22.4 Dictation Speed Letter

Dear Dr. Doyle Will you be available for a brief meeting in my office on June 15 at three in the[1] afternoon? I would like for the two of us to talk over a research project that will allow us to increase[2] our business by more than $20,000.

At our meeting we can at least get our initial thoughts together.[3] If you cannot join me on June 15, would June 18 be better? Please call my secretary and let him know[4] the day you are available.
Lloyd Davis   [87 words]

22.5 Minutes Taken During a Meeting

Student Accounting Club Meeting
    The meeting was held on July 6.
    The meeting began at noon.
    President[1] Ann Johnson presided over the meeting.
Committee Facts
    The social committee is planning a meeting[2] at which we can welcome new members.
    The financial secretary said that the books had been audited by one of the[3] school officials.
    There was no new business and no old business.
    Without further discussion, the meeting[4] concluded two hours later.   [84 words]

LESSON 23

23.1

1 Please buy 12 pounds of grain and 15 feet of rope.
2 He will meet the bus at 5 o'clock.
3 Do not bother to call me after 2 a.m.
4 Do you know of an investment that will pay at least 10 percent?
5 The room is only 5 feet wide.

¶ Notes for Placing a Phone Call

    Call Ralph and tell him about the weather.
    There is a 90 percent chance it will snow today. We could get as much as 2 feet[1] of snow.
    His plane was scheduled to arrive at 11 a.m.
    It is now scheduled to arrive[2] at 2 p.m.
    It could arrive as late as 3 o'clock.   [51 words]

23.2

1 Our new sales representative has a pleasing manner.
2 Many people have mentioned that they liked the meeting.
3 Mr. Royal has mentioned that you are a good money manager.
4 Can Roy mentally solve that math problem within a minute?

5 The men and women of our book club meet monthly.

¶ Personal Note

Dear Steve   Our college food service organization has hired a new manager, Ruth Doyle.

Within a month Mrs.[1] Doyle will be hiring college men and women to work in food service. She mentioned that she is looking for people who[2] have an easy personal manner in dealing with other people, who can be trusted to handle money,[3] and who are available to work about 40 hours a month.

It sounds like a great opportunity for you;[4] let me know if you decide to apply. Floyd   [88 words]

23.3

1 Edward does not feel awkward.
2 Despite our financial losses, we will proceed "onward and upward."
3 Forward my check by 2 p.m.
4 Attend the conference; then talk to me afterward.
5 Ms. Woodward finds her career to be rewarding.

¶ Retirement

Dear Edward   After a rewarding career as a teacher, I am retiring at the end of the season.[1] One of the special rewards of teaching has been all of the fine people I have met.

In June[2] I am looking forward to traveling. Afterward, let us get together. Betty   [53 words]

23.4   Dictation Speed Letter

Dear Mrs. Lloyd   I am glad to be able to tell you that the sales in the region handled by Miss Edwards increased in April.[1] While the April increase is not a large one, it does show that Miss Edwards is starting to do a good job of selling.[2]

I hope you will have an opportunity to write to Miss Edwards to tell her that we are pleased with the job[3] she is doing. Very truly yours [66 words]

23.5   Insurance Claim

Dear Mr. Woodward   According to our telephone conversation this afternoon, I am putting my[1] financial claim in writing.

At about 6 a.m. a rainstorm hit our part of the state. By 10 a.m.[2] the water was high enough that we had to leave our lake home. At about 4 p.m. it was safe to inspect the[3] damage.

I estimate that repairs to the home and replacement of furniture will cost $5,500.[4] Very truly yours   [83 words]

LESSON 24

24.1

1 We think she is responsible for the success of the book.
2 We are sending you a request to arrange a meeting.
3 I think he is a responsible student.
4 Please send the agenda between 1 p.m. and 5 p.m.
5 I have heard nothing from her regardless of my requests.

¶ Business Letter

Dear Mr. Benton   As editor of <u>Business Magazine</u>, I am wondering if you would allow us to do[1] a story about you. I would like to cover the things which have been responsible for your success.

If you are[2] willing to comply with my request, please send me a letter regarding the date when we might get together.[3] Yours very truly   [62 words]

24.2

1 Ms. Jennings put her savings into restoring old buildings.
2 There are listings for job openings in the paper.
3 I am writing the proceedings of each of our meetings regarding earnings.
4 What are your feelings about the findings of the committee?
5 The proceedings at the meetings are fair.

¶ Cost Savings

To: Janet Jennings
From: Peter Anderson

At one of our staff meetings last week I recall that somebody[1] mentioned that our earnings had increased in the month of March. I do not have a copy of the proceedings of that[2] meeting. Can you get me a copy of the findings?   [50 words]

24.3

1 There is no possibility I will have the authority to issue a quality control check.

2 The majority of our security staff have the ability for the job.

3 I need to hire a person with a lot of ability in office facility planning.

4 The best quality of her personality is her sincerity.

5 Lee has the responsibility and authority in quality control.

¶ Memo

To: Helen Lee

From: Fred Davis

We need to hire a new person to be in charge of data processing at our[1] Dallas facility. Would you please write a job announcement?

The individual we are looking for must[2] be dependable and have a good personality.

[46 words]

24.4 Dictation Speed Letter

Dear Miss Jennings   I am requesting that you send me your latest price list for the books in the book series called "Market[1] Management." I am looking forward to receiving this price list as soon as possible. Very truly yours[2]   [40 words]

24.5 Business Memo

To: Ann Wheeler

From: Sarah Golden

Things have not gone well since we hired Harry Doyle for our territory in the West. Here are some of the things I am[1] concerned about:

1. The majority of our customers do not like his personality.

2. I am[2] concerned about his dependability. Many of our best customers say that they have not seen him since he joined[3] our staff.

3. Several customers mentioned new items that we are planning to release in the future.

Please talk[4] with Harry about these issues. Let him know that he needs to make some changes in his performance.   [97 words]

LESSON 25

25.1

1 Shipping is increasing at all West Coast ports.

2 The report of James Sporting Goods was issued yesterday.

3 All airports in the region are closed because of the storm.

4 The news reporter will do a story about the sports at our school.

5 We have an assortment of portable heaters.

¶ Business Meeting

Fred   Ms. Mary Allen, president of Allen Sporting Goods Company, will be visiting our resort on[1] June 23. I will meet Ms. Allen at the airport. However, the weather reports are not good. If the[2] airport is closed, Ms. Allen will plan to arrive on June 27. I am looking forward to[3] having Ms. Allen visit our sport shop. John   [68 words]

25.2

1 Gloria appreciates her creative associate, Ms. Garcia.

2 Mr. Garcia is doing creative work in areas of research.

3 Your associate has several areas of knowledge which we appreciate.

4 The creation of new items often represents an opportunity for business growth.

5 Gloria created the campaign design, but I planned it out.

¶ Advertising Material

Dear Madam   This letter acknowledges your letter of May 23 to our general manager, Ms. Gloria[1] Lane. Gloria left yesterday afternoon on a business trip, and your letter has been referred to me.

We are[2] currently working on several areas. Advertising copy has been written and is now being[3] edited for your approval. Artwork has been created too.

We believe that we will be able[4] to send these things to you within three weeks. Very truly yours   [89 words]

25.3

1 Beth will meet me at the football game on Saturday, May 17.

2 Gloria will have a birthday party on Tuesday, January 19.

3 We sent you requests for payment on October 3, November 5, and December 5.

4 February 9 will be the first Monday of the month.

5 Let us get together some Friday evening in August or September.

¶ College Schedule

Dear Theresa   I am happy to tell you that I have just registered for my college classes. School begins[1] on September 2 and ends on December 19. My math class meets at 8 a.m. on Monday, Wednesday, and[2] Friday. My physical education class meets at 10 a.m. on Tuesday and Thursday. The history course I am[3] taking meets at 1 p.m. on Monday, Wednesday, and Friday.

Please let me know your schedule for this semester.[4] Perhaps you can come up to see me some Friday or Saturday. Sincerely   [94 words]

25.4   Dictation Speed Letter

Dear Mrs. Mead   When you were in our place of business last Saturday, you requested that we send for a price list[1] for Smith office furniture. I am sorry to inform you that the Smith Company has gone out of business.[2]

Please stop in again so that we can show you the lines of office furniture which we have available. Very truly yours[3]   [60 words]

25.5   Department Merger

Dear Mrs. Richards   Last November my associate, Gary Boyd, and I devised a plan to merge the sales[1] division with the advertising division. We think that the plan we have developed will enable our company[2] to realize savings in the future in the area of overhead costs.

Would you be able to spend about[3] two hours with us to listen to our plan? Would Tuesday, January 5, be a possible date?[4] Very truly yours

[82 words]

LESSON 26

26.1

1 The manufacturer should have called by this time.
2 We will meet with the gentlemen from the insurance company very early in the morning.
3 Where can we buy insurance for our manufacturing facilities?
4 Our insurance company insures anything of value anywhere in the country.
5 We will insure the goods your company manufactures anytime.

¶ Insurance Policy

To: Tom Edwards
From: Susan Harvey
It is time to renew our insurance policy on our manufacturing[1] facilities. It is vital that we reduce our manufacturing costs in every way. Do you think[2] we can do anything about our insurance costs?

If you have any other thoughts on ways that we might reduce our[3] manufacturing costs, please feel free to discuss them with me any morning this week.   [75 words]

26.2

1 Mr. Adams encourages students enrolled in his class.
2 It is unlikely that our engineers will be unable and unwilling to solve the problem.
3 My teacher encourages us to read reports that contain unrelated and innovative research.
4 We cannot force you to work if you are unwilling to do so.
5 We will have to wait to get someone to unload the supplies.

¶ Payment Collections

Gentlemen   Our company is concerned about your unpaid account. We wrote to you on January 16 and[1] again on February 18 but have not received any reply.

Until we hear from you, we[2] must assume that you are simply unwilling to pay your bill. This is unfair to us since we have bills of our own[3] to pay.

We encourage you to answer this letter. Unless we hear from you by April 16, we will take legal[4] action. Very truly yours   [84 words]

26.3

1 We have not visited Yale in many years.
2 I have not removed the yellow grass in my yard.
3 The money in my savings account yields 6 percent.
4 Lee is buying yellow yarn to make a sweater.
5 We do not yet know if we will have a sale on yarn at the end of the year.

¶ Furniture Manufacturer

Ladies and Gentlemen   Our corporation has just purchased all of the outstanding stock of the Yale Company.[1] Yale is a leading manufacturer of outdoor furniture for yards and patios. Yale Company has[2] yielded 6 percent in each of the last three years.

The former Yale Company will now operate as Yale[3] Manufacturing Company. Very truly yours
[67 words]

26.4   Dictation Speed Letter

Dear Leo   Could you mail me the name of the woman who was appointed credit manager of the Boyd Toy Manufacturing[1] Company last week? I made a note of her name, but I cannot find it anywhere. I would appreciate your[2] help at this time because I would like to write to her sometime early in the new year. Fred   [55 words]

26.5   Personal Note

Dear Mrs. Tyler   The old year is leaving us and the new one will be here in less than three weeks. This year has been[1] a good one for us in the insurance business. We should be able to finish this year with a net profit[2] of $100,000, which is 10 percent above the net profit of last year. This fine year was possible[3] because of people like you. We appreciate the business from your insurance agency.

If there is anything we can[4] do for you in the coming year, please call on us at any time. Cordially yours   [94 words]

LESSON 27

27.1

1 Can you clarify the modifications in our specifications?
2 We will specify the new records classification system.
3 I received the justification for modifying the specifications this morning.
4 I do not know the identification of the signature on this letter.
5 What justification can you possibly have for classifying the research?

¶ Library System

To: Gary Bennett
From: Edna Day
I have just received notification that you have completed[1] the work on our new library classification system.

I like the way you have provided[2] identification of each of the problem areas within our library. I, too, like the way you have[3] provided justification for each of your recommendations and the specifications for new material. Your work on this project is sincerely[4] appreciated.   [82 words]

27.2

1 I have misplaced the page with the mistake.
2 We cannot afford to have mistakes such as misprints in our material.
3 If we print misleading material, we may be sued.
4 Our staff should not be making such mistakes.
5 The mystery book is misleading.

¶ Thank-You Letter

Dear Mr. Bernstein   I appreciate the fact that you took the time to write to me to point out the mistake[1] in our magazine. We did indeed misplace the last word on page 57 of our October issue.

We do not[2] print misleading articles. We have a fine staff of editors, but despite their best efforts mistakes can occasionally[3] occur. Very truly yours
[64 words]

27.3

1 Our new hardware shop is on Broadway at Times Square.
2 We quoted a low price for insuring their hardware store.
3 David intends to quit our staff by the end of the year.
4 We can always quote a lower price.
5 Floyd quickly quoted facts about our hardware sales.

¶ Insurance Quotes

Dear Mrs. Woodward   I appreciate your writing to me to quote your insurance rates for our new place of[1] business. Since moving into our new hardware store on Broadway, we have had quite a few quotes to review. We had to[2] quit reviewing quotes and make a decision.

Despite the fact that we cannot accept your

quoted rates, it is[3] reassuring to know that we qualify for insurance with your company. Very truly yours [78 words]

27.4 Dictation Speed Letter

Dear Mrs. Willis We were glad to have your recent purchase. If any mistakes were made in the content of our shipment,[1] please let us know. Let us hear from you, too, if you have any problems with the operation of the goods you have[2] purchased. Cordially yours [45 words]

27.5 Factory Plan

Dear Miss Moreno I am attaching a copy of the specifications that we have drawn up for the[1] construction of our new factory in Peoria. Please have one of the members of your staff study the[2] specifications and make whatever changes are needed.

I would appreciate it if you could send them[3] quickly — no later than Tuesday, January 4. Very truly yours [73 words]

LESSON 28

28.1

1 We correspond regularly with customers to thank them for the products they order.
2 Thank you for your order of February 10 for our products.
3 Thank you for the opinions on the equipment.
4 Ann never attends our regular morning meetings regarding updating equipment.
5 Just thank her for ordering the products.

¶ Lost Shipment

Dear Mr. Johnson Thank you for answering my letter of February 20 asking about our order of[1] December 16. In your correspondence you said that our order must have been lost in shipment. We have been[2] ordering products from you regularly, and never before has a shipment become lost.

In order to track[3] down the missing goods, we have reviewed the records of our truck driver. In our opinion, the products we ordered[4] never left your plant. Could you perhaps check your own shipping records again? Cordially yours [96 words]

28.2

1 We expect the expert from the export company to arrive at 3 o'clock.
2 The extra credit portion in the exam was extremely easy.
3 We expanded the contract when it expired.
4 We expect to examine the shipment to see if it is exactly what was ordered.
5 The exact cost of the medical exam is extremely expensive.

¶ Study Notes
Material About Economics Exam
Our exam will be held on Wednesday, September 10. The exam[1] at this time will cover exports.

We need to be able to write exact quotes from the experts mentioned in class.

We need[2] to be able to figure exact costs and expenses in at least one case problem.

We should expect the exam[3] to take the entire class time. [65 words]

28.3

1 Dear Ms. Edward Thank you for your reply to my letter of August 16.
2 We will wait for your reply. Sincerely yours
3 Please let me know what time we can meet. Very sincerely yours
4 Dear Ms. Woodward Please check the attached invoice to make sure it is exactly what you ordered.
5 I look forward to seeing you in September. Very cordially yours

28.4 Dictation Speed Letter

Dear Ms. Miller Thank you for your letter expressing appreciation for the quality of our products.[1] We value the opinions of people who regularly order our products.

I will keep your letter in our files.[2] Maybe we will be able to use it in an advertising campaign. Very truly yours [52 words]

28.5 Relocation

Dear Paul I am sorry to inform you that I will be moving from the city to join an export company[1] located on the West Coast. It is necessary, therefore, for me to resign my position on the city[2] council. This is my official notification that the November meeting will be the last meeting I will be able[3] to attend.

I want you to know that working with you has been quite exciting. Thank you for all your help.[4] Very sincerely yours   [84 words]

LESSON 29

29.1

1 Ms. O'Brien, the trial lawyer, spoke to her client, Ms. Ryan.
2 I must talk with my client prior to the trial.
3 I will go to the appliance store for a dryer.
4 We place reliance on the riot police to quiet the mob.
5 The science class was quiet prior to the exam.

¶ Business Letter
Dear Mrs. O'Brien   We are proud to welcome you as a new client of Science Magazine. I am sure that you will[1] find advertising in the pages of Science Magazine to be profitable.

Thank you once again,[2] Mrs. O'Brien, for being willing to advertise in Science Magazine. Yours very truly   [58 words]

29.2

1 Ryan Enterprises has several international interests.
2 Our school provides entertainment in the evenings that interests many international students.
3 The committee interfered with the plans.
4 We entered the room and interrupted the interview with Mrs. O'Brien.
5 Introduce me after the interview.

¶ Job Interview
Dear Mr. Ryan   This is just a quick note to confirm that everything is in order prior to your job[1] interview.

When you arrive at our building, you will notice that we have two entrances on Broadway. Please use the[2] south entrance.

I am eager to learn more about the courses you have taken in international business.[3] I am sure you are equally interested in learning more about our company, International[4] Enterprises. Very truly yours   [87 words]

29.3

1 There is a flight every hour between Chicago and New York City.
2 Los Angeles, California, is an exciting place for an American vacation.
3 I will fly from Philadelphia, Pennsylvania, to Denver, Colorado, on Wednesday, October 23.
4 We will open branch offices in Georgia and Florida.
5 Mr. Rosen was president of a company in St. Louis, Missouri.

¶ Geography Class Notes
Notes on Ports and Shipping
The first primary ports of the United States were Boston and Philadelphia.[1] Later, New York became the busiest port. On the West Coast of the United States, San Francisco was the[2] first major port. Los Angeles and Seattle are primary West Coast ports.

On the Mississippi River,[3] St. Louis and New Orleans have been shipping centers for many years.   [70 words]

29.4   Contribution Appreciation

Dear Dr. O'Brien   Thank you for your very generous cash gift for the National Science Association.[1] Our Association is not supported by any government agency. We are so pleased with your cash gift[2] that I just had to write a personal note to tell you of my sincere appreciation. Very truly yours[3]   [60 words]

29.5   Letter of Condolence

Dear Mrs. Glenn   In the paper yesterday morning, I read of the death of the president of your company,[1] Helen Jennings. I am extending to you my regrets on behalf of my organization, International[2] Enterprises.

I was a client of Mrs. Jennings for many years. Mrs. Jennings will always[3] be remembered as a leader in the field of entertainment broadcast media. Sincerely yours[4]   [80 words]

30.1

1 The property deed is probably enclosed in the envelope.
2 What envelope do we usually use for this size enclosure throughout?
3 We will probably find the same error in the newspaper.
4 He recognized that the envelope has an unusual stamp.
5 Beth will probably not recognize the problem.

¶ Newspaper Advertising

To: Carlos Vega
From: Richard Cohen

Your plan that we sell advertising in the student newspaper is[1] interesting. Throughout the years the newspaper has been considered the property of the school and has represented[2] an expense to the school.

Maybe the time has come to recognize that the newspaper does not have to be supported[3] by the school.

Selling advertising space in a student newspaper is not unusual. Enclosed in the envelope[4] is a list of people to invite to the October 27 meeting of the newspaper staff to discuss this matter. [99 words]

30.2

1 We appreciate your cash contribution to the art field.
2 We have a number of contributors to our magazine.
3 Our newspaper is now being distributed in every city.
4 An attribute we value is honesty.
5 What is the total distribution of your magazine?

¶ Distribution Routes

Dear Scott   Thank you for your contribution to our recent convention of distributors of National Products[1] Corporation. Your presentation on ways to develop new distribution routes was appreciated.[2] Everyone is saying that the convention this year was a success. Certainly much of this success can be attributed[3] to you. Sincerely   [64 words]

30.3

1 I am grateful for the successful career I have.
2 It is doubtful that Mark is helpful.
3 Julie is thankful she worked carefully.
4 Hopefully the party will be successful and I will have a delightful time.
5 I am grateful for the helpful and useful advice you have so carefully given me.

¶ Research Report

David, I hope that you will find the research report helpful in successfully completing your paper. Hopefully,[1] this report will help you to complete the project. It is doubtful that very many people know of this useful[2] reference material. Fred

[46 words]

30.4   Dictation Speed Letter

Dear Gary   Enclosed with this letter you will find an advertisement from our local newspaper. The advertisement[1] is for some property west of the city.

You will note that the asking price for this property is[2] $28,000. It is doubtful that the owners will be able to get $28,000 for it[3] today. Hopefully, the enclosed newspaper clipping will be helpful. Very truly yours   [75 words]

30.5   Survey Report

Dear Mr. Klein   It was a pleasure to receive your letter in response to our survey. I am pleased to say that we have[1] enjoyed an unusually good rate of response to our survey. Many people went to the extra[2] effort of adding their own helpful comments.

Your letter, with its helpful comments, can only make our final[3] report more useful and complete. Thank you for your contributions to our survey. Very truly yours   [78 words]

30.6   Message

Marvin Boyd called to say that he will meet you at 12:15 p.m. for lunch. He will come to your[1] office. Sandra   [22 words]

LESSON 31

31.1

1 I welcomed your prompt reply.
2 The unconfirmed rumor seemed to be true.
3 I was informed that the picture would be framed promptly.
4 The suspect claimed to be unjustly blamed.
5 She was confirmed as a member and welcomed to the club.

¶ Letter of Recommendation

Dear Ms. Green   It is my pleasure to recommend Mr. Jack Haley for a position with Davis Company.[1] In his former position, Jack promptly named the right committees and welcomed every challenge that came his way.[2] He seemed to enjoy solving problems quickly.

Jack Haley should prove to be a fine member of your staff. Very truly yours[3]   [60 words]

31.2

1 Do not mix the boxes containing tax forms and index cards.
2 Ms. Fox will prepare your income tax.
3 Tax forms are kept in boxes.
4 Do not index the cards in the blue box.
5 The fixed rate of interest is 10 percent.

¶ Storage of Records

To the Staff   Starting in January we will be accepting boxes of records for inactive storage.[1] You will receive a standard-size file box. Each box is given a file number, and you will receive an index card[2] containing that same number.   [45 words]

31.3

1 She already went shopping almost two hours ago.
2 Our prices are already too high and cannot be altered.
3 Janet does not offer options, although she does not agree.
4 Almost every member of our organization wants another option to the plan.
5 James is always willing to help, although he may disagree.

¶ Accounting Club

Kenneth   Already it is time for the Accounting Club to make plans for the school year. Although things went well last year,[1] we almost ended the year with no money. Let us get together to discuss what we can present to the[2] members at the first meeting. Dave   [45 words]

31.4   Dictation Speed Letter

Dear Madam   It makes no difference whether your staff flies 200 miles, 10,000 miles, or farther. Yale Airlines[1] will promptly take them where they need to go. Your company officials will not need to worry about[2] reservations.

If you need to know more about Yale Airlines, we will be glad to have our well-informed sales[3] representative visit you at your request. Yours very truly   [74 words]

31.5   Company Shareholder

Dear Ms. Booth   I am pleased to learn, Ms. Booth, that you are a new shareholder of the Smith Office Products Company.[1] As you may already know, we are the largest[2] manufacturer of file boxes and index cards.[2]

You will be kept informed of the operations of our organization through quarterly and annual reports. Soon[3] you will be receiving a copy of the annual report and also a copy of our company magazine.[4] It is issued in January, April, August, and December. Yours very truly   [97 words]

LESSON 32

32.1

1 I understand that your progress in shorthand is satisfactory.
2 The suggestion to include progress reports was considered worthless.
3 Mike suggests that Bill be included in the planning because of his experience.
4 I do not understand why the book report did not include a short summary.
5 There is a shortage of worthwhile suggestions to satisfy the manager.

¶ Sales Suggestion

Dear Bob   One of our sales representatives has suggested that we include a book of short stories in our sales list.[1] She reports that such a book will satisfy a very real demand.

It is my experience that this sales[2] representative makes good suggestions. I think it would be worth reviewing this suggestion. Judy [57 words]

32.2

1 A requirement is to fill out this inquiry form.
2 Each student is required to take two years of history.
3 Most things of value are not easy to acquire.
4 Send your inquiry about the requirements to our personnel office.
5 They need to acquire some data about the requirements.

¶ Business Letter

Dear Mr. Phillips   I am writing to inquire about the requirements for becoming a real estate agent.[1] I would like to acquire a real estate license sometime in the near future.

I will appreciate your reply[2] to this inquiry. Very truly yours [50 words]

32.3

1 I do not belong to the Franklin Bank.
2 Frankly, I do not know if Mr. Strong is a banker.
3 Ray did not give a blank check to Lincoln Center.
4 Frank is one of the younger people to be hired by the bank.
5 Our organization will hold a meeting sometime this spring at the Franklin Center.

¶ Letter

Dear Miss Franklin   Your request for me to give a speech at your spring meeting arrived just a day too late. I have[1] already accepted an opportunity to give a speech at a meeting of the Bankers Association on[2] Saturday, April 15. Therefore, I will not be available.

I suggest that you ask Frank Strong. Dr. Strong is[3] an outstanding young leader in the area of computer research. I am sure, Miss Franklin, that this meeting[4] will be a great success. Very truly yours [87 words]

32.4   Dictation Speed Letter

Dear Fay   Thank you for your suggestion that we include a calendar of events with the May issue of our club[1] newsletter. I realize that this will increase the printing costs of our newsletter.

Despite the cost, I think it will be[2] worth it if this is what it takes to make our organization strong. Give me some time to make up a rough draft[3] of the calendar, and then I will share it with you. Frank [70 words]

32.5   Advertising Solicitation

Dear Miss Adams   The Lincoln Times is no longer just a morning newspaper. It is now a 24-hour[1] newspaper with regular issues every morning, afternoon, and evening. Each issue brings you the[2] latest news.

This change in our policy means that every day your advertisements have three opportunities to[3] reach potential customers. Your advertising in the Lincoln Times will probably bring more customers into[4] your store than any other advertising medium. Sincerely yours [92 words]

LESSON 33

33.1

1 George made a donation of $300.
2 Do you have permission to alter some of the conditions?
3 I cannot accept your invitation to meet you at the station.
4 Did you read the Monday edition of the newspaper?
5 I know James will make a fine addition to our news station!

¶ Student Newspaper

Dear Mark   I was pleased to receive your invitation to write an article for the Tuesday edition of our student[1] newspaper. I will agree to write the article only on the condition that I may use the word processing equipment[2] in the newspaper office. I cannot meet this deadline without the help of automation.

Do I have[3] permission to use the word processor? Franklin [71 words]

33.2

1 Fred has several books he read during his boyhood.
2 Childhood memories may affect our lives daily.
3 There is the likelihood that the train will be on time.

4 There is a fire station in each of the neighborhoods in the city.

5 The Franklin Center offers a course in parenthood.

¶ Physical Fitness

Dear Parent Lifelong habits of physical fitness should begin in childhood. Physical fitness can[1] reduce the likelihood of childhood illness. Please encourage your children to take part in the physical[2] education activities offered in your neighborhood. Very truly yours   [54 words]

33.3

1 What was the result of the meeting?

2 The college has adult evening classes.

3 Mary consulted with the new members.

4 Frank took the rejection of his plan as the ultimate insult.

5 Ultimately we will develop new guidelines.

¶ Sales Lead

Dear Miss Grant   At the last meeting of the Adult Education Association you told me that the Davis[1] Book Company was interested in computerizing its accounting operations. I consulted with our[2] sales representative in the Dallas area, and she immediately called on them.

The first result of[3] her call was a series of rewarding meetings with our experienced consultants. The ultimate result[4] was a new, highly profitable account for our organization.

Thank you, Miss Grant, for this[5] valuable sales lead. Sincerely yours   [109 words]

33.4   Dictation Speed Letter

Dear Mr. James   Yesterday I heard some news that will make you happy. Davis College has adopted our book Business[1] Management and has placed an order for 200 copies. The teachers selected this textbook after[2] making a thorough and detailed study of all the books on the market today.

I am sure that as the editor[3] of Business Management you will be pleased with this news. Frances Drake   [73 words]

33.5   Additional Copies Requested

Dear Miss Wiley   This morning I learned that the supply of the book Business Consulting will shortly be[1] exhausted. I estimate that we now have in the

neighborhood of 3,000 copies. This number will, in my[2] opinion, last us only through December.

Therefore, I request that you manufacture another[3] 30,000 copies immediately. We know from experience that it usually takes several months to[4] print that large a number. Yours very truly   [87 words]

34.1

1 The business letter does not contain an appropriate closing.

2 We need to print large quantities of programs.

3 Many executives wish they knew the product.

4 Adam does not object to studying the subject of computer programming.

5 Scott knows how to use that particular computer program.

¶ Communications Course

Ladies and Gentlemen   On Saturday, February 3, the School of Business will offer a one-day course for[1] executives who wish to better their communication skills. This course is appropriate for any[2] executive in any type of business. The main objective of the program is to help executives to write[3] and to dictate better letters. A large quantity of programs are being sent for members of your staff interested[4] in the subject of communication skills. Very truly yours   [91 words]

34.2

1 Mr. Rossi is determined that the southern region increase sales.

2 Steven returned to Western State College during the fall term.

3 Do not return your order blank to our eastern office.

4 The termination of our 3 o'clock flight will be in the southern terminal.

5 Air travel would increase if our terminal buildings were more modern.

¶ Printing Needs

Dear Mr. Worth   I am to determine what quantity we should print of Modern Science.

On the basis of our[1] past experience, I believe we

should be able to sell 50,000 copies in the first year. About[2] 20,000 copies could be sold in the western region and about 35,000 copies could be sold[3] in the northern region.

If sales turn out better than we expect, we can have larger quantities[4] printed. Sincerely yours

[84 words]

34.3

1 You have my gratitude for giving me a copy of the constitution.
2 Frank has an aptitude for computers.
3 Western Airlines is going to institute an air-travel plan.
4 Most people look for a positive attitude in all workers.
5 Your failure to make payments on time constitutes a breach of contract.

¶ Future Plans

Dear Rose I am planning to attend the Norris Computer Institute. At your suggestion, I took an aptitude[1] test, and the test showed that I would be good at computer programming. The results of the aptitude test gave[2] me the direction I needed.

You have my gratitude, Rose, for suggesting that I take the aptitude test.[3] Sincerely   [62 words]

34.4 Dictation Speed Message

Dear Fred Janice called and said that she wishes to meet you for dinner tonight. She is returning from her business trip[1] this afternoon. Eileen is having trouble fitting into the organization, and you may have to[2] terminate her contract. William

[44 words]

34.5 Approval of Constitution

Dear Ms. Worth We are pleased with your determination to complete the new constitution for our organization.[1] All of us on the executive board owe you our sincere gratitude.

Copies of the new constitution[2] are being sent to our members along with the agenda for our next meeting. The main objective will be to[3] vote on the new constitution. Yours very truly   [70 words]

35.1

1 This particular situation cannot continue.
2 The second period class has been canceled.
3 The financial situation of our organization is quite serious.
4 The class took a genuine interest in her theory of economics.
5 Previously we tried various aspects of your plan.

¶ Student's "To Do" List

1. Continue to collect information on various economic theories.
2. Try to talk with Professor[1] Dunn at the end of the class period.
3. By October 16 try to complete all the various[2] assignments previously started.
4. Check with Beth to see if she has a genuine interest in working[3] together on a project.

[64 words]

35.2

1 We will patiently await your payment.
2 Are you aware that sales in our division are ahead of the rest of the company?
3 I will be away from my office in July.
4 George has been awake since 4 a.m.
5 We will await the arrival of the football coach before we begin the awards ceremony.

¶ Vacation Schedule

To the Staff While I am away on vacation for two weeks, David Valdez will be managing the[1] division. Our production is currently ahead of schedule, and it should be a good time for me to be[2] away.

Problems may arise which cannot await my return. Mr. Valdez is aware that he is to make decisions[3] on my behalf.   [63 words]

35.3

1 Frank did not knowingly erase the computer disk.
2 Barbara willingly gave her time to the class.
3 Printing ink is quite interestingly our most profitable product.

343

4 This product has become increasingly difficult to manufacture.

5 The roles are exceedingly complex, but the actors are performing convincingly.

¶ Executive Training

Dear Mr. Jackson Enrolling in our executive training course will do several things for you:

1.[1] You will learn to express your theories and thoughts interestingly and convincingly.

2. You will build your[2] confidence, and you will find that you will be able to obtain exceedingly satisfactory results in the[3] management of people.

If you would like more information about this exceedingly practical course, phone[4] or write us today. Very truly yours [87 words]

35.4 Dictation Speed Letter

Dear Ms. Frank You have my sincere appreciation, Ms. Frank, for the part you played in our executive[1] conference in Albany yesterday afternoon. All of us felt that you presented your theories of management[2] exceedingly well and quite convincingly. I am sure, Ms. Frank, that everyone benefited from the presentation[3] of your subject matter. Sincerely yours [67 words]

35.5 Years of Service

Dear Mrs. Goldman If my memory serves me correctly, on Friday, December 16, you will complete[1] 25 years as a professional of the Johnson Recreation Planning Company. Throughout the years, your[2] contribution to our company has been exceedingly valuable.

You have my best wishes, Mrs.[3] Goldman, for many more increasingly productive and happy years with us. Sincerely yours [78 words]

LESSON 36

36.1

1 Carlos will celebrate his anniversary next month.

2 Your request comes at a most inconvenient time.

3 Paul is very reluctant to discuss this subject in public.

4 Which item is next on our agenda?

5 Linda has gone to work for Southern State Incorporated.

¶ Plans to Incorporate

Dear Judy It is hard to believe that only three years have passed since you began your own company. I am glad to[1] hear that you are ready to incorporate.

Thank you for your offer to sell me shares of stock in your[2] company. I am reluctant to buy right now. Making this type of investment would not be convenient at this time.[3]

Thank you for giving me this opportunity. Sincerely yours [73 words]

36.2

1 The superintendent should be able to supervise the sales division.

2 Barbara does a superior job of supervision.

3 Our old product line will be superseded by a superior new product design.

4 The authority of the plant superintendent does not supersede that of the vice president.

5 Bob is doing a superb job as supervisor of your department.

¶ Job Opening

Fred You might be interested to know that we will have a job opening for a new supervisor[1] in our product development lab. As you know, the work we do in our lab is of superior quality.[2] To be the supervisor of this lab represents a superb opportunity for a person having[3] your background.

I suggest you apply as soon as the job is announced to the general public. Sincerely [77 words]

36.3

1 We will soon circulate a new copy of our company regulations.

2 You are to be congratulated on formulating a new plan.

3 We need to formulate a better way to circulate our articles.

4 Interest rates are regulated and should be calculated correctly.

5 Congratulations! Your newspaper has achieved an outstanding circulation.

¶ Company Policy

Greg I understand you wish to take a printing calculator home with you. Company regulations[1] do not allow any of us to remove calculators or other office equipment from the building. It has been[2] several years since this policy was formulated. Copies of the policy were circulated to[3] members of the staff before you were hired. It did not occur to me to tell you about the regulation. George[4]

[80 words]

36.4

1 Are you a frequent traveler on our airline?
2 The frequency of use of the calculator is low; consequently, it remains in good condition.
3 Frequently her remarks are eloquent.
4 What will be the consequences of the new guidelines?
5 Mrs. Franklin frequently visits our clothing shop.

¶ Publication of Article

Dear Mrs. Sanchez   Thank you for the magazine article you sent us recently. Your writing style is eloquent; I always enjoy reading your articles.[1] We will probably print your article sometime in the spring.[2]

You have been having articles accepted by our magazine with very high frequency. Consequently,[3] we would like to hire you as a contributing editor.

If this proposal interests you, contact me so[4] that we may discuss the details. Very truly yours

[88 words]

36.5   Dictation Speed Letter

Dear Mr. Samuels   Thank you for your letter inquiring about the cost of leasing a new car from us.[1] This is such a frequent inquiry that we have printed a brochure on the subject. A copy is enclosed.[2] Leasing a new car from us is exceedingly cost effective. Pay a visit to our offices as soon as[3] it is convenient for you to do so. Yours very truly

[73 words]

36.6   Contribution Request

Dear Mrs. Strong   Your letter asking the Davis Calculator Company to contribute calculators to your[1] school has been referred to me.

We frequently receive requests for contributions of equipment to public schools.[2] We have had to formulate a policy, however, of making donations only in the state of Illinois,[3] where our home office is located.

I hope you will understand our position. Sincerely yours

[77 words]

37.1

1 The membership of our organization has increased.
2 Thank you for your leadership during the last year.
3 James is considering ownership of his own small business.
4 Elaine has excellent relationships with her fellow workers.
5 I appreciate your help and friendship.

¶ Club Membership

Dear Miss Gordon   According to the Office of the Dean, you have the grade point average to qualify you for[1] membership in the Accounting Club. I am sure you will find membership interesting and enjoyable.

Please[2] consider sending the attached application blank to our membership committee. Very truly yours

[57 words]

37.2

1 Ms. Adams is impressed by the new employees.
2 The Empire Import and Export Company will employ you.
3 All of our employees are impressed with the improvement courses.
4 The impact of your import products is most impressive.
5 I am embarrassed to say that our employees did not act in an impartial manner.

¶ Profitability Statements

To: Leslie Baker
From: Arlene Jones
I am most impressed with the financial statements of your Import and Export[1] Division. Your division has shown the most improvement in profitability.

You and all of the[2] employees of your division deserve my most sincere congratulations. Let me repeat most emphatically,[3] I am impressed with your performance.

[65 words]

37.3

1 Miss Bridges has been transferred to our Los Angeles office.
2 Business is transacted today by the computer transmission of data.
3 Can you provide me with a translation of this letter?
4 It is more productive to transcribe from shorthand notes than dictation tapes.
5 The first type of big business in America was the transportation industry.

¶ Purchase Request

Mr. Ryan   The company treasurer just transmitted to me your note requesting permission to purchase[1] a transistor radio for Mr. Frank Dwyer.

The transistor radio you wish to purchase costs over[2] $250. I am reluctant to approve such a request, but I will do so in view of the[3] impressive contribution Mr. Dwyer has made to the Empire Transportation Company. Forward your[4] purchase request to me. I will have our purchasing department complete the transaction. James French

[99 words]

37.4   Dictation Speed Letter

Dear Miss Gates   I noticed that the name of David Smith was omitted from the list of auditors who were selected[1] to go to the July meeting of national credit people in Memphis. I know we agreed that the list should be[2] limited to five auditors, but I seem to recall that Mr. Smith was included in those five. If he[3] was omitted in error, he should be added to the list. Ray Baker   [72 words]

37.5   Rising Costs

Dear Professor West   You will recall that on April 5 you invited us to give you a price on the painting[1] of your home. On the basis of a detailed survey that we made, we quoted you a price of $3,000[2] provided the work could be started on or before June 12. Today is June 30, but we have not heard from you.[3] Because of rising costs, we cannot do the work at the quoted price if we do not hear from you by July 10.[4] Please call us today, Professor West, and authorize us to proceed. Yours very truly

[96 words]

38.1

1 The electronics industry assumes a significant role in the world economy.
2 A significant amount of data is transmitted electronically today.
3 I think it would be a good idea to send a memorandum to all branch managers.
4 It is very important that you speak up at the meeting on this subject.
5 The opinions of Marco and Mary are of equivalent merit.

¶ Business Communication

To: Scott Sanchez
From: Diana Boyd
Thank you for taking the time to speak with me about the importance of our[1] communicating with our branch offices more quickly. As our business becomes more and more worldwide, the speed of[2] communication becomes increasingly significant.

Since each of our branch offices has at least one[3] computer, the concept of electronic mail is entirely possible. We will begin a cost study[4] immediately.

[83 words]

38.2

1 Keith says his grades have risen steadily.
2 We are temporarily out of envelopes.
3 I readily agree that science is a difficult subject.
4 Can we temporarily handle all incoming calls?
5 A large family could easily travel in that car.

¶ Jet Travel

Dear Mr. Bates   Thank you for writing to inquire about the prices and models of the Empire Jet. The Empire[1] Jet is easily the finest business jet manufactured today.

Our Model 102 is in stock and[2] readily available to you. By owning an Empire Jet, your executives can be on their way to[3] important meetings speedily.

Please read the enclosed brochure and then invite one of our sales representatives[4] to show you how easily you may join the happy family of Empire Jet owners. Yours very truly   [97 words]

38.3

1 The cost of the subscription to <u>Suburban Magazine</u> is substantial.
2 Service will extend to several suburban area subdivisions.
3 The contractor plans to submit plans for a new subdivision next week.
4 Ellen does not subscribe to the <u>Suburban Daily</u>.
5 Many subscribers submitted an article.

¶ Newspaper Delivery

Dear Mr. and Mrs. Samuels   Your name has been submitted to us as the parents of a child who can be a[1] newspaper carrier. The <u>Daily Tribune</u> is a new newspaper selling its first subscriptions. We have many[2] subscribers in your subdivision.

If your child would like to deliver newspapers on a daily basis, please[3] submit the attached application form. Cordially yours   [70 words]

38.4   Dictation Speed Letter

Mrs. Casey   Our auditors have just finished a detailed study of our sales records. This study indicates[1] that our sales drop sharply in June and July. This study is not only surprising but astonishing.

Please go check[2] into the matter in detail with your sales staff and advise me what steps are needed to solve our problem. Alice[3] Tracy
[61 words]

38.5   Magazine Article

Dear Roy,   It was a pleasure receiving the manuscript you submitted to our magazine. Your article speaks[1] out on issues that are important today and will make a significant contribution to the appeal[2] of our magazine.

Your article will be printed in our January issue. Upon printing your article,[3] we will send you a check for $300. You may consider this letter to be the equivalent[4] of a contract. Very cordially yours
[87 words]

38.6   Reminder

Jim   Someone from your dentist's office just called. Do not forget your appointment next Wednesday. It is at 10:30 a.m.[1] Nancy
[21 words]

39.1

1 Ruth has my sincere apology.
2 The advance of technology has been most impressive.
3 Our school is investing in the equipment for a new biology laboratory.
4 Do you plan to major in either sociology or psychology?
5 You deserve an apology for the inconvenience.

¶ Note of Apology

Mr. West   I sincerely apologize for being late to my sociology class. In the previous[1] class period our psychology class was involved with technological testing which ran late. Again,[2] sincere apologies.
Lee Baker   [46 words]

39.2

1 Please return the self-improvement plan in the self-addressed envelope.
2 Allan wrote the entire report himself.
3 James does not consider himself to be selfish.
4 The members of the Congress have voted themselves a pay increase.
5 I am giving myself more self-confidence through a self-improvement course.

¶ Letter

Dear Mr. Kinney   The National Management Institute is offering a self-improvement course to acquire[1] self-confidence. Over 10,000 people have already given themselves self-confidence and, in turn,[2] self-esteem.

Attached is a list of dates when our self-improvement course will be offered at locations near you.[3] Why not select a location, and return the enclosed registration form in the self-addressed envelope.[4] Yours very truly   [83 words]

39.3

1 Our psychology class is studying human behavior in society.
2 We handle a variety of office products.
3 Sam is feeling a great amount of anxiety about his presentation.

4 Our company has received notoriety over our legal problems.

5 The Accounting Society as several new members.

¶ Accounting Presentation

Miss Best   Thank you very much, Miss Best, for inviting me to speak to your Accounting Society. I will[1] discuss with the members of your society the wide variety of job opportunities which are[2] available. I will also talk about the favorable job market and help to relieve some of the[3] anxiety about finding a job. Dr. Jonathan Edwards   [69 words]

39.4   Dictation Speed Letter

Dear Dr. Best   I would like to have your reaction to a research project I recently finished. Will you be[1] available for a brief meeting on this research project on July 15? If you will not be available[2] on that date, will it be possible for you to see me on July 21 or 22?

Let my[3] secretary know, Dr. Best, the date you prefer. Sincerely yours   [72 words]

39.5   Retirement Plan

Dear Mrs. Mendez   Under the new Self-Employment Retirement Law, self-employed people now have the[1] opportunity to claim a deduction of up to 15 percent of their gross income. If you fit into the[2] self-employed classification, you should set up a retirement plan for yourself to relieve the anxiety[3] for your retirement years.

Why not stop in at our bank soon to set up a retirement account? Very truly yours[4]   [80 words]

LESSON 40

40.1

1 Our new magazine will be published in the fall.

2 This publication will not be ordinary.

3 The statistical material in the report is questionable.

4 She is an extraordinary character and a privilege to work with.

5 The circulars were not delivered because of extraordinary circumstances.

¶ Publication Announcement

Dear Sir   This letter is to announce the publication of an extraordinary new magazine. Careful[1] statistical analysis of our intended readership has shown us the type of magazine to publish.[2]

There is no question that Advertising Today will have wide circulation among advertising executives.[3] Plan on becoming a subscriber today. Very cordially yours   [73 words]

40.2

1 Ms. Cunningham recently moved to Jacksonville.

2 Janet Washington will be our new manager in Greensburg.

3 David will take the afternoon flight from Lexington to Nashville.

4 Our history book contains an interesting account of the Battle at Lexington.

5 Which cities are closest to Pittsburgh, Harrisburg, and Louisville?

¶ Comparison Shopping

Dear Mr. Washington   Many think that the Burlington Store in Greensburg is very expensive. This is[1] definitely not the case. We invite you to make price comparisons between our store and any other store[2] in Greensburg.

As you will see by the enclosed circular, the prices in our Greensburg store are quite reasonable,[3] just as they are in our two stores located in Jacksonville and Lexington.

Please visit our store soon, Mr. Washington.[4] Sincerely yours   [83 words]

40.3   Speed Dictation Memo

Ladies and Gentlemen   My purpose in writing you this short note is to ask you the name of the person who[1] prepared your personnel booklet. We plan to issue a similar booklet for our manufacturing company[2] next year. We like your personnel booklet so well that we would like to persuade the person who prepared it to help[3] us with ours. As a personal favor, would you tell me where I can reach this person. Thank you for your help. Sincerely[4]

[80 words]

40.4   Payment Request

Dear Ms. Buckingham   Thank you for your prompt reply to our letter requesting your payment of $1,200[1] for the quantity of electronic products you purchased for your Pittsburgh manufacturing plant last June. Quite[2] naturally, we are sorry that you cannot send us your check immediately. However, your justification[3] for the delay is satisfactory. Under the circumstances, we will willingly allow you an[4] extension of 30 days. We look forward to receiving your check for $1,200 on or before May[5] 10. Sincerely yours   [103 words]

LESSON 41

41.1   Expiration of Insurance

Dear Ms. Ford Have you forgotten that your insurance policy expired last week? It must have slipped your mind because[1] I am sure you would never let this insurance policy lapse. Will you please take three or four minutes to complete[2] the enclosed form and return it together with your check in the envelope that is enclosed. Sincerely yours[3]   [60 words]

41.2

Martin   recently   Rogers   applied   credit
reference   determine   attached   complete
greatly   appreciate   promptness   Dear Mrs.
with our   that will   to me   as soon as possible
Cordially yours

41.3   Credit Reference

Dear Mrs. Martin Recently Mr. David Rogers applied for a charge account with our department store. He[1] gave us your name as a credit reference. Can you give us any information that will help us determine how[2] much credit we should extend to Mr. Rogers?

I have attached a form for you to complete. Please fill out the form[3] and return it to me as soon as possible. We will greatly appreciate your promptness. Cordially yours[4]   [80 words]

41.4   Communications Bulletin

Dear Dr. Cummings Every week we send out a communications bulletin that is of assistance to[1] people in business. Each bulletin has several sam-
ples of effective letters, as well as suggestions[2] on how to compose them. You can use these suggestions to your advantage whenever you have to write business[3] or social letters of your own.

Fill out and mail the enclosed card if you would like to receive free copies of our[4] communications bulletin. Sincerely yours   [90 words]

41.5   Finance Update

Dear Mr. Harris Our latest financial statement is enclosed for your review. This year has been a difficult[1] one for our organization. We lost several sales representatives in three states. We have had no success[2] finding adequate replacements. I am satisfied with our progress in spite of these difficulties. Our[3] sales were 15 percent under last year. I am confident we will make considerable progress next year.[4] Let me know if there are any other facts you wish. Yours very truly   [91 words]

LESSON 42

42.1   Purchase Request

Dear Ms. Wells It was a pleasure to receive your order for various items in our line of office[1] products. May we ask that you fill out the enclosed form and return[2] it to us since this represents your first order with us. This will help our credit department to handle your account.

We hope that you will be satisfied with our[3] goods. We look forward to doing business with you. Cordially yours   [73 words]

42.2

enclosed   copy   prepared   Brown   serve   contract
agrees   review   office   systems   approval   initial
contact   questions   Sincerely   Dear Mr.   of the
I have   to do   let me   if you have

42.3   Contract Review

Dear Mr. Lang Enclosed is a copy of the letter I have prepared to be sent to Mrs. Brown. This letter[1] will serve as a contract by which Mrs. Brown agrees to do a review of our office systems.

Please look over[2] the letter and let me know if it meets with your approval. Then initial it and keep a copy for your files.[3] Feel free to contact me if you have any questions. Sincerely   [78 words]

42.4 Appreciation Letter

Dear Mr. Tarkington   The computer you installed in our store several months ago is working perfectly.[1] We are so satisfied with it that I just had to write to tell you about it.

The computer has saved me much time[2] during the first few months of operation. I find it much easier to keep track of my inventory and to[3] bill my customers.

Thank you for determining exactly the type of computer that is needed for my[4] business. Yours truly   [83 words]

42.5 Income Tax

Dear Mr. Hastings I almost forgot that the enclosed income tax report for the federal government is[1] due in a week or two. I should have referred it to you long ago. I was engaged in making an objective[2] study of our insurance coverage and did not remember the report. Let me know if you need any other[3] information from me. I will be glad to furnish it.

I hope that my delay causes you no[4] difficulty. Cordially yours   [84 words]

LESSON 43

43.1 Magazine Article

Dear Ms. Drake   Thank you very much for sending me the magazine article on writing more effective[1] collection letters. It is just the kind of item we are looking for as a nice change of pace from our[2] articles on creative writing.

At this time I would like to ask you to be patient and give me several[3] months in which to find an issue that will best accommodate your article. Very truly yours   [76 words]

43.2

Benson   guest   speaker   shorthand eager   presentation   how   into   office   remind September 13   9 a.m.   join   proper arrangements   Dear Miss   thank you for

43.3 Speaker Presentation

Dear Miss Benson   Thank you for agreeing to be a guest speaker in our shorthand class. We are all eager to hear[1] your presentation on how shorthand fits into the office of the future.

This is just to remind you that the[2] date on which you will visit us is September 13. Our class begins at 9 a.m.

Please let me know[3] if you would like to join us for lunch following our class. I will make the proper arrangements for you.[4] Sincerely   [82 words]

43.4 Investment Planning

Dear Mr. Gates   Our research department has just developed an investment plan that may enable you to[1] increase the return from your holdings considerably. May I present this plan to you on my next visit to[2] Chicago during the week of January 15? I am sure that you will be interested in the unique[3] character of many of the features of this plan.

I will call you when I arrive on January 18.[4] I hope you will be able to spare me about 30 minutes. Sincerely   [95 words]

43.5 Telephone Techniques

Dear Mr. Davis   The New York Telephone Company has offered to give a seminar on telephone[1] techniques in our office on Tuesday, Wednesday, and Thursday, May 5, 6, and 7. I want all the members of your staff to[2] attend one of these sessions.

The purpose of the seminar is to review proper ways to use the telephone.[3] I feel all of us will profit by the advice and information that will result from this session.

Please advise[4] your staff that it has been scheduled for the May 7 session. It will be held promptly at 10 o'clock.

Call me if you[5] have any questions or concerns about this seminar. Very truly yours   [114 words]

LESSON 44

44.1 Memo

To: Personnel Committee
From: Bob Myers
Subject: Committee Meeting

There will be a meeting of the[1] Personnel Committee on October 8 at 3 p.m.

Enclosed is a copy of the agenda for the[2] meeting. Please let me know if you have any additional items you would like to have discussed and whether[3] you will be able to attend. Your immediate response regarding your attendance will be greatly appreciated. [79 words]

44.2

Barnes time other board outline difficult unusual encountering Wilson College understood necessary financial

44.3 Wilson College

Dear Mr. Barnes Thank you for the time you and the other members of the board let me have to outline the[1] difficult and unusual space problems we are encountering at Wilson College. I left with the opinion[2] that the board understood our problems and that they would take the necessary steps to provide us with the financial[3] assistance we need. Sincerely yours [67 words]

44.4 New Office

Dear Mr. Temple You will be glad to know that our management has decided to open a sales office in[1] Camden so that we can better serve our customers in the East. We are opening that office on[2] December 12. An official announcement will appear in the Camden papers tomorrow.

The office will be[3] managed by Mrs. Helen Hugo. She was our special representative in Maine for several years.

We recommend that[4] after December 12 you send all orders and correspondence direct to Camden. In that way we will always[5] obtain immediate acknowledgment of orders and answers to any questions. Yours very truly [119 words]

44.5 Book Exhibition

Dear Mr. Moore Your letter telling us that you plan to exhibit your books at the Eastern Association[1] for Education meeting on April 16 has been referred to me.

If you wish, you can send to us all the[2] material that you plan to use at the exhibit. We will then store it for you until the date of the[3] meeting. This

is a service that we are glad to provide without charge to the exhibitors.

Please let me know if there is[4] any other information we can give you. Yours sincerely [91 words]

LESSON 45

45.1 Purchase Order

Gentlemen Thank you for the order we received from you yesterday for bond paper and office supplies. We were[1] delighted to receive it because it was the first one we have received from your firm. The order has been processed.[2] You should have it soon. It is our sincere hope that this will be the first of many orders you will send us.

We also[3] manufacture paper products of all types. You will find that our prices are the lowest in the industry.[4] Yours very truly [84 words]

45.2

Dwyer opened $1,000 promptly charged perhaps simply overlooked status it has been let me is in

45.3 Credit Account

Dear Mr. Dwyer It has been six months since I opened a charge account at your store. Since that time I have charged[1] over $1,000 worth of goods. You sent me a bill each month during the first four months. I paid each promptly.[2]

You have not sent me a bill for the past two months even though I have charged over $2,200.[3] Perhaps you have simply overlooked sending me a bill.

Please let me know whether the status of my account is in[4] good order. Yours truly [84 words]

45.4 Credit Reference

Dear Mrs. Baker Very often I have written to someone to ask why we have not received payment for items[1] purchased on account. That is not why I am writing to you today.

Today we received the final payment[2] from you for the furniture you purchased from us last year. There was not one time you sent us a late payment.

Your[3] excellent credit record at our store means

that there is no credit limit on your next purchase. We will be glad[4] to serve as a credit reference for you should the need arise. Cordially yours

[94 words]

45.5 Credit Collection

Dear Ms. Gates   There are several ways for an organization to ask for payment of overdue accounts. We are[1] therefore asking you to send your remittance of $480 for the leather goods you purchased in[2] September, October, and November. If you cannot pay the entire amount at this time, I suggest[3] you send us a partial payment and try to make definite arrangements to pay the rest. Sincerely yours

[79 words]

LESSON 46

46.1   New Sales Office

Dear Mr. Hanson   We are pleased to announce that we will open a sales office in Westport so that we can[1] better serve our customers in this area. We are opening that office on November 10. An official[2] announcement will appear in the Westport papers on November 8.

After November 10 please send all orders[3] and correspondence direct to the Westport address, which is given in this letterhead. Yours very truly

[78 words]

46.2

community   adult   education   program
excelled   nation   6 p.m.   approximately   teacher
as you know   in our   let me   if you

46.3   Adult Education Program

Dear Mr. Moore   Our community, as you know, has an adult education program that is excelled[1] by very few cities in the nation.

Our evening classes meet on Wednesday and Thursday evenings from 6 p.m.[2] until 8 p.m. for approximately 20 weeks. We have an opening at the present time for a[3] shorthand teacher in our evening program. Please let me know if you would be interested in teaching this program.[4] Sincerely yours

[81 words]

46.4   Credit Card

Dear Madam   I am pleased to write you that your application for a credit card at the Worth Ladies Shop has been[1] approved. It is a pleasure to send you the enclosed card. Hereafter when you buy clothes or accessories at our[2] shop, simply show your credit card to the sales clerk. This will enable him or her to process the sale quickly.

We[3] feel sure you will find shopping at the Worth Ladies Shop a pleasure. We sincerely hope that we will see you often.[4] Yours truly   [82 words]

46.5   Public Relations

Dear Ron   It was a pleasure to visit your company last fall. I want you to know how much I appreciated[1] the time you took to explain how your information system works. I was very interested to learn that[2] your company regularly provides classes for your executives in which they are taught how to dictate effective[3] business communications.

If at any time in the near future business brings you to San Francisco,[4] please let me know. Yours very truly   [86 words]

LESSON 47

47.1   Membership Survey

Dear Member   Will you please take just a minute or two to answer the enclosed questionnaire. Your answers to the four[1] short questions will help us to determine where we need to improve our services to our members.

Will you please[2] renew your membership now? Your membership will not expire for a few months. It is nevertheless a good[3] idea to renew it now. You will be helping your organization by responding to my two requests. Sincerely[4]   [80 words]

47.2

Maxwell   Ms.   reference   applied   particularly
ability   pertinent   regarding   decision   envelope
convenience   replying   I would   I should have

47.3   Reference Request

Dear Mr. Maxwell   Ms. Sue Nash has given me your name as a reference. She[1] has applied for an executive secretarial position in my office.

352

I am particularly interested in learning about her[2] communication ability. I would also like to have any other pertinent information you[3] think I should have regarding my decision to hire Ms. Nash.

I have enclosed an envelope for your convenience[4] in replying. Sincerely [85 words]

47.4 United Way

Dear Ms. Mann I have been named the campaign chairperson for the United Way Drive. There is something you can do to[1] help the United Way in your community.

Please send United Way pledge cards through your company mail to[2] all the members of your staff. This allows us to reach the working people in our city while spending a very[3] small amount of money on postage.

Please let me know if you will be able to help us this year. Yours very truly[4] [80 words]

47.5 Business Memo

To: Ray Martin
From: Jack Lopez
Subject: Personnel Vacancies
We have been having difficulty finding sales[1] representatives to fill two territories. The first includes the cities of Jacksonville, Dallas, and[2] Burlington. The other territory includes the cities of Boston and Lexington. These jobs have been open[3] for more than five months.

I hope you can take action on these vacancies immediately. If you have any leads, please[4] let us know. [82 words]

LESSON 48

48.1 Insurance Payment

Dear Mrs. Adams The Legal Department has determined that our company is legally obligated[1] to pay the expenses of Mr. Philip Gates. Mr. Gates was injured on the job in our Washington plant. The[2] total cost of his medical bills is $3,800. Would you please issue Mr. Gates a check[3] for $3,800 as soon as possible.

If you have any questions or need additional facts, please[4] call me. Very truly yours [86 words]

48.2

Bentley subscription advertising next current subscriber avoid special value available limited with the you can of this Yours truly

48.3 Magazine Subscription

Dear Mr. Bentley Subscription prices for Eastern Advertising Magazine will be increasing with the next issue.[1]

As a current subscriber you can avoid the increase by extending your present subscription now for one or two[2] years at the current rate.

Subscribe today and take advantage of this special value. This offer is available for[3] a limited time only. Yours truly [69 words]

48.4 Communications System

Dear Peter I would like to express our appreciation for the helpful assistance you gave our public relations[1] department in reorganizing its methods of handling our worldwide communications[2] system. The successful solution of what has been a difficult and expensive operation was the result of[3] your assistance. We were extremely pleased with the way you dealt with our staff. Your services are valuable to[4] publishing companies like ours. Sincerely yours [88 words]

48.5 Publishing Opportunities

Ladies and Gentlemen I have just received an advertising pamphlet published by the public relations[1] department of the Worth Publishing Company. It lists the unusual opportunities in the publishing[2] world. The person responsible for this booklet must be a recognized leader in the publishing industry[3] and should be commended for the work.

I do not ordinarily give advertising matter to my business[4] students. I would be happy to do so in the case of your booklet if you will let me have 50 copies.[5] Sincerely yours [102 words]

49.1 Late Payment

Dear Mr. West   We were glad to open a charge account for you at the State Street Store. Part of our agreement when[1] we opened this account was that you would pay your bills within a reasonable time after you received them.

Our[2] records show that during July and August your food purchases amounted to $250.[3] We have not yet received your check.

Please send us a check today. An envelope is enclosed for your convenience.[4] Cordially yours
[81 words]

49.2

Hughes   sincerely   kindnesses   Houston Wednesday   opportunity   worthwhile   especially The Common Market   several   thank you for your   to me   I was   I can   has been

49.3 Public Relations Visit

Dear Ms. Hughes   Thank you very sincerely for your many kindnesses to me when I visited your printing plant[1] and office in Houston on Monday, Tuesday, and Wednesday. I found the opportunity to visit your operations[2] very worthwhile. I was especially pleased to see our latest book, The Common Market, in print! After visiting[3] your plant, Ms. Hughes, I can see why your organization has been selected to print several of our most[4] important books. Sincerely yours   [86 words]

49.4 Guest Speaker

Dear Mr. Harrington   I have been requested by the board of directors to obtain a speaker for the[1] regular yearly meeting of the New York Legal Association. In my opinion the best person for this[2] assignment is Dr. Fred H. Davis. Dr. Davis has been successful in banking and in newspaper[3] publishing. He is a recognized expert on world affairs, and he is held in high regard in both[4] political and financial circles. Yours very truly   [87 words]

49.5 Time Management

Dear Mrs. Parks   Most people seem to feel that there is never enough time to do all the things that need to be done[1] in professional life. Are you one of these people? Would you like to have a better way of doing your work so that[2] you would have more time for other things?

All you have to do is send for a copy[3] of our new book, Managing Your Time. Send for your copy today. A handy order blank is enclosed.[4] Very truly yours   [84 words]

50.1 Article Publication

Dear Dr. Day   The editor of our magazine, Janice Hastings, has asked me to inform you that your[1] article will be published in our technical publication.

I have been thinking for some time that we should publish[2] an article of this type, and I am very glad that your article will appear in our magazine. You have done[3] a very complete job of reporting on the technical aspects of computer printers. Thank you for a job[4] well done. Yours truly
[83 words]

50.2

Billings   income   federal   government   due   almost slipped   referred   involved   objective   insurance coverage   furnish   I should have   I was I will be glad   Sincerely yours

50.3 Tax Report

Dear Mr. Billings   The enclosed income tax report for the federal government is due in a week or two, and it[1] almost slipped my mind. I should have referred it to you a long time ago. I was involved in making an objective[2] study of our insurance coverage, and I almost forgot about it. If you need any other information[3] from me, I will be glad to furnish it. Sincerely yours   [71 words]

50.4 Equipment Needs

Dear Dr. Baxter   The program information concerning your speaking engagement for the convention to be held in Miami[1] on Saturday, April 16, is enclosed. So that we can assure you have the equipment needed for your[2] presentation, we have enclosed forms for you to list the equipment you will need in your meeting room. Please fill out the[3] forms and return them to me immediately.

I am looking forward to hearing your presentation[4] in April. Sincerely yours   [84 words]

50.5   Presentation Preparation

Dear Mike   Thank you for consenting to provide assistance to our guest speaker, Frank Jennings. Mr. Jennings will[1] arrive at 9 p.m. on Friday, December 3. Please pick him up at the Western Airlines terminal[2] building at the airport.

Mr. Jennings will need seating for 75 people, a podium, and a[3] microphone in his meeting room. Please see to it that his needs are met.

Thank you for your willingness to help.[4] Very truly yours   [82 words]

LESSON 51

51.1   Insurance Renewal

Dear Mr. Parker   If you have not recently increased the amount of insurance you carry on your property,[1] you are probably not adequately insured. That means that in case of a fire you will have to pay for part[2] of the price of rebuilding.

Take this opportunity to have one of our insurance agents call on you if your[3] policy has not been reviewed in the past five years. Sincerely
[72 words]

51.2

Paul   yesterday   morning   colleague   resigned accepted   position   Sawyer Computer   up resigning   must   analyst   shortly   could not

51.3   Available Employment

Dear Paul   Yesterday morning I learned that my friend and colleague, Tom Woods, had resigned and had accepted a position[1] as manager of the Sawyer Computer Company. While he was happy here, he felt he could not pass up[2] this opportunity.

His resigning has caused problems for the company, but we must carry on. We plan to[3] name the new analyst shortly. Sincerely yours   [69 words]

51.4   Finance Committee

Dear Steve   I will be glad to serve as a member of the finance committee for our organization. I[1] understand that I am to begin my work on this committee with the first meeting to be held in February.[2] Would it be possible, Steve, for you to give me copies of the budgets for the current year and the budgets for[3] several recent years? I would find this most helpful.

I look forward to the opportunity to help our[4] organization in this way. Yours truly   [86 words]

51.5   New Employee

Dear Alice   You will be pleased to know that Tom Best has joined our staff. As you know, Tom made a fine reputation for[1] himself during the time that he was in charge of the service department at the Carson Center in Los Angeles.[2] Recently, however, the Carson Center was sold.

Tom closed its service department and joined our organization[3] on November 3.

The next time your car needs service, please let us know. Very truly yours   [76 words]

LESSON 52

52.1   Business Meeting

Dear Mr. Jackson   Thank you for agreeing to meet with me in your Chicago office. I will be arriving on[1] Western Airlines Flight 67 at 3 p.m. on September 7.

I am looking forward to[2] presenting the information which the members of my staff and I have developed for your company. I know[3] you will be pleased with what you see.

I hope after our meeting you will be free to be my guest for dinner.[4] Very truly yours   [81 words]

52.2

Burlington   talking   possible   editor   responsible experience   advertising   marketing   declined salary   figure   ideas   as you know   I have been would have been   for this   if you have   let me

52.3 Job Vacancy

Dear Mr. Burlington   As you know, I have been talking with May Baker about a possible position as an[1] editor. She would have been a good person for this responsible job because of her experience in[2] advertising, publishing, and marketing. She has, however, declined the job because of the salary figure.[3]

If you have any other ideas, please let me know. Very truly yours   [72 words]

52.4 Transportation Costs

To: Sandra Gordon
From: Bob Case
Subject: Publication of Transportation Costs
Enclosed you will find a booklet[1] that was recently published by the National Oil Company in Oakland, California.

This report shows[2] the railroad industry in a very good light, and I would like to use parts of the report in our own[3] advertising. Please write to National to inquire whether we may obtain publishing rights to this booklet and[4] get back to me as soon as possible.   [86 words]

52.5 Business Letter

Dear Mr. Lexington   Yesterday I forwarded to you the plan prepared for the location of the new[1] furniture, fixtures, and office equipment for our two floors in the Hancock Building.

After you and your managers[2] have had an opportunity to study the plan, I would like to discuss it with you. Any time between 10 a.m.[3] and 4 p.m. on Thursday, June 5, will be satisfactory for me. Very truly yours   [78 words]

A P P E N D I X

BRIEF FORMS

The number indicates the lesson in which the brief form or brief-form derivative was introduced.

a 4
about 12
accompany 16
acknowledge 20
acknowledged 20
acknowledges 20
acknowledgment 20
advantage 18
advantages 18
advertise 18
advertises 18
advertising 18
afford 8
after 12
afternoon 12
am 4
an 4
and 18
anniversary 36
any 26
anybody 26
anyone 26
anything 26
anytime 26

anyway 26
anywhere 26
appropriate 34
appropriately 34
appropriation 34
are 4
at 4
be 8
became 8
because 8
before 8
began 8
being 8
believe 8
beside 8
between 24
business 22
businesses 22
businesslike 22
but 10
by 8
can 8
cannot 8
character 40

characters 40
circular 40
circulars 40
circumstance 40
circumstances 40
communicate 16
communicated 16
communication 16
communications 16
companies 16
company 16
convenience 36
convenient 36
conveniently 36
correspond 28
corresponded 28
correspondence 28
correspondent 28
correspondents 28
corresponds 28
could 10
depart 18
difficult 22
difficulties 22

difficulty 22
direct 16
directed 16
direction 16
directly 16
director 16
disadvantage 18
doctor 14
doctors 14
Dr. 14
during 14
electric 38
electrical 38
electricity 38
electronic 38
electronically 38
enclose 30
enclosed 30
enclosure 30
envelope 30
envelopes 30
equip 28
equipment 28
equipped 28
equivalent 38
ever 16
every 16
everywhere 16
executive 34
executives 34
experience 32
experienced 32
extraordinary 40
for 8
force 8
forced 8
forget 8
forgive 8
form 8
forms 8
from 12
general 20
generally 20
gentleman 26
gentlemen 26
glad 12
gladly 12
good 8
goods 8
govern 20

government 20
have 8
his 8
hour 4
however 20
I 4
idea 38
ideas 38
immediate 18
immediately 18
importance 38
important 38
in 4
include 32
included 32
includes 32
including 32
inclusion 32
inconvenience 36
inconvenient 36
inconveniently 36
incorporate 36
incorporated 36
inform 8
insurance 26
insure 26
insured 26
insuring 26
is 8
it 4
manufacture 26
manufactured 26
manufacturer 26
memorandum 38
morning 26
mornings 26
Mr. 8
Mrs. 12
Ms. 22
never 28
newspaper 30
next 36
not 4
nothing 24
object 34
objected 34
objection 34
objective 34
objects 34
of 4

office 14
offices 14
once 14
one 14
opinion 28
opinions 28
opportunities 20
opportunity 20
order 28
ordered 28
ordering 28
orders 28
ordinarily 40
ordinary 40
organization 20
organize 20
organized 20
our 4
out 22
outcome 22
outside 22
outstanding 22
over 22
overhead 22
overlook 22
overnight 22
part 18
particular 34
particularly 34
partly 18
partner 18
party 18
present 20
presented 20
presently 20
privilege 40
privileges 40
probable 30
probably 30
product 28
production 28
products 28
program 34
programmed 34
programmer 34
programming 34
programs 34
progress 32
progressed 32
progressive 32

PHRASES

The number indicates the lesson in which the phrase was introduced.

about the 12	from the 12	I would be 8
about them 12	from you 12	I would not 5
about this 12	from your 12	I would not be 8
about you 12	has been 11	if the 10
about your 12	has been able 11	if you 9
after the 12	have not 8	if you are 9
are in 5	he will 8	if you can 9
are not 5	he will be 8	if you cannot 9
as soon as 16	here are 14	if you have 9
as soon as possible 16	here is 14	if you will 9
as the 10	I am 5	if your 9
as you 9	I am glad 12	in it 5
as you know 9	I can 8	in order 28
as your 9	I can be 8	in our 5
at this time 26	I cannot 8	in the 10
be glad 12	I cannot be 8	in this 10
by the 10	I could 10	in which 10
by this time 26	I could not 10	is in 10
by you 8	I do 9	is not 10
by your 8	I do not 9	is the 10
can have 8	I have 8	is there 14
can you 8	I have not 8	is this 10
Cordially yours 12	I have not been able 11	it has been 11
could not 10	I hope 19	it is 8
Dear Madam 12	I hope that 19	it was 14
Dear Miss 12	I hope that the 19	it will 5
Dear Mr. 12	I hope the 19	it will not 5
Dear Mrs. 12	I know 9	let me 16
Dear Ms. 28	I may 9	let us 16
Dear Sir 12	I may be 9	next month 36
did not 10	I may have 9	next time 36
do not 9	I might 9	next year 36
do you 9	I might be 9	of course 16
do you know 9	I need 9	of our 5
for me 9	I think 24	of the 10
for my 9	I was 14	of them 10
for our 8	I will 5	of these 10
for that 10	I will be 8	of you 8
for the 10	I will be glad 12	of your 8
for this 10	I will have 8	on our 9
for you 8	I will not 5	on the 10
for your 8	I will not be 8	on this 10
from our 12	I would 5	one of our 14

one of the 14
one of them 14
send the 24
send us 24
send you 24
sending you 24
should be 10
should have 10
should not be 10
Sincerely yours 28
some of our 19
some of the 19
some of them 19
thank you 28
thank you for 28
thank you for the 28
thank you for your 28
thank you for your letter 28
thank you for your order 28
that are 10
that will 10
there are 14
there is 14
there was 14
there will 14
they are 14
they are not 14
they will 14
they will be 14
this is 10
this is the 10
this will 10
this will be 10
to be 11
to do 16
to have 11
to make 16
to me 16
to take 9
to the 10

to us 16
to you 9
to your 9
up to date 14
Very cordially yours 28
very much 26
Very sincerely yours 28
Very truly yours 12
we are 9
we are not 9
we can 8
we cannot 8
we do 9
we have 9
we have not 9
we have not been 11
we have not been able 11
we hope 19
we hope that 19
we hope that the 19
we hope the 19
we hope you will 19
we know 9
we may 9
we may be 9
we might 9
we might be 9
we might have 9
we need 9
we think 24
we will 8
we will be 8
we will have 9
we will not 9
we will not be 9
we will not have 9
we would 8
we would be 9
we would have 9
we would not 8

we would not be 9
we would not have 9
when the 12
which is 10
will not 5
will you please 14
with our 12
with the 12
with you 12
with your 12
would not be 9
you are 8
you are not 8
you can 8
you can be 8
you can have 8
you cannot 8
you have 8
you have been 11
you have not 8
you have not been able 11
you might be 9
you might have 9
you will 8
you will be 8
you will be able 11
you will have 8
you will not 8
you will not be 8
you would 8
you would be 8
you would have 8
you would not be 8
you would not have 8
your order 28
Yours sincerely 28
Yours very sincerely 28
Yours very truly 12

INDEX TO WORDS

The number indicates the lesson in which the theory word was introduced.